CAREER DIRECTIONS

The Path to Your Ideal Career

Fifth Edition

Donna J. Yena
Johnson & Wales University

Mc Graw Hill

Connect Learn Succeed™

CAREER DIRECTIONS: THE PATH TO YOUR IDEAL CAREER
Published by McGraw-Hill, a business unit of The McGraw-Hill Companies, Inc., 1221 Avenue of the
Americas, New York, NY, 10020. Copyright © 2011 by The McGraw-Hill Companies, Inc. All rights reserved.
No part of this publication may be reproduced or distributed in any form or by any means, or stored in a data-
base or retrieval system, without the prior written consent of The McGraw-Hill Companies, Inc., including, but
not limited to, in any network or other electronic storage or transmission, or broadcast for distance learning.

Some ancillaries, including electronic and print components, may not be available to customers outside the
United States.

This book is printed on acid-free recycled paper.

1 2 3 4 5 6 7 8 9 0 WDQ/WDQ 0

ISBN 978-0-07-337515-1
MHID 0-07-337515-2

Vice president/Editor in chief: *Elizabeth Haefele*
Vice president/Director of marketing: *John E. Biernat*
Senior sponsoring editor: *Alice Harra*
Director of development: *Sarah Wood*
Developmental editor: *Jenae Grossart*
Editorial coordinator: *Vincent Bradshaw*
Senior marketing manager: *Keari Green*
Digital developmental editor: *Kevin White*
Director, Editing/Design/Production: *Jess Ann Kosic*
Senior project manager: *Jane Mohr*
Production supervisor: *Nicole Baumgartner*
Senior designer: *Srdjan Savanovic*
Senior photo research coordinator: *Jeremy Cheshareck*
Cover design: *Daniel Krueger*
Interior design: *Kay D Lieberherr*
Typeface: *10/12 Times Roman*
Compositor: *Laserwords Private Limited*
Printer: *Worldcolor*
Cover credit: *©Iconica*
Credits: The credits section for this book begins on page 300 and is considered an extension of the copyright page.

Library of Congress Cataloging-in-Publication Data
Yena, Donna J.
    Career directions : the path to your ideal career/Donna J. Yena.—5th ed.
        p. cm.
    ISBN 978-0-07-337515-1 (alk. paper)
    1. Vocational guidance. I. Title.
HF5381.Y46 2011
650.1—dc22
                                            2009051325

The Internet addresses listed in the text were accurate at the time of publication. The inclusion of a Web site
does not indicate an endorsement by the authors or McGraw-Hill, and McGraw-Hill does not guarantee the
accuracy of the information presented at these sites.

www.mhhe.com

Dedication

This book is dedicated to the thousands of students and the teachers who have applied the techniques in this book as a tool for planning and launching successful careers for the past 25 years. I want to especially thank my husband John, whose experience in his 40 years as a leader in career education has provided me valuable guidance, support, and inspiration to ensure this text continues to benefit the career success of the students it serves.

About the Author

With 30 years of experience in career development and human resources, Donna Yena brings a practitioner's perspective to this book. Her experience as Vice President of Career Development at Johnson & Wales University, along with her background as a manager, instructor, and curriculum designer, contribute to the advice and techniques found in *Career Directions: The Path to Your Ideal Career* and the *Career Directions Handbook.*

Yena developed and implemented a series of career management education courses for students at Johnson & Wales University, while responsible for experiential education programs for more than 3,500 students at four campuses. For 30 consecutive years, 98 percent of Johnson & Wales University graduates were employed within 60 days of graduation, under Yena's leadership. Yena is one of the University's certified DACUM (Developing a Curriculum) facilitators. She currently serves as a member of the Board of Governors for the World Association of Cooperative Education and is a member of the Society for Human Resource Management; the Women's Foodservice Forum; and NACE, the National Association of Colleges and Employers.

Yena is a nationally recognized speaker on career development, job placement, and student success. She has led seminars for school professionals and their students across the country and has published numerous articles on a range of job search and career development topics.

Brief Contents

Contents

Preface

WELCOME TO *CAREER DIRECTIONS: THE PATH TO YOUR IDEAL CAREER*

The fifth edition of *Career Directions* is designed to assist career seekers, both in and out of the classroom, from a wide variety of diverse backgrounds. This book is equally ideal for those who are decided or undecided about their career paths, those who are in a career transition, or those who are returning to school with plans to start a new career or reenter the workforce. A major goal of your education is to prepare you for a satisfying career. Being prepared to manage your career from internship and co-op experiences to your first career position and beyond increases the likelihood that you will achieve your career goals. Filled with both updated and new content and features, the fifth edition of *Career Directions* blends the basics of career planning and searching with resources contemporary to today's workplace.

Updated sources and theories, new case studies, real-world examples, and exercises and activities have been added to the fifth edition, making it a comprehensive and current resource for the modern career seeker. Successful job search techniques vary, and as you customize your search to meet your own individual career goals, you will need to decide which online and traditional career resources will work best for you. For example, the use of recruitment technology can be very different between small, local companies and mid-size, large, regional, or national companies. Many companies are now looking to online social networking sites to recruit new hires. Becoming well-versed in resources such as Facebook, Twitter, MySpace, and activities such as blogging will put you ahead of other candidates and increase your chances of connecting with a potential employer. In addition to two new chapters covering networking and internships and co-ops, these are just a few examples of the updated content found in the fifth edition.

The information provided to you in *Career Directions* spans the needs of a wide variety of job seekers. Students in career schools, four-year colleges, and community colleges can all benefit from using this book in career development courses and career workshops. The book can also be used independently for those who want to direct their own career planning and job search efforts. *Career Directions* provides instruction and resource materials that will help you find your internship or co-op job or your first position after graduation or help guide you through a career transition.

CAREER DIRECTIONS HANDBOOK

Since the job search process varies by industry, researching industries and potential career paths is imperative throughout your career planning and searching activities. The text, *Career Directions: The Path to Your Ideal Caree*r, is designed to help you assess, plan, take action, and attain your desired career path, and the updated *Career Directions Handbook* is carefully designed to assist you in this process.

The *Career Directions Handbook* is a current and comprehensive tool that is now conveniently available both in print and online. Packed with valuable information, the *Career Directions Handbook* will arm you with knowledge, statistics, career possibilities, and over 1,000 specific job descriptions spanning a multitude of industries. Included industries range from technology, to health care, to business, to everything in between! Knowing your industry options, corresponding career paths, specific job descriptions, and what you can expect for each one in terms of salary and job outlook will give you a realistic perspective of your options.

Whether you have already pinpointed a specific industry in which you are interested or you are still unsure about the career path you desire, the *Career Directions Handbook* offers a wealth of information. With this information, you will be prepared over other career seekers in the hiring pool. When you are prepared, and know what you want in a career, it translates into confidence during interviews and throughout your life.

Acknowledgments

I would like to acknowledge the tremendous efforts and guidance of the entire McGraw-Hill Higher Education team whose vision, partnership, and expertise contributed to the development of this fifth edition. Particular thanks go to Jenae Grossart and Vincent Bradshaw for the talent, commitment, and diligence they demonstrated in shepherding this new edition to completion. I would also like to extend my gratitude to Alice Harra and Sarah Wood for your continued support and belief in this book; to Keari Green for your marketing efforts in ensuring the value of this book is communicated to students and instructors alike; to Jane Mohr and Janean Utley for your efforts behind the scenes regarding schedule coordination and production; to Srdjan Savanovic and Daniel Krueger for your work on the cover and interior design; and to Destiny Hadley and Marcy Lunetta for your work on citations and permissions, respectively.

McGraw-Hill and Donna Yena would like to acknowledge all the instructors who reviewed this and previous editions. Their continued insight and input contribute directly to the development and success of this text.

5th Edition Reviewers

Amanda C. Baker, *Johns Hopkins University*

Amy Buoscio, *Northwestern College*

Lois A. Citron, *New York Career Institute*

Jack Colocousis, *Bryant & Stratton College*

Laurie M. Dressel, *DeVry University*

Lani Drobnock, *McCann School of Business and Technology*

Denise Berg Eldred, *SOLO Marketing Group*

Alexandra Spaith Evans, *Miller-Motte College*

Sam Giamas, *Bryant & Stratton College*

Gladys S. Green, *State College of Florida*

George Huisman, *IntelliTec Colleges*

Deborah Kosydar, *McCann School of Business and Technology*

David M. Leuser, *Plymouth State University*

Debbie Liddel, *Pinnacle Career Institute*

Stephen G. Makosy, *Bryant & Stratton College*

Rita M. Murphy, *Plaza College*

Amy M. O'Donnell, *The University of Toledo*

Christopher C. Old, *Sierra College*

James Rubin, *Paradise Valley Community College*

Yogeswari S. Saddanathan, *Gwinnett College*

Maria E. Sofia, *Bryant & Stratton College*

Pat Sorcic, *Bryant & Stratton College*

Dr. Dee Strbiak, *DeVry University*

Belen Torres-Gil, *Rio Hondo College*

Donna Townsend, formerly of *Baker College of Clinton Township*

Dr. Gail L. White, *DeVry University*

Earl Wiggins, *Miller-Motte College*

The fifth edition of *Career Directions: The Path to Your Ideal Career* is designed to ensure that students will not only learn fundamental strategies of career success, but also will be able to put those basics into action through real-world cases, examples, and a multitude of activities.

"A refreshing change from my current textbook, with more contemporary topics."

Belen Torres-Gil, Rio Hondo College

Career Directions is

1. **Identify** how world trends are affecting the workplace

2. **List** the 21st century skills employers consider critical to career success

3. **Recognize** the value of your education in the workplace

It is important for you to have an awareness of the world around you as you prepare for today's workplace. Now more than ever, societal and economic trends will affect your job and your work environment on a regular basis. This chapter discusses how world trends are reshaping your world of work by focusing on the major challenges today's workers face and how businesses and people are responding to these changes. The chapter also focuses on the skills you will need for success in the millennial workplace. A major part of your own professional development will depend on your ability to respond and adapt to some of these changes.

LEARNING OUTCOMES outline the focus of the chapter and provide a roadmap for the material ahead. Each is tied to a main heading in the chapter, as well as to the chapter summary, to help reiterate important topics throughout.

CASE STUDY

CASE STUDIES located at the beginning of each chapter introduce students to chapter topics through real-world scenarios. Related Discussion Questions are provided at the end of each case to encourage classroom discussion.

"It encompasses real world application, engages active learners, and is at an appropriately rigorous level."

Maria E. Sofia, Bryant & Stratton College

CASE STUDY

Maria attended community college immediately following her graduation from high school. While pursuing her degree in communications, Maria completed an internship at a local hospital in their public relations office. As an intern, Maria was part of a team that helped to develop a local ad campaign to recruit more members of the community into the hospital's volunteer program. Her work included meeting with college students and local business groups to explain the importance of the volunteer program and share the positive feedback about the experience from current volunteers. Her goal after graduation was to work in a small advertising firm where she could further develop her writing and presentation skills and learn more how to promote a variety of different products and services.

Discussion Questions

1. What skills did Maria need to apply to work successfully with her coworkers who were so different from her?

2. Why do you think Maria was selected to create the campaign for the nutrition products?

3. What else could Jim do to increase his value to the firm in a competitive job market?

. . . a comprehensive and engaging way for students to explore, identify, and achieve their ideal career paths.

REAL LIFE STORIES exemplify chapter topics, and allow students to connect the material to current businesses, well-known individuals, and their own lives. These stories range from companies like American Girl, LLC, to people such as Lance Armstrong, to everyday individuals who have had experiences similar to those that students might face.

Real Life Stories

Laura Murphy

Dissatisfaction with several entry-level positions and work for a car rental company led Laura Murphy to pursue a more rewarding career. She went back to school and obtained an associate degree in nursing. She became a travel nurse and eventually assumed a nursing position at a medical center's high-risk and delivery center. She also worked with new mothers, like herself, to adjust to parenthood.

Laura moved on to work as a full-time school nurse which allows her to spend time with her two children. She believes nursing offers a wide variety of career paths for those seeking a personally rewarding career with many opportunities.[1]

Source: Reprinted with permission. Winter 2005 *Alpha Phi Quarterly.* Copyright © 2005.

---

[1] T. Riemer Jones, et. al. (2005). "Values-Based Career Moves." *Alpha Phi Quarterly* 117(1). Retrieved August 31, 2009, from www.alphaphi.org/pdfs/Quarterly/2005Winterp.1-10.pdf.

ACTIVITIES provided throughout each chapter encourage immediate application and practice of the topics covered.

"Easy to read; full of activities to make students begin thinking."

Debbie Liddel, Pinnacle Career Institute

"I like the variety of exercises. They are thought-provoking and allow the student to personally connect with the content."

Earl Wiggins, Miller-Motte College

ACTIVITY 2.1

Choosing Values

...es affect most of the choices we make every day. The career you choose should be com-...ole with your values. The following words describe some common values. From the list, ...ct 10 that are most important to you and then rank them 1 to 10, with 1 being the most ...ortant:

...lues	Most Important	Rank (1 = most important)
...ing a difference		
...grity		
...ness		
...ng		
...utation		
...iduality		
...ice		
...er		
...ness		
...sity		
...ce		

PROGRESS CHECK QUESTIONS facilitate class discussion and encourage students to pause and reflect on key topics as they progress through each chapter.

> **"The Progress Check Questions are on target, thought-provoking, and can be used effectively as the basis for classroom (or online) discussion."**
>
> *David M. Leuser, Plymouth State University*

Progress Check Questions

1. Do you think your strongest personality traits are always an advantage to you? why not?
2. How do you think your personality traits affect your career choice?

Real Life Stories

Lance Armstrong

Lance Armstrong's extraordinary athletic career is an example of how one can draw upon strong personality traits to set ambitious goals and overcome potential obstacles that co prevent achieving those goals.

At age 22, Lance Armstrong became the youngest winner of the World Championship bicycle road racing. He went on to break a record, winning the Tour de France for seven c

---

NOTES	Sample Goal Statements

Vague Goal Statements	SMART Goal Statements
1. I want to save my money.	1. I will save 10 percent of my income to pay for my professional certification test to be taken next spring.
2. I want to be happy with my job.	2. By January, I will have my resume updated with the eight transferable skills from my current job with the goal of having a new job by April.
3. I want to work for a progressive company.	3. I want to work for a company that has customized career paths that will allow me to move to a senior financial analyst's position in five years.
4. I want to find an internship in my field.	4. I want a teaching internship to earn the 13.5 credits I need to qualify me my student teaching for by September.

NOTES BOXES highlight material directly related to chapter topics, providing reinforcement and enhancement of the subject matter.

CHAPTER SUMMARIES review the Learning Outcomes outlined at the beginning of the chapter, bringing the material full-circle, encouraging retention, and preparing students for the next chapter.

CHAPTER SUMMARY

By exploring the career paths overview in this chapter, you have had career planning foundation and establish direction for your job searc

Beginning with knowing the difference between a job and a c First, it helps you decide which of the two is a better choice for you a can change your course at any time in the future, it is best to have a time with a series of unrelated jobs if you later decide you want to p

Understanding how jobs relate to different career paths is key career moves as you work your way along your career path. The n available to you will always be changing along with periods of growth the rate at which companies are able to create more or new job oppo in the market. Being knowledgeable about current trends in job gro important. It will ensure you know whether you have a strong futur

REFLECTION EXERCISES at the end of each chapter allow students to think critically about what they have learned and respond through an application-based exercise.

"The exercises are very useful and lend themselves to group discussion or activity."

James Rubin, Paradise Valley Community College

CAREER PATHS AND CAREER DECISION MAKING

Based on what you have learned about career paths in this chapter, identify two potential career paths you think you would like to pursue:

_____

To try to decide which career path might best suite you, answer the following questions. What am I trying to decide between my two options?

_____
_____

What do I need to know?

_____
_____

Why do I need to know it?

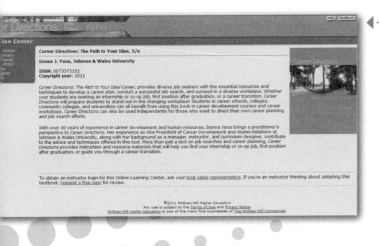

ONLINE LEARNING CENTER

The Online Learning Center (OLC) is a website that follows the text chapter by chapter with digital supplementary content. The instructor's side of the OLC contains useful resources to aid in planning and teaching the course, including the Instructor's Manual, PowerPoint presentations for each chapter, a Test Bank, and an Asset Map. The Asset Map fully integrates the text with all coordinating supplements. It is designed to assist instructors in organizing and teaching the course efficiently and comprehensively.

As students read the book, they can go to the student side of the OLC to take self-grading quizzes, review material, access relevant Web links, and view and print examples and relevant forms. The information center includes the book's table of contents, preface, sample chapter, description of supplements available, and information about the author. The OLC for *Career Directions* is located at www.mhhe.com/yena5e.

WHAT'S NEW

NEW THROUGHOUT THE TEXT!

NEW to this edition: Case Studies

NEW to this edition: Real Life Stories

NEW to this edition: Progress Check questions in each chapter

NEW to this edition: Reflection Exercises included at the end of each chapter

UPDATED Chapter Summaries throughout

CHAPTER 1: THE MILLENNIAL WORKPLACE

- 21st century skills employers consider critical to career success
- The value of your education in the workplace
  - New: Activity: Understanding the Value of Your Degree
- Coverage of today's economy: mortgage crisis 2007, Obama stimulus package 2009; new job growth trends: green jobs, education, credit management, researching job growth trends
  - New: Activity: Researching Job Growth Trends
- More diversity coverage and examples
- Entrepreneurship job growth
- New: Three Real Life Stories
- Generational differences in the workplace
- Social and professional networking trends

CHAPTER 2: SELF-ASSESSMENT

- Know what 21st century skills employers want
- New: Activities covering values, interests, personality traits, skills, emotional intelligence
- New: Three Real Life Stories
- New: Emotional intelligence
- Discussion of emotional intelligence and importance to career success
- Expanded discussion of job matches for some personality types.

NEW! CHAPTER 3: GOAL SETTING AND CAREER DECISION MAKING

- New: Practice writing goals
- New: Apply career decision-making skills

- New: Real Life Story
- New: Discussion of possible influence of ethnicity, age, and gender on personal definitions of career success with activities:
  - New: Activity: Age and Career Success
  - New: Activity: Gender and Career Success
  - New: Activity: Ethnicity and Career Success
  - New: Activity: Write Your Career Success Statement
- Setting goals for self-improvement—expanded discussion and activities
  - New: Activity: Use SMART approach to practice writing goal statements

CHAPTER 4: PERSONAL DEVELOPMENT

- New: Real Life Story
- Communication skills: conversation skills, telephone skills, writing, listening skills
  - New: Activity: Write a SMART Goal to Improve a Speaking Skill
  - New: Activity: Write a SMART Goal to Improve a Writing Skill
- Advice on personal finances: saving, budget, debt management, credit score, retirement planning
  - Activity: Write a SMART Goal for Personal Finance Skills
- Expanded discussion of time and stress management
  - New: Activity Write a SMART Goal to Improve Time and Stress Management Skills
- Expanded discussion of grooming and dress

CHAPTER 5: CAREER PATHS OVERVIEW

- Job versus career discussion has been expanded
- New: Activity: Job versus Career, helps students gain a better understanding of the difference between the two and how it relates to their personal values, interests, and definitions of success
- Where the Jobs Are: expanded public sector list
- Career path examples include hospitality, information technology, retail services, health care
  - New: Activity: Identifying Career Paths
  - New: Activity: Researching Career Paths using the Career Voyages website
- New: Two Real Life Stories

CHAPTER 6: YOUR CAREER PORTFOLIO

- New list of employer expectations replaces 17 Pathways to Success
  - Updated activity skills developed through coursework to include 21st century skills examples
  - Updated Activity: Skills Developed Outside the Classroom
- New: Real Life Story
- New: Addition of a portfolio time line helps students plan their portfolio development from the preparation to presentation stages
- Types of portfolios expanded to include e-portfolios

NEW! CHAPTER 7: CAREER NETWORKING

- Types of networking: person to person, networking events, career fairs, conferences, and workshops
  - Activity: Create a List of Career Network Contacts
  - Activity: Create a Calendar of Networking Events
  - Activity: Create Your Career Network Card
- New: Real Life Story
- How to network: plan, establish rapport, connect, follow-up, build relationships, networking online, social networking
  - Example: Networking at a Career Fair
  - Activity: Create Your List of Online Networking Resources

NEW! CHAPTER 8: INTERNSHIPS AND CO-OP PROGRAMS

- Importance of internships and co-ops to the student and employers
- Finding the right program
  - Day in the Life of Accounting Intern Leah
  - Day in the Life of Ad Sales Associate, Carla
  - Day in the Life of Merchandising Co-op Student, Anthony
- New: Two Real Life Stories
- Learning Goals
  - Activity: Writing Learning Goals
  - Activity: Write a SMART Learning Goal for Co-op and Internship Experiences
  - Activity: Reflect on Your Accomplishments
- Your Success with the Program

CHAPTER 9: SOURCES OF JOBS

- Streamlined to include discussion of the visible job market and hidden job market
- New: Real Life Story

CHAPTER 10: RESUMES AND JOB APPLICATIONS

- New: Determine when to use different resume styles
- New: Organize information for your resume
- New: Real Life Story
- New: Practice the use of power words in your resume
- New: Resume samples have been added
- New: Section on electronic (e-resumes) and paper resumes
  - New samples of e-resumes
  - New Activity: Create Your Own E-resume

CHAPTER 11: LETTERS

- New samples include networking letter and career changer letter
- New: Real Life Story
- New samples of e-cover letters

CHAPTER 12: SUCCESSFUL INTERVIEWS

- Reorganized for clarity: before the interview, during the interview, after the interview
- Information about telephone calls now includes new examples of self-introductions
- Information on researching companies now includes resources for researching companies online, researching small companies, and using blogs and message boards
  - New Activity: Company Research Profile
- New: Real Life Story
- Updated information on group interviews and tips, typical questions asked, 21st century skills questions, ethics, improper questions and how to respond, and questions to ask during an interview
  - New Activity: Prepare and Practice Responses to General Questions
  - New: Sample responses to some general and 21st century skills interview questions.

CHAPTER 13: ACCEPTING OR REJECTING A JOB

- New: Real Life Story
- New: Introduction of new topic of salary negotiation and the dos and don'ts of salary negotiation
  - Activity: Practice Salary Negotiation

CHAPTER 14: GROWING YOUR CAREER

- Preparing for your first day on the job
- Identifying the purpose of industry orientation and training programs
- Recognizing the importance of periodic review and assessment of your performance

- Determining strategies to get promoted and recession-proof your job
- New: Real Life Story

CHAPTER 15: CONTEMPORARY ISSUES IN THE WORKPLACE

- Coverage of employee assistance programs
- Identifying how health-related issues affect you in the workplace
- Recognizing family care issues that affect you in the workplace
- New: Real Life Story
- Discussion of laws that protect employees from workplace discrimination
- Expanded discussion of personal ethics and discrimination issues including misuse of technology at work and why people make unethical decisions

Career Planning

The Millennial Workplace

After completing this chapter you will:

1 **Identify** how world trends are affecting the workplace

2 **List** the 21st century skills employers consider critical to career success

3 **Recognize** the value of your education in the workplace

It is important for you to have an awareness of the world around you as you prepare for today's workplace. Now more than ever, societal and economic trends will affect your job and your work environment on a regular basis. This chapter discusses how world trends are reshaping your world of work by focusing on the major challenges today's workers face and how businesses and people are responding to these changes. The chapter also focuses on the skills you will need for success in the millennial workplace. A major part of your own professional development will depend on your ability to respond and adapt to some of these changes.

CASE STUDY

Maria attended community college immediately following her graduation from high school. While pursuing her degree in communications, Maria completed an internship at a local hospital in their public relations office. As an intern, Maria was part of a team that helped to develop a local ad campaign to recruit more members of the community into the hospital's volunteer program. Her work included meeting with college students and local business groups to explain the importance of the volunteer program and share the positive feedback about the experience from current volunteers. Her goal after graduation was to work in a small advertising firm where she could further develop her writing and presentation skills and learn more about how to promote a variety of different products and services.

When Maria graduated, the job market was extremely tough. She spread the word about her qualifications and skills by posting her Web resume online and was contacted by three employers whom she was unfamiliar with for interviews. Her first choice was to obtain a position with an agency she applied to that had a well-established reputation in the large Hispanic community where she lived in. Maria took Spanish courses while at the community college and felt confident speaking the language. Many of the employees that worked with her were older than Maria and had more knowledge and experience. There were four other recent college graduates. Her fellow workers came from various ethnic backgrounds and most had been with the firm for some time. One of her assignments was developing an advertising plan for a line of nutrition products which she did not know a lot about. Maria had built an online network to keep in touch with friends, teachers, and colleagues from the hospital and the community college. She used her network to reach out to a few former teachers and colleagues at the hospital to gain advice on how to go about the project and to learn more about the product. Jim, one of her older colleagues at the firm, knew a little about the product but had never created an ad campaign targeted to a Hispanic community.

Maria involved Jim in the project along with two other colleagues who had experience with creating ad campaigns targeted to different ethnic groups. When the project was near completion, she was able to test the ad campaign with members of the community by conducting focus groups in Spanish. The product was very successful, and Maria was assigned to work with Jim and several other more experienced colleagues to develop an online community of contacts that could either provide leads or product information for future projects.

Discussion Questions

1. What skills did Maria need to apply to work successfully with her coworkers who were so different from her?
2. Why do you think Maria was selected to create the campaign for the nutrition products?
3. What else could Jim do to increase his value to the firm in a competitive job market?

1.1 WORLD TRENDS EFFECT ON THE WORKPLACE

The workplace is constantly changing in response to world events and trends. Changes in the economy, an aging and more diverse population, entrepreneurial opportunities, and technological advances are all examples of such events and trends. Being aware of what is shaping the workplace can help you better prepare for career opportunities that lie ahead.

ECONOMIC CONDITIONS

The state of the economy is a significant factor to consider in your career planning. Fluctuations in the economy influence the number and types of jobs that grow or decline. The economy is shaped by many conditions converging at both a national and international level at any given time. For example, globalization affects job growth. As the world becomes more global, buying from other countries is a more common practice and more work is outsourced. The application of technology reduces the dependence on labor in many sectors. The health of the financial markets also drives economic conditions. Healthy financial markets grow and create jobs.

Unstable financial markets result in a decline in job growth. An example of this was the mortgage crisis that started in the United States at the end of 2007. Inappropriate financial regulations and practices allowed excessive debt accumulation. Low-income households defaulted on mortgage payments, and home foreclosures rose. Banks stopped lending to each other because of the need to finance foreclosures. When banks are reluctant to lend, firms delay investment decisions and job creation and growth decline.

Banking crises typically have long-lasting effects on employment. What started as a crisis in the U.S. housing market expanded into a global recession presenting labor market challenges worldwide. In China, factory job losses rose. In Europe and the United States firms cut hours and benefits. Significant job losses in the United States started in the financial services and construction sectors and grew to include a majority of industries. The stock market collapse led to a decrease in individual wealth held in pensions, and older workers ready for retirement chose to stay in the workplace beyond their anticipated retirement age.

In 2009, President Obama signed the American Recovery and Reinvestment Act which called for the government to invest money in key initiatives to stimulate the economy by creating new jobs in new industries. One of these initiatives is a focus on the creation of green jobs, which are jobs that have a positive impact on the environment. These jobs are responsible for providing products or services that help lower prices or create greater efficiency so that consumers can spend less and rely on products over long periods of time. Jobs that build products or provide services that conserve energy or enable use of alternative energy sources are an example. These may include making buildings more energy efficient, or electric power renewable, or building energy-efficient vehicles. Green jobs require a wide range of skills from management, accounting, architectural, and marketing to more skilled trades such as construction and manufacturing.

Another area of job growth impacted by the recent economy includes jobs in education. When unemployment is high, many return to school to either retrain for new jobs in the future or to qualify for better jobs in their current career field once the employment market regains strength. Jobs in credit management also grow in tough financial times. For example, credit counselors are in greater demand to help people stop accumulating debt that they can't pay and to help them establish a plan to pay existing debt. Another example is the demand for financial counselors, sometimes called prevention counselors, that help people create a financial plan to avoid home foreclosure. There is no question that economic trends have a direct impact on the workplace. It is important for you to monitor economic trends and how they are affecting the job market in your career field so that you can adjust your career plan if needed to respond to current market conditions.

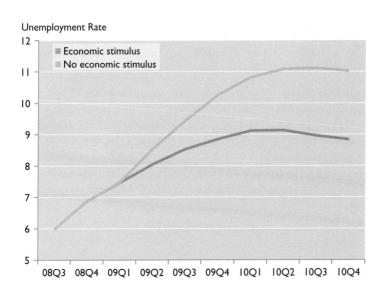

FIGURE 1.1

Stimulus Job Growth

Source: BLS
      Moody's Economy.com
Zandik, Mark. "Economic Stimulus Impact on the Economy." Moody's Economy.com. West Chester, PA. 2009.

ACTIVITY 1.1

Researching Job Growth Trends

Working with a group, create a plan for how to research trends in job growth based on economic conditions. List three sources of information that you think are the most informative (*e.g., Occupational Outlook Handbook, local newspaper, financial reports online similar to Moodyseconomy.com*).

1. _____

2. _____

3. _____

List some key economic indicators of job growth to follow and why they are important (*e.g., stock market, housing market, outsourcing*).

_____

_____

_____

_____

Progress Check Questions

1. How would you describe the current job market where you live?

2. How might current conditions in the job market influence your career decisions?

DIVERSITY

Workforce diversity is described by a variety of dimensions such as ethnicity, race, age, or gender as well as by secondary influences such as religion, socioeconomics, and education. For companies that compete globally, a diverse workforce has distinct advantages. Work teams with different backgrounds and experiences bring different views on problem solving, team building, marketing, and a variety of other areas that are important to enhancing individual and company performance.

> "*By 2050, there will be no majority race.*"
> ACRN—The American Career Resource Network[1]

Different groups have different needs, and they want their needs to be recognized and met as much as possible. Employers that provide more customized approaches to employee recruitment and training, coaching, retention, and benefits plans are better able to attract and retain a diverse workforce.

Ethnicity and Race   A landmark study, Workforce 2020,[2] points to the impact that greater ethnic diversity in the labor market is having on changing the workplace. Kraft Foods is an example of a company responding effectively to its diverse workforce. Through the development of diversity network groups, Kraft uses employee councils to build employee development.

Through 10 employee councils (African-American Council, Hispanic Council, Asian-American Council, Women in Sales Council, Black Sales Council, Women in Operations,

[1] ACRN America's Career Resource Network. (2009). "The Economic Challenge." Retrieved March 12, 2009, from http://cte.ed.gov/acrn/econchal.htm.

[2] R. W. Judy and C. D'Amico. (1997). "Workforce 2020: Work and Workers in the 21st Century." Retrieved September 1, 2009, from www.eric.ed.gov/ERICDocs/data/ericdocs2sql/content_storage_01/0000019b/80/16/bb/41.pdf.

Hispanic-Asian Sales Council, Rainbow Council, Professional Support Council, and the African-American in Operations Council) Kraft takes an active role in mentoring and supporting its diverse workforce.[3] One example of its work includes outreach to college and university internship programs to source new talent in addition to internal professional development programs.

Companies that are open to creating formal and informal opportunities for workers to network in groups with both similar and different ethnic backgrounds build better communication channels among employees and a sense of community that can enhance employee satisfaction and retention.

Age   Age diversity at work is the inclusion of employees of all age groups in the workplace. There are many benefits of various age groups working together. Each age group brings diverse skills and strengths. Older workers bring historical perspective on traditional approaches to workplace issues. Younger workers who bring an understanding of the modern market may be better equipped to identify and apply technology solutions and may be more flexible in considering multiple viewpoints and solutions to business problems. All age groups can learn new ideas and new ways of thinking from each other.

Although there are advantages to age diversity in the workplace, there is also the potential for some unique challenges. Older workers may need more technology training, while younger workers may need more training in product knowledge. Different age groups may have different attitudes toward their work environment. For example, older workers may see the corner office as a sign of status. Younger workers typically prefer more open team work spaces or informal meetings at offsite locations like Starbucks.

In some companies, older workers who choose to work beyond their planned retirement age may find themselves working for recent college graduates. There are many ways in which companies can customize programs and services to maximize the strengths of each age group.

Gender   Gender diversity refers to the proportion of males to females in the workplace. The number of females in the workplace continues to grow. By 2016–17, women are projected to earn more doctorate degrees as well as first professional degrees than men.[4] Companies continue to find progressive ways to attract and retain women to build gender diversity throughout the organization. For example, Deloitte and Touche's National Diversity Council provides a national network of people to support women in a variety of ways. A women-to-women mentoring program supports efforts to attract women to the firm.[5]

Particular focus on career advancement opportunities is designed to support the growth and retention of talented women within the company. Another network provides information sharing for female professionals who are also mothers.

In addition to mentoring programs for women, many companies offer coaching and mentoring to men who may be adapting to working with and for more female executives.

[3] Kraft Foods. (2009). *Kraft Foods'* "Diversity Vision." Retrieved March 12, 2009, from www.brands.KraftFoods .com/careers/ourCulture/diversity/htm.

[4] Catalyst Inc. (2009). "U.S. Labor Force, Population & Education." Retrieved September 1, 2009, from www .catalyst.org/file/143/qt_us_percent20labor_force_pop_ed.pdf.

[5] Deloitte and Touche USA LLP. (2009). "Championing Diverse Workplaces." Retrieved August 27, 2009, from www.deloitte.com/view/en_CA/ca/about/diversity/article/4052388a90ffd110VgnVCM100000ba42f00aRCRD.htm.

FIGURE 1.2

The Aging Workforce

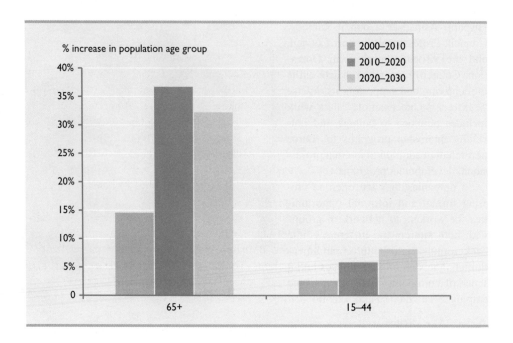

There are still gender gaps in mid- and upper-level management in many companies. One reason is that many women choose to leave and reenter the workplace at different points in their lives to care for their children or parents. This often slows down the career advancement that may have occurred with steady employment. A survey of U.S. college graduates by *Harvard Business Review,* showed that 37 percent of women voluntarily stopped working at some point in their career as opposed to 24 percent of men. Voluntary decisions to take a break during one's career is a major cause of the gender gaps that still exist today.[6]

GENERATIONAL DIFFERENCES

Employers are concerned about the loss of talent that will come with the retirement of the baby boomers in their companies. At the same time, more baby boomers are rethinking their retirement age and seeking out opportunities to continue to work and be productive at their jobs. In response, some employers provide incentives for employees about to retire to stay engaged with their work beyond their planned retirement age. More employers also rehire retirees from other companies recognizing the benefit of their knowledge and experience.

With older workers remaining active at work, companies are addressing ways to connect the four generations of workers that now comprise their workplace. Each generation has a different definition of success based on the value they place on family, work, personal fulfillment, and the use of technology. In progressive organizations, training and development integrates the talents each group brings and mentoring occurs up, down, and across the organization to maximize everyone's talent.

Progress Check Questions

1. How would you describe the type of experiences you have had interacting with diverse groups, and what did you learn from those experiences?

2. How many generations are living in your family? What are some things that all the generations have in common?

[6] S. A. Hewlett, C. B. Luce, P. Shiller, and S. Southwell. (February 24, 2005). "Hidden Brain Drain: Off-Ramps and On-Ramps in Women's Careers." *Harvard Business Review.* Retrieved February 24, 2005, from www. harvardbusinessonline.hbsp.harvardedu/relay.jhtml?name.

ENTREPRENEURSHIP

Entrepreneurial careers are projected to grow as large corporations downsize and demand increases for more customized services to meet the needs of diverse populations. The trend for college graduates to pursue this career path is connected to the broader trend for millennials to pursue work that is satisfying and challenging. Young entrepreneurs are frequently motivated to achieve work-life balance and contribute to the community, which often drives them to own and operate their own businesses. Older workers often choose owning and operating their own business as an alternate career path after gaining experiences and accumulating the financial resources needed to start a company. Being able to apply knowledge and skills acquired over years of work experience in new and creative ways can provide increased career and personal satisfaction.

Those choosing this career path must be prepared to meet internal and external challenges. Internal challenges include supporting product development, hiring and training the right employees, managing cash flow, and ultimately making a profit. External challenges include financing and government regulations. Technology has made it easier to start and manage new start-up companies. Online tools provide readily accessible resources such as articles, forums, blogs, on-demand seminars, podcasts, and professional advisors to provide prospective entrepreneurs with the preparation and networks needed to be successful. Entrepreneurs must have a strong knowledge base of the field, an extensive network inside and outside the field, a strong commitment, and a willingness to take risk.

Real Life Stories

The American Girl Doll

The American Girl doll was founded by Pleasant T. Rowland. Rowland was an elementary school teacher who developed innovative teaching materials focused on the integration of reading with other language arts. Her interest in creative and educational toys for her own children led her to writing children's books. She had a vision that she could create educational products that would make learning fun for children. She expanded her work to developing other educational products including dolls and toys that successfully integrated learning with play. Her first attempt to present a new doll with clothing representing an era in history and a children's book that told the story of that era was not successful. She persisted in believing that her product had value. Her repeated efforts finally resulted in mothers embracing the new product line. Its appeal as an educational product led to a rapid success of the American Girl Doll throughout the country and later around the world. Rowland started with a concept that she believed in and applied her teaching and writing skills and her experience as a mother in a new and creative way. Rowland has been honored as one of the 12 outstanding entrepreneurs in the United States by the Institute of American Entrepreneurs.[7]

SitePoint.com

At the age of 15, Matt Mickiewicz launched SitePoint.com, which grew to become one of the best-known resources for Webmaster/Web developers on the Internet. Matt started SitePoint.com with the simple goal of providing educational resources to Web developers to help them grow their businesses and careers. SitePoint.com publishes three separate e-mail newsletters focusing on design and development and a wide range of business topics. A fourth newsletter targets a community of developers who participate in online forums.

Matt began his career by building a one-page resource site that outlined useful tools and software for building a Website. The demand for the information grew rapidly, and Matt realized that there was an opportunity to build a full-service online educational site for those interested in developing and improving Websites. As the business grew, Matt noticed the trend for viewers

[7] FundingUniverse. (2005). American Girl, Inc. Retrieved September 1, 2009, from www.fundinguniverse.com/company-histories/American-Girl-Inc-Company-History.html.

to print tutorials they were most interested in. Matt saw this as an opportunity to take the most popular tutorials and publish them in a print-on-demand book on the Website. Later, he added another feature called the Marketplace where Websites can be bought and sold. The Website has become a leading resource for Web developers throughout the world and has received up to four million unique visitors and 27 million page views each month.

When talking with others interested in opening their own business, Matt advises that it is important to set modest goals at the start and be patient. Finding investors that believe in your product and building a customer base can be a tedious process and requires perseverance. He also stresses the importance of creating value for your product and services and creating a niche by focusing on something you know you can consistently do well. Finally, he stresses the importance of being constantly tuned in to new opportunities and being prepared to act on them to stay current and sustain long-term success.[8]

Kinko's

Paul Orfalea, founder of Kinko's Inc., realized as a student that he had the ability to see the big picture when presented with challenging situations. He enjoyed analyzing and thinking creatively about ways to solve problems. He developed a self-confidence that enabled him to feel comfortable taking risks and learning from his successes or failures. When Paul discovered that he had dyslexia and attention deficit hyperactivity disorder (ADHD), he understood his restless tendency and his need to learn more from hands-on experience and networking with others than from reading or writing about how to do things. In college, he noticed that the copier machine in the library was in constant demand and that copy machines were not otherwise available to the general public. Paul saw an opportunity to create his own copy service and started his business at a stand near a college campus. Paul developed a steady customer base of mostly college students but did not have the financial resources to grow his business.

He encouraged local investors to share ownership with him, and within 10 years, he had established a network of 80 stores. Keeping his eye open to customer demand, he started a 24-hour service at his stores that enabled students, businesses, and travelers to access his service when they needed it. Kinko's grew to 1,200 locations and 23,000 employees in 10 different countries. When advising college students about becoming an entrepreneur, he does not attribute his success to any particular type of copy machine or technology. Instead, he talks about how he focused on his strengths and saw his disabilities as learning opportunities.[9]

FIGURE 1.3

Entrepreneurial Job Growth Trends

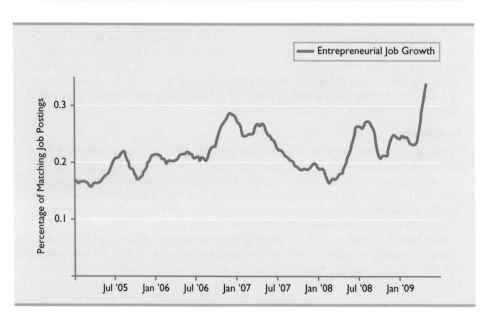

[8] Young Entrepreneur Forums. (2009). Entrepreneur Resource Center. Retrieved August 27, 2009, from www.youngentrepreneur.com/. . ./interview-with-matt-mickiewicz/.

[9] FundingUniverse. (1997). Kinko's Inc. Retrieved September 1, 2009, from www.fundinguniverse.com/company-histories/Kinkos-Inc-Company-History.html.

NOTES | Most Popular Options for Entrepreneurs

- Start and manage own business.
- Work in an existing firm.
- Take over a family business.
- Buy an existing franchise.
- Help bring new ideas to a corporation.

SOCIAL AND PROFESSIONAL NETWORKING

Social and professional networks have reshaped the workplace in a variety of ways. Employers have found some distinct advantages to incorporating the use of social and professional networks to enhance many business practices. The following are the most frequent benefits cited by employers.

Recruitment: Searching social and professional networks has become a useful way for companies to find relevant candidates, actively seeking employment, for any position by searching for applicants with skills that best match those the company is looking for. Connecting with potential candidates through these online networks is also a way to reach out to qualified individuals who may not be aggressively searching for a job but would consider the right career move if the opportunity became available.

Candidate screening: Many companies rely on social networking sites to screen job applicants. In a survey of 31,000 employers conducted by Career Builder.com, interviewers said that information found on online networks about applicants influenced their hiring decision.[10]

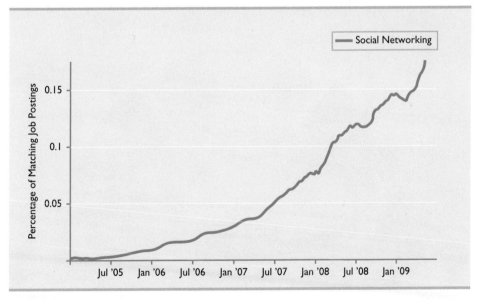

FIGURE 1.4

Growth in Social Networking

---

[10] H. Havenstein. (March 9, 2008). "Careers IDGNS Internet IT Management Sites Social Networking Software and Web 2.0." *ComputerWorld.* Retrieved February 2, 2009, from www.thestandard.com/news/2008/09/12/one-five-employers-uses-social-networks-hiring.

Social learning: Seventy percent of learning in most companies is social learning, much of which occurs through company online networks.[11]

Generation Y: Because Gen Y'ers have grown up with social networks as part of their daily experiences, companies realize the need to adapt to the communication and learning styles of their evolving workforce of Gen Y'ers.

It is important for you to be aware of how online networks are used in the workplace so that you can use these Internet resources in the most productive ways as part of your job search and career progress.

In Chapter 7, you will learn ways to use social and professional networks in ways to enhance your job search, including how your online profile and communication can help you build and maintain a professional reputation with employers.

Progress Check Questions

1. What are some of the traits that Pleasant Rowland, Matt Mickiewicz, and Paul Orfalea share that make them successful entrepreneurs?

2. What social and professional networks do you use now? What is the main thing you use them for?

1.2 WORKPLACE KNOW-HOW AND 21ST CENTURY SKILLS

The relationship between the employment community and educators is extremely important. Companies need graduates who have the skills necessary to make positive contributions to their business. When employers hire, they expect you to have basic workplace skills. Being able to demonstrate those skills to employers will be a great advantage to you when applying for a job. These skills also help you stand out when being considered for a new position or promotion. The Partnership for 21st Century Skills is an example of one way the business community and educational leaders are working together to improve the success of graduates in the workplace.

FIGURE 1.5

21st Century Skills

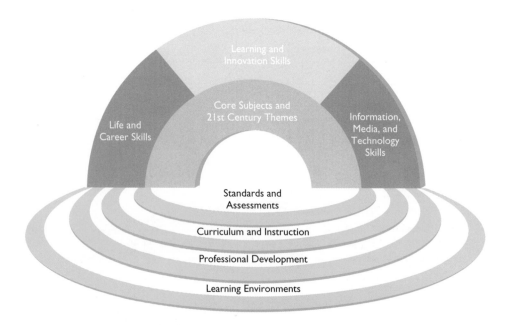

[11] P. Clayton. (2009). "Career Advancement, Employment Trends, Recruitment Leadership Podcast." *Trend Watcher: Informal Learning.* Retrieved March 20, 2009, from www.totalpicture.com/. . ./trendwatcher-informal-learning.html.

THE PARTNERSHIP FOR 21ST CENTURY SKILLS

The Department of Education and the business community conducted a survey of 431 employers to identify the critical workplace skills graduates need.[12] Employers cited the knowledge, applied skills, and emerging content areas necessary for graduates to succeed in the workplace. While a wide range of knowledge and skills were cited, employers ranked the following four skill areas as most important:

- Professionalism and work ethic
- Oral and written communications
- Teamwork and collaboration
- Critical thinking and problem solving

NOTES   Knowledge

English language (spoken)	Government/economics
Reading comprehension (in English)	Humanities/arts
Writing in English (grammar, spelling, etc.)	Foreign languages
Mathematics	History/geography
Science	

NOTES   Applied and Transferable Skills*

Critical thinking	Leadership
Oral communications	Creativity/innovation
Written communications	Lifelong learning/self-direction
Teamwork/collaboration	Professionalism/work ethic
Diversity	Ethics/social responsibility
Information technology application	

*_Applied skills_ refer to those skills that enable entrants to use the basic knowledge acquired in school to perform in the workplace. _Transferable skills_ refer to those skills that enable workers to use the basic knowledge acquired in school, on the job, or through life experiences to perform in the workplace.

NOTES   Emerging Content Areas

Expectations of personal responsibility for health, finances, and career on the rise:

Health and wellness choices
Personal financial responsibility
Entrepreneurial skills
Economic issues and the role of the U.S. and global economy
Economic and cultural effects of globalization
Informed citizenship
Importance of non-English skills[13]

---

[12] Partnership for 21st Century Skills. (2004). "Most Young People Entering the U.S. Workforce Lack Critical Skills Essential for Success." Retrieved August 27, 2009, from www.21stcenturyskills.org/index.php?option=com_content&task=view&id=250&Itemid=64.

[13] The 21st Century Skills Partnership. (2006). "Are They Really Ready to Work?" Retrieved March 29, 2006, from www.21stcenturyskills.org/. . ./FINAL_REPORT_PDF09-29-06pdf[0].

In Chapter 2, Self-Assessment, you will assess your knowledge and applied skills and preparedness in emerging content areas. In Chapter 3, Goal Setting and Career Decision Making, you will set goals for self-improvement.

In Chapter 12, Successful Interviews, you will learn about interview questions that target particular 21st century skills and practice suggested answers to these questions to maximize your success with your interviews. Throughout the text, you will learn more about how emerging content areas impact your career success and how to further develop yourself in these career-critical areas.

....

Progress Check Questions

1. Why do you think applied and transferable skills are so important to employers?
2. Why do you think there is an increase in the importance of personal responsibility for finances, health, and career?

....

SCANS (SECRETARY'S COMMISSION ON ACHIEVING NECESSARY SKILLS)

The SCANS report is now more than 20 years old, and new jobs created in the current and future economy require a broader view of the different skill sets required for career success. SCANS highlighted many of the same skills and knowledge as the 21st Century Partnership study. However, the 21st century workplace study's focus on emerging content areas better reflects the aspects in an effort to provide opportunities for the work-life balance.[14]

The 21st century skills required to succeed in this more blended environment include one's ability to demonstrate responsibility for personal finances and health. In addition, there is greater emphasis placed on the need to build communication skills that allow one to adapt to more diverse work environments. For example, non-English-speaking skills are identified as a critical skill. Finally, there is equal importance given to acquiring the necessary knowledge for career success as is given to the importance of applied skills.

Many believe that in the past, there may have been an overemphasis on applied skills over knowledge. While critical thinking and problem solving are necessary skills, problems cannot be analyzed or solved without the knowledge to think with. In the 21st century skills movement, skills and knowledge are considered to be inseparable components of career success.

THE SPELLINGS REPORT

NOTES

In 2006, The Spellings Report began the discussion about the need to implement a plan that would improve the success rates of college graduates in the workplace. Too many graduates were entering the workplace without the skills employers said were important to career success. The decline in literacy among college graduates was one of the greatest skill deficiencies. It was most notable because the fastest growing jobs require it.

Following the Spellings Report, the 21st Century Skills Report outlined a plan to improve what we expect of graduates and how well we prepare students to have the necessary skills well beyond their first job.[15]

[14] U.S. Department of Labor. (2009). "Secretary's Commission on Achieving Necessary Skills." Retrieved August 27, 2009, from http://wdr.doleta.gov/SCANS/.

[15] U.S. Department of Education. (2006). "A Test of Leadership: Charting the Future of U.S. Higher Education." Retrieved September 1, 2009, from www.ed.gov/about/bdscomm/list/hiedfuture/reports/pre-pub-report.pdf.

1.3 EDUCATION AND THE WORKPLACE

The American Career Resource Network (ACRN) has reported that 65 percent of the fastest growing occupations in the United States require some form of postsecondary education including either an associate's degree, vocational certification, or bachelor's degree.[16] In most career fields there are incremental earnings per year as a result of degree attainment. Typically, associate degree graduates earn more per year than high school graduates. That annual additional salary grows for bachelor degree and master degree graduates. The U.S. Census Bureau Website is a reliable source for the most current information on earnings by degree attainment.

The value of a college degree holds strong through fluctuations in the economy. In fact, college graduates have been reported to have a much lower unemployment rate than the nation as a whole. For example, in April 2009, when unemployment rates were soaring,

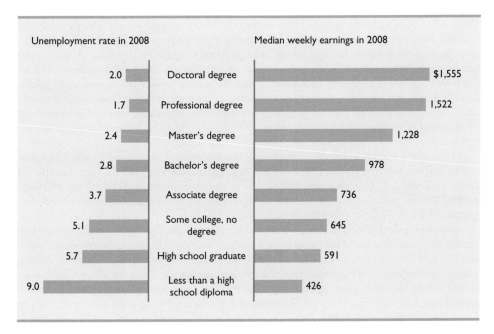

FIGURE 1.6

Education Pays

ACTIVITY 1.2

Understanding the Value of Your Degree

You can do research using the Bureau of Labor Statistics Website, which provides information about your possible earning potential for three different jobs that you might be interested in that utilize the degree you will earn. List (1) the job title, (2) potential earnings, and (3) required education.

1. _____

2. _____

3. _____

Based on what you found, are you interested in one job more than another? _____
Did you become interested in any other jobs with greater earning potential if you pursued an additional degree? _____

[16] ACRN America's Career Resource Network. (2009). The Economic Challenge. Retrieved March 12, 2009, from http://cte.ed.gov/acrn/econchal.htm.

the national unemployment rate was 8.5 percent while the unemployment rate for college graduates was 4.3 percent. A spread between college graduates' and overall unemployment has held constant through every recession since at least the 1970s.[17]

Progress Check Questions

1. How can your education impact your career success in the field you have chosen?

2. If your field requires any special certifications or licenses, do you know what will be needed to keep them current as you progress through your career?

CHAPTER SUMMARY

There will always be external factors that change the workplace and the skills and experiences needed to be successful in your career. We have seen how swings in various aspects of the economy, from the stock market to the housing market, can significantly impact the career opportunities available to you at any given time. As a result of these periodic changes, there will be opportunities for you to develop new skills and perform different and challenging work. Keeping your skills current through formal education or informal learning, such as through professional associations, workshops, seminars, and online learning tools, will continue to be important to your career success and advancement. You should make it a habit to monitor these trends so that you can anticipate ups and downs in the job market and in particular career areas.

Your ability to work with individuals from diverse backgrounds is essential for you to be effective in whatever role you play in your company. Whether members of your work groups differ by ethnicity or race, age, or gender, you will need to be open to different ways of solving problems, working through processes, and accommodating work-life situations and different learning and management styles.

Developing entrepreneurial skills is as important to your work in a large corporation as it is to starting your own business. In the global market in which so many U.S. companies compete, companies that perform best often do so on their ability to think and market creatively, take risks, develop strategic partnerships, and stay closely aligned with customer needs. These are all traits of the successful entrepreneurs discussed in this chapter as well as most others who chose entrepreneurial career paths. Learning these skills can be important to your ability to add value to your company in a way that stands out from others.

The importance of developing relevant workplace skills and keeping them current is critical to your career success in both good and bad economic times. Stay knowledgeable about the skills employers say they need. Plan on constantly developing and growing those skills in school, at work, or through other life experiences. In Chapter 2, you will get started by assessing how well prepared you are to demonstrate the 21st century skills employers say are important. Assessing your skills is only the first step. In Chapter 3, Goal Setting and Career Decision Making, you will learn to set goals for self-improvement in areas that are not currently your strengths, to improve your chances for better career opportunities. In Chapter 2, you will also learn to assess yourself in other areas important to your career success. Understanding the process of self-assessment is very important because it is something that you will need to do periodically to successfully manage your career.

[17] C. Romans. (2009). "Your Money. CNN Transcripts, CNN.com." Retrieved April 11, 2009, from www.transcripts.com/TRANSCRIPTS/0904/11/cnnitm.0.1.html.

MILLENNIAL WORKPLACE IMPACT ON YOUR CAREER DECISIONS

Based on what you learned in Chapter 1, what level of influence do you think each of the following will have on your career decisions? Mark an "X" on the line under your choice.

	None	Somewhat	High
World Trends			
Economy			
Diversity			
Generational differences			
Entrepreneurship			
Social and professional networking			
Workplace Know-How and 21st Century Skills			
Knowledge			
Applied skills			
Emerging content areas			
Education and the Workplace			
Employment rates and your degree			
Earnings and your degree			

1. Which of these are most in your control? Discuss why.

_____

_____

2. How do those that you consider not in your control affect your career decisions?

_____

_____

Self-Assessment

After completing this chapter, you will:

1 **Identify** the factors involved in understanding yourself

2 **Determine** how your values influence your career choice

3 **Recognize** interests that influence your career choice

4 **Define** how your personality traits relate to your career choice

5 **Describe** how well your skills compare with 21st century skills employers want

6 **Explain** how emotional intelligence is related to your self-assessment

This chapter focuses on helping you better understand yourself in relation to your career planning. Knowing yourself is an important first step toward a successful career because your job should be compatible with who you are. When you choose a job that is a good match, you are likely to stay in the job longer and be more satisfied with your decision. Self-assessment is the process of identifying your values, interests, personality traits, knowledge, and skills. Once you have a better understanding of yourself in each of these areas, you can think about how each of them can influence the career choices you make now and in the future. In this chapter, you will identify your values, interests, personality traits, and skills. In the process, you will focus on the 21st century skills employers have identified as important for career success in the workplace and you will learn what emotional intelligence is and the role it can play in your career success.

CASE STUDY

Carlos enrolled in a paralegal studies program at the nearby community college. He had graduated with honors from high school. He thought he chose the right college program, but wasn't really sure. His father was a policeman and Carlos admired the work that he did. He often talked to Carlos about going to college and how important it was to follow a career in which you could make a difference to others. Carlos was reminded of how fortunate he was to be part of a close family unit, unlike so many families in his community.

One of his instructors referred Carlos to a professional career counselor in the nearby area who could help him assess whether he was choosing the right career field for him. The counselor was trained to administer and interpret a variety of career assessment tests. When he met the counselor after completing his tests, Carlos learned some things about himself that would help him feel more comfortable with his career choice now and in the future.

The tests basically confirmed that Carlos had the personality and skills to be successful as a paralegal. He also learned about other career options that matched his personality and skills. The personality test revealed that Carlos was self-directed, motivated, reliable, and had characteristics that indicated a good work ethic. It also revealed that Carlos was a compassionate person and often put others' needs in front of his own. Carlos agreed with this, telling his counselor that he often had difficulty saying no to others.

His skills tests showed that Carlos had above average writing skills and strong analytical and problem-solving skills. That was aligned with his interest in and skill with researching and processing complex information.

His counselor told Carlos that his test results supported his choice to pursue a career as a paralegal, but reminded Carlos that he need not limit his thinking to that career field.

His results showed he was suited for other careers that also matched his personality and skills. During their discussion, Carlos talked about his strong desire to do work that would help to improve the local community and make it a more attractive place for people to live and work. He also said that he really thought he would enjoy learning more about the law, how cases were prepared and presented, and how legal decisions were made. His counselor asked Carlos if he had ever considered being a lawyer. Carlos was surprised by the suggestion at first. He later did not rule out the possibility as a long-term career goal. His counselor advised him to get started as a paralegal and use that experience to further develop his verbal presentation skills, legal knowledge, and ability to persuade and influence others. Carlos would also need to practice being firm and decisive in his professional dealings with others. He was now convinced that his career choice as a paralegal was the right decision and that someday he might consider other career paths that maximized his professional skills and interest in the law.

Discussion Questions

1. What personal values influenced Carlos's career choice?
2. In what areas did Carlos need to improve if he wanted to consider a career as a lawyer? Do you believe that these are areas he could improve in through experience as a paralegal? Why or why not?
3. Do you think that your values, interests, and personality or your skills will determine your long-term career path?

 ## 2.1 UNDERSTANDING YOURSELF

Knowing what you enjoy doing, how you like to spend your free time, or what motivates you to accomplish your goals is part of understanding who you are. As you consider what your values are, what interests you, and what some of your personality traits are, you can begin to build your own career profile which will help you market yourself to employers during your job search. Adding a list of your workplace skills and your education and experience will ensure your career profile is complete. You will find the information about yourself that you keep in your career profile to be helpful when you prepare to network, write your resume, promote yourself during an interview, or decide whether a job offer is a good match for you.

NOTES	My Career Profile

My values
My interests
My personality traits
My skills

2.2 YOUR VALUES

Your values are the standards you choose to live by. Your values affect most of the choices you make every day. The sum total of your personal values or standards make up your value system. Values themselves are not right or wrong. What is an acceptable choice for one person may be unacceptable for you because of your value system. For example, one person may feel little or no obligation to spend time helping others through some sort of community work. For you, community service may be very important because one of the standards you have set for yourself is helping others. The following are some examples of values:

- Time with family
- Financial reward
- Community service
- Professional position
- Personal relationships
- Social status

One way to identify your values is to ask yourself, What is important in my life? The answer may tell you a lot about the values you have. The examples listed may reflect some of your values. There are probably some you would like to add or subtract from the list. Knowing what is important to you makes you aware of your own value system.

ACTIVITY 2.1

Choosing Values

Values affect most of the choices we make every day. The career you choose should be compatible with your values. The following words describe some common values. From the list, select 10 that are most important to you and then rank them 1 to 10, with 1 being the most important:

Values	Most Important	Rank (1 = most important)
Making a difference		
Integrity		
Fairness		
Caring		
Reputation		
Individuality		
Service		
Power		
Openness		
Diversity		
Justice		
Commitment		
Equality		
Teamwork		
Independence		
Respect		

Achievement		
Contribution		
Professionalism		
Wealth		
Authority		
Membership		

VALUES AND YOUR CAREER CHOICE

Your values can influence your career choices in many ways. For example, if you value independence and individuality, you may decide to work with a small, entrepreneurial company where you might have more freedom to work in a less structured environment. If you value teamwork and diversity, you may be better suited for a larger company. You can also choose companies in your job search that match your values. Service to the community or diversity are two examples of company values that might match your own personal values.

Not only do your values influence the type of company you may choose, but they can also influence your choice of job. If you value nights and weekends with your family, you will probably require a job that does not include much overtime or weekend work. Frequent travel may be something you prefer to avoid. If your job choice is to be a loan officer in a bank, you will generally find spending time with your family will be possible because this job generally has a standard work week and little, if any, travel.

Try not to make a career choice that conflicts with your values. For example, if you are considering a career in sales, you may need to travel and work some nights and weekends. Perhaps if you rethink what is important to you, you may realize that time with your family, rather than a standard schedule, is what really counts and that good planning gives you the free time you want while you pursue a sales career.

Progress Check Questions

1. How do you think your values affect your career choice?
2. Do you think your values will change at different stages of your life and career? Why or why not?

Real Life Stories

Laura Murphy

Dissatisfaction with several entry-level positions and work for a car rental company led Laura Murphy to pursue a more rewarding career. She went back to school and obtained an associate degree in nursing. She became a travel nurse and eventually assumed a nursing position at a medical center's high-risk and delivery center. She also worked with new mothers, like herself, to adjust to parenthood.

Laura moved on to work as a full-time school nurse which allows her to spend time with her two children. She believes nursing offers a wide variety of career paths for those seeking a personally rewarding career with many opportunities.[1]

---

[1] T. Riemer Jones, et. al. (2005). "Values-Based Career Moves." *Alpha Phi Quarterly* 117(1). Retrieved August 31, 2009, from www.alphaphi.org/pdfs/Quarterly/2005Winterp.1-10.pdf.

2.3 YOUR INTERESTS

Interests are the activities you choose because you enjoy them. Your interests may lean toward individual or group activities. Most people enjoy some combination of the two. Some of the interests you enjoy the most may become hobbies. Having a variety of interests and hobbies helps you grow and develop, while at the same time, provides a good source of fun and relaxation.

INTERESTS AND YOUR CAREER CHOICE

How you spend your free time says a lot about you—your likes, dislikes, and motivation. This information can provide you with leads to the career that is best for you. For example, if you spend free time as an officer in a club or organization, you may have an interest in a job that puts your leadership skills to work.

ACTIVITY 2.2

Identifying Your Interests and Hobbies

Interests affect most of the choices we make every day. The career you choose should be compatible with your interests. The following words describe some common interests and hobbies. From the list, select 10 that are most important to you and rank them 1 to 10, with 1 being the most important.

Interests/Hobbies	Most Important	Rank (1 = most important)
Computer games		
Photography		
Movies		
Writing a journal		
Cooking		
Traveling		
History		
Exercise/fitness		
Sports		
Reading books		
Listening to music		
Collecting items		
Drawing/sketching		
Painting		
Dancing		
Theater		
Writing		
Playing a musical instrument		

An interest in writing while pursuing a career in culinary arts may mean that you are suited for a career as a food writer. Pay attention to what you enjoy doing, and you may discover interests that apply to a variety of career areas. Career interest inventories can help you find out more about yourself and how your interests relate to different careers, including making matches with occupational groups and specific occupations.

Progress Check Questions

1. How do you think your interests affect your career choice?
2. Do you think the current career you are considering matches your interests?

Real Life Stories

Denzel Washington

The American actor Denzel Washington is an example of a person who launched a successful career based on his longtime interest in acting.

As a camp counselor for the American Boys and Girls Club of America, Denzel had his first experience with acting, appearing in a small theater production for kids. As an adult, his interest in acting did not surface again until he went to college and explored a few different career interests. He started in a premed program and then switched his major to political science. Finally, he decided that neither of these career paths interested him. He then majored in journalism, thinking that he would pursue a writing career. While in college, his acting abilities became apparent after appearing in two student productions. After receiving his degree in journalism, he immediately pursued acting roles that eventually led to his successful acting career. Denzel says that although it took him awhile to discover what he really wanted to do while he was in college, he learned a lot about himself in the process.

"I found what I liked and what I didn't like. I became aware of my own study habits and I eventually found the thing I loved."[2]

Denzel Washington's story demonstrates how your interests can play a major role in your career decisions. His story also demonstrates the importance of learning from the decisions you make along the way, even if they do not turn out to be the final path you take.

NOTES | Values and Interests Tests

DISC profile tests are often used in career planning to assess behavior, personal interests, attitudes, and values. DISC is an assessment tool to help you learn your behavior patterns and to what degree you use each dimension of behavior in a situation. The DISC tests allow you to discover your general behavioral style in regard to four dimensions: dominance, influence, steadiness, and conscientiousness.

DISC profiles can tell you a lot about your own communication style, how you relate to others, and how you might respond to different situations.

DISC profiles evaluate how you respond (according to four behavioral dimensions) to the four *P*'s:

*P*roblems (dominance)

*P*eople (influence)

*P*ace (steadiness)

*P*rocedures (conscientiousness)

DISC testing does not detect right or wrong behaviors; rather, it helps you understand how you instinctually react when confronted with conflict or challenges. DISC attitudes, personal interests, and values reports can help you discover your strengths.

Source: www.discprofile.com.

---

[2] R. Hazell. (October 2000). "Education Is the Pathway for Success in the Mind of Denzel Washington." *The Black Collegian Online.* Retrieved September 1, 2009, from www.black-collegian.com/issues/1stsem00/denzel2000 -1st.shtml.

2.4 YOUR PERSONALITY TRAITS

A personality trait is a distinguishing quality or characteristic that belongs to you. The sum total of your unique personality traits makes up your personality. Developing an effective personality is critical to your career success.

    The career you choose should be compatible with your personality traits.

ACTIVITY 2.3

Identify Your Personality Traits

From the list, select 10 that you think best describe you and then rank them 1 to 10, with 1 being what you consider to be your strongest personality trait. Your strongest personality trait may be either an asset or drawback to your career success.

Personality Traits	Your Strongest	Ranking (1 = your strongest)
Adaptability		
Artistic		
Egotism		
Conformity		
Loyalty		
Objectivity		
Positivism		
Selfishness		
Conventional		
Selflessness		
Honesty		
Extroversion		
Moodiness		
Creativity		
Empathetic		
Enterprising		
Assertiveness		
Social		
Defensiveness		
Aggressiveness		
Risk taking		
Seriousness		
Tolerance		
Investigative		
Passiveness		
Impulsivity		
Realistic		
Persistence		
Confidence		

Progress Check Questions

1. Do you think your strongest personality traits are always an advantage to you? Why or why not?

2. How do you think your personality traits affect your career choice?

Real Life Stories

Lance Armstrong

Lance Armstrong's extraordinary athletic career is an example of how one can draw upon strong personality traits to set ambitious goals and overcome potential obstacles that could prevent achieving those goals.

At age 22, Lance Armstrong became the youngest winner of the World Championships in bicycle road racing. He went on to break a record, winning the Tour de France for seven consecutive years, but every race he competed in did not always result in victory. For example, starting well in his first ever Tour de France, a 21-stage race, he won the eighth stage of the race, but later fell to sixty-second place and eventually pulled out.[3]

He came in last in his first professional event in Spain, rebounding two weeks later to finish second in a World Cup race in Zurich, Switzerland. When he was a runner up at the Tour du Pont, he continued to train hard for the next year's event, which he won. Perhaps his most challenging situation was learning that he had cancer, which he thought would be terminal. After undergoing the rigorous medical procedures he needed to treat his illness, he did not give up his ambition to continue racing.[4] Soon after completing his treatments, he went back to endurance training, cycling five days a week for two to five hours a day.

He attributes his continued success as a racer after overcoming his obstacle with cancer to his focus on continuing to work harder at training and never giving up on his belief that he could return to racing and experience new victories. Lance Armstrong's story is filled with examples of personality traits that helped him stay focused on his goals and achieve success.

ACTIVITY 2.4

Develop Your Personality Traits

List five of the preceding personality traits you would like to develop, and write a goal to develop them.

Example	Plan
Confidence	*I will offer my opinions more often in class even when they are different from those of others.*
1. _____	_____
2. _____	_____
3. _____	_____
4. _____	_____
5. _____	_____

---

[3] "Lance Armstrong Biography." (2009). Retrieved June 27, 2009 from www.biography.com/articles/Lance-Armstrong-9188901.

[4] M. Hitti. (2005). "Inside Lance Armstrong's Remarkable Success." Retrieved June 27, 2009, from www.webmd.com/fitness-exercise/news/20050616/inside-lance-armstrongs-remarkable-success.

PERSONALITY AND YOUR CAREER CHOICE

The best way to understand the connection between your personality and your career choice is to complete an assessment, with the help of a career counselor, to see how closely your choice matches your personality.

The following examples show possible job matches for some personality types.

Artistic   People who like to express themselves through work. These individuals prefer working with forms, design, colors, words, and patterns and mostly dislike structured tasks and rules.

Good Career Choices

Editor

Graphic designer

Drama teacher

Landscape architect

Producer

Conventional   People who prefer rules, procedures, schedules, and instructions and pay attention to detail. These individuals enjoy working with data.

Good Career Choices

Accountant

Actuary

Building inspector

Cost estimator

Financial planner

Technical writer

Enterprising   People who see the big picture are more likely to take risks and enjoy completing projects from beginning to end. These individuals are typically leaders.

Good Career Choices

Advertising sales agent

Financial officer

Management analyst

Program director

Sales representative

Sales manager

Investigative   People who enjoy problem solving, pay attention to detail, and use logic more often than imagination when approaching their work. These individuals usually prefer to work alone.

Good Career Choices

Computer systems analyst

Librarian

Optometrist

Science teacher

Software engineer

Statistician

Realistic People who are hands-on, logical, and results driven. These individuals like finding solutions to problems.

Good Career Choices

Diagnostic medical sonographer

Electrician

Highway patrol pilot

Locksmith

Engineer

Orthodontist

Social People who enjoy working with and helping others. These individuals work well in teams or one-on-one and are usually good communicators.

Good Career Choices

Family practitioner

Personal coach

Personal trainer

Counselor

Community service leader

Teacher

These are just examples of how certain personality traits may match certain types of jobs.

There is a wide range of assessments available to you to help you better understand which careers may best match your personality type. Employers often use these assessments before hiring candidates to match the right person with the right job.

Personality assessments also provide helpful information for your career planning process. Some personality types are better suited for certain careers than others.

While there are certainly exceptions to general patterns, there are many examples of personality types that match well with certain types of jobs.

The Keirsey Temperament Sorter and the Myers-Briggs Type Indicator (MBTI) are two frequently used personality assessments.

Once you complete either assessment you can obtain a report that describes how your results relate to career paths that you might be well suited for. It can be fun to explore how your personality type matches your career interests. More importantly, having this information provides a solid foundation for your career planning and can help you feel more confident as you make your career decisions.

If you decide that you are interested in taking one of these assessments, be sure to work with a qualified professional who can help you through the process of taking the assessment and interpreting your results. Check with your career services department, or an instructor, for guidance on individuals at your school who may be qualified to administer and interpret the assessments. You may also consider working with a private career counselor.

In Chapter 5 you will become aware of career trends and major areas of projected job growth. The *Career Directions Handbook* contains detailed information on career paths and related jobs in a wide range of career fields. You can use the results of your assessment with the information in the *Career Directions Handbook* to research and consider career paths that might best match your personality.

2.5 YOUR SKILLS

Skills are abilities that have been acquired by training or experience. An ability is something you are able to do and is usually innate as opposed to learned. You can learn skills in the classroom, at work, or through a variety of life experiences. As you are career planning and conducting a job search, you will want to focus on assessing how many skills you have developed that are important to employers. The most important workplace skills are technical and transferable or applied skills. Technical skills are the knowledge and capability to perform specific, operational tasks related to a job.

Applied or transferable skills are skills that can be transferred from one job to another. Your transferable skills will enable you to explore a wider variety of career choices and will help you stand out with employers whether you are applying for your first job, changing careers, or interested in career advancement. You should think about transferable skills as the key to career mobility throughout various phases of your career.

It is important to know your technical and applied/transferable skills as you build your career profile. You will refer back to the list of skills you identify for yourself when you write your resume, search for jobs online using key words, and communicate your strengths in an interview or cover letter. Skills may build throughout your career as you acquire more experience. Some skills you will use right away; some you will use in the future.
The following are some examples of technical and applied/transferable skills.

Technical Skills

analyzing	calculating	devising	interpolating	tabulating
assembling	computing	drafting/drawing	operating	taking dictation
auditing	correlating	extrapolating	photocopying	transcribing
balancing	costing	forecasting	programming	typing
bookkeeping	designing	inspecting	repairing	word processing
budgeting				

Transferable/Functional Skills

acknowledging	consolidating	endorsing	obtaining	recommending
administrating	consulting	establishing	organizing	recruiting
advising	contracting	evaluating	persuading	requesting
answering	controlling	executing	planning	responding
anticipating	cooperating	expediting	praising	scheduling
appraising	corroborating	explaining	preparing	selecting
arranging	counseling	facilitating	presenting	selling
assigning	deciding	following-up	prioritizing	summarizing
assuring	defending	improving	problem solving	supporting
authorizing	delegating	initiating	proposing	updating
collaborating	discussing	innovating	questioning	validating
communicating	disseminating	integrating	reassuring	writing
conferring				

21ST CENTURY SKILLS

The results of a study, conducted by four organizations with over 400 employers, provides relevant information about the key skills needed to succeed in the emerging, 21st century workplace. The four organizations that conducted the study include The Conference Board, Corporate Voices for Working Families, Partnership for 21st Century Skills, and the Society for Human Resource Management. The main summary of the findings indicate that, by far, employers rated applied/transferable skills as very important to career success, more than basic knowledge and technical skills. This does not mean the knowledge and technical skills are not important; it rather points to the fact that applied/transferable skills most enable workers to succeed in the global economic playing field in which U.S. companies compete.[5]

[5] The Conference Board. (2009). Retrieved August 31, 2009, from www.conference-board.org/Publications/describes.cfm?id.

FIGURE 2.1

The Partnership for 21st Century Skills

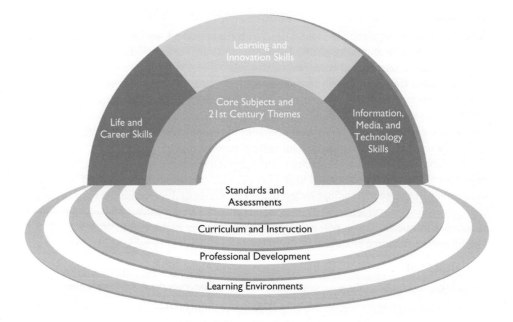

"Our nation's long-term ability to succeed in exporting to the growing global marketplace hinges on the abilities of today's students."
          J. Willard Marriott, Jr., Chairman and CEO, Marriott International, Inc.[6]

NOTES | **21st Century Applied/Transferable Skills**

Critical thinking/problem solving: Exercise sound reasoning and analytical thinking. Use knowledge, facts, and data to solve workplace problems. Apply math and science concepts to problem solving.

Oral communications: Articulate thoughts and ideas clearly. Have public speaking skills.

Written communications: Write memos, letters, and complex technical reports clearly and effectively.

Teamwork/collaboration: Build collaborative relationships with colleagues and customers. Be able to work with diverse teams. Negotiate and manage conflict.

Diversity: Learn from and work collaboratively with individuals representing diverse cultures, races, ages, gender, religions, lifestyles, and viewpoints.

Information technology application: Select and use appropriate technology to accomplish a given task. Apply computing skills to problem solving.

Leadership: Leverage the strengths of others to achieve common goals. Use interpersonal skills to coach and develop others.

Creativity/innovation: Demonstrate creativity and inventiveness at work. Integrate knowledge across different disciplines.

Lifelong learning/self-direction: Be able to continuously acquire new knowledge and skills, monitor one's own learning needs, and learn from one's mistakes.

Professionalism/work ethic: Demonstrate accountability and effective work habits, e.g., punctuality, working productively with others, time management, workload management.

Ethics/social responsibility: Demonstrate integrity and ethical behavior. Act responsibly with the interests of the larger community in mind.

---

[6] Corporate Voices for Working Families. (July 2008). "Tomorrow's Workforce Ready or Not–It's a Choice the Business Community Must Make Now." Retrieved June 20, 2009, from www.cvworkingfamilies.org/system/files/2008WorkforceReadiness-ReadyorNot.pdf.

Emerging Content Areas

Health and wellness choices: Make appropriate choices concerning health and wellness, e.g., nutrition, stress reduction, work-life effectiveness.

Personal financial responsibility: Exercise personal financial responsibility, e.g., balancing a checkbook, budgeting skills, and retirement planning.

Entrepreneurial skills: Use entrepreneurial skills to enhance workplace productivity and create career options.

Economic issues: Understand economic issues and the role of business in the U.S. and global economy.

Globalization: Demonstrate understanding of global markets and the economic and cultural effects of globalization.

Informed citizenship: Participate effectively in community and government as an informed citizen.

Importance of non-English language skills: Use non-English language skills as a tool for understanding other nations, markets, and cultures.

The degree to which you have already developed many of the 21st century skills employers need depends on your age and the amount of experience you have had. Even if you are younger and have limited experience, you will find that you have applied many of the preceding skills to some degree. By completing the inventory of the following skills, you will recognize skills you have applied and target the skills you still need to develop.

ACTIVITY 2.5

21st Century Skills Inventory

From the list of skills provided, give examples of times when you applied one or more applied skills.

Once you have written your examples, choose three to five applied skills you think you still need to develop. You will refer back to this list later in chapter 3 when you practice goal setting for self-improvement.

Skills	Examples of Times When You Applied These Skills
Critical Thinking/Problem Solving	
Exercised sound reasoning and analytical thinking to solve problems	_____
Applied math and science concepts to problem solving	_____
Oral Communication	
Articulated thoughts and ideas clearly and effectively	_____
Demonstrated public speaking skills	_____
Written Communication	
Wrote memos or letters clearly and effectively	_____
Wrote complex technical reports clearly and effectively	_____
Teamwork/Collaboration	
Built collaborative relationships with classmates, colleagues, or customers	_____
Worked with diverse teams	_____
Diversity	
Learned from and worked collaboratively with individuals representing different cultures, races, ages, gender, religions, lifestyles, and viewpoints	_____
Information Technology Application	
Selected and used appropriate technology to accomplish a given task	_____
Applied computing skills to problem solving	_____
Leadership	
Leveraged the strengths of others to achieve common goals	_____
Used interpersonal skills to coach and develop others	_____

Creativity/Innovation

Demonstrated creativity and inventiveness   _____

Integrated knowledge across different disciplines   _____

Lifelong Learning/Self-Direction

Continuously acquire new knowledge and skills   _____

Monitor my own learning needs   _____

Learn from my mistakes   _____

Professionalism/Work Ethic

Demonstrated personal accountability   _____

Demonstrated effective work habits, e.g.,

   Punctuality   _____

   Working productively with others   _____

   Time management   _____

   Workload management   _____

Ethics/Social Responsibility

Demonstrated integrity and ethical behavior   _____

Acted responsibly with the interest of the greater   _____
community in mind

Emerging Content Areas

Health and Wellness Choices

Made appropriate choices concerning health and wellness, e.g.,

   Nutrition   _____

   Exercise   _____

   Stress reduction   _____

   Work-life effectiveness   _____

Personal Financial Responsibility

Exercised personal financial responsibility, e.g.,   _____

   Balancing a checkbook   _____

   Budgeting skills   _____

   Retirement planning   _____

Entrepreneurial Skills

Used entrepreneurial skills to enhance workplace   _____
productivity and create career options

Economic Issues

Understand economic issues and the role of business   _____
in the U.S. and global economy

Globalization

Demonstrated understanding of global markets and the   _____
cultural effects of globalization

Informed Citizenship

Participated effectively in government and community   _____
as an informed citizen

Non-English language skills

Used non-English language skills as a tool for understanding   _____
other nations, markets, and cultures

   Go back and circle three to five of the applied skills and three emerging content areas you think you still need to develop.

21ST CENTURY SKILLS AND YOUR CAREER CHOICE

You may find that you are interested in a career that uses the skills you already have, or you may wish to develop new skills that will set you in a different career direction. For example, if you have good listening skills and interpersonal skills, you may have what it takes to be a front desk manager at a hotel. You may learn specific computer skills for the hotel's reservation system. By combining the skills you already have and the ones you want to develop, you can begin to make yourself a stronger job candidate. If you are unsure about whether you will fit into a career field that interests you, remember there is a wide range of jobs that may suit you within each field.

If you tend to have many hands-on technical skills, such as programming or graphic design, you may enjoy a variety of positions in the technology industry. If you have great social skills, such as working well as a team member or teaching, and prefer using them on a daily basis, you may enjoy a job that focuses more on dealing with people. Within every career field, jobs range from high people orientation to high task orientation. The travel/tourism field is a good example. If you are in a travel/tourism program in school and you find that many of your good skills are interpersonal ones, you will probably enjoy a job as a tour escort, where you are dealing with people a lot. If you find your personal and technical skills to be stronger than your interpersonal skills, you may enjoy a job as a data analyst in the travel industry. The tour escort spends most of his or her time working with the public, individually and in groups, while the data analyst may independently review population trends in a city and write recommendations on whether or not to build a new hotel or restaurant there. Both jobs are in the travel/tourism industry, but each requires a different type of person.

Progress Check Questions

1. Which applied/transferable skills do you think are the most difficult to develop?
2. Which of the emerging content areas do you currently have under your control?

 ## 2.6 EMOTIONAL INTELLIGENCE

Emotional intelligence is your ability to identify, assess, and manage your emotions. An important part of your self-assessment is being aware of how your emotional intelligence impacts your career success. People who manage their emotional intelligence well are better able to work productively in teams, take a logical approach to problem solving, manage stress, and build positive relationships. Emotional intelligence is important to working with and managing a diverse workforce. While your emotional intelligence is influenced by your values, interests, and personality, it is your value system that primarily drives the behavior associated with emotional intelligence.

ACTIVITY 2.6

Understanding Your Emotional Intelligence

Assessing how you think about and react to a variety of situations can help you better understand your own emotional intelligence. Once you have an overall sense of your emotional intelligence, you can work on improving areas you need to develop to enhance your performance in the workplace.
   Provide answers to each of the following questions.

1. How well do I take criticism?

_____

_____

2. How well do I communicate constructive criticism to others?

_____

_____

3. How well do I tolerate uncertainty?

_____

_____

4. Do I control my negative emotions well?

_____

_____

5. Am I open to suggestions from others?

_____

_____

6. Do I see opportunity in difficult situations?

_____

_____

7. Do I demonstrate confidence in most situations?

_____

_____

8. Am I dependable in an emergency?

_____

_____

9. Am I comfortable in most new situations?

_____

_____

10. Do I exercise self-discipline in most aspects of my life?

_____

_____

11. Can I usually control my anger?

_____

_____

12. How well do I deal with disappointment?

_____

_____

13. Am I concerned about disappointing others?

_____

_____

14. Do I think about the long-term consequences of my decisions and/or behavior?

_____

_____

15. Do I consider opinions that differ from mine when making decisions?

_____

_____

MANAGING YOUR EMOTIONAL INTELLIGENCE

Learning to manage your emotional intelligence may require lots of practice because it may require you to change the way you think and react to some situations on a daily basis.

Being aware of what you are feeling and thinking can help you control your emotions. Try to set aside some time each day to think about situations you are dealing with at work or home, and ask yourself the following questions:

What am I thinking right now?

What am I saying to myself?

What am I feeling about the situation? (e.g., am I excited, frustrated, unsure, angry?)

How am I feeling physically? (e.g., tired, hungry?)

By taking a pause before acting on a situation, you can better understand the emotions that might positively or negatively impact your behavior. Once you get into the habit of using this simple technique at the beginning or end of each day, you will become better able to apply this reflective process while you are actually in situations throughout the day which will improve your ability to exercise your emotional intelligence on a regular basis.

Progress Check Questions

1. In what kinds of situations do you need to manage your emotional intelligence the most?
2. Is there a time when your use of emotional intelligence determined a positive outcome for you?

The foundation of a successful career plan and job search is understanding who you are.

We have seen that there are a variety of self-assessment resources that you can use to gain a clearer picture of your likes and dislikes, strengths and weaknesses, and the careers you might best be suited for. By completing a number of activities to learn more about yourself, you have identified key characteristics that you can now use to determine your best career paths. You have seen how matching your values, interests, personality traits, and skills is key to your career success and satisfaction.

Your skills are integral to your ability to perform your job well. By exploring skills that range from technical to applied and transferable, you are better aware of how different types of skills contribute to your career growth. When you develop a wide range of skills, you expand your career choices and prepare yourself for career advancement opportunities and for changing your career, should you decide to do so. You should constantly assess your skills and set goals to improve them or learn new skills to ensure your skills are always relevant to changes in the job market. This is also one of the best ways to recession-proof your career during an unstable economy.

SELF ASSESSMENT AND CAREER DECISION MAKING

Take time to reflect on each of the following items based on the work you have completed in Chapter 2. Make two or three entries in each section that best represent you at the current time. This will be a start of your career profile that you should regularly review and update as your priorities change and you learn new skills. You can refer to your profile throughout various phases of your job search as you prepare your resume or prepare for a job interview.

MY CAREER PROFILE

My career goals: _____

My values: _____

My interests: _____

My personality traits: _____

My skills: _____

Goal Setting and Career Decision Making

After completing this chapter you will:

1   **Develop** your definition of career success

2   **Identify** and write goals for self-improvement

3   **Apply** career decision-making skills

Your career success will largely depend on your ability to reassess yourself on a continuous basis to evaluate your career progress and determine areas you still need to develop. However, simply being aware of areas to develop is not enough to achieve career success. Successful careers are built on setting goals and making effective career decisions on an ongoing basis.

Your goals and decisions need to be directed toward your larger definition of what career success means to you. Career success means something different to everyone. Your personal definition will be influenced by your values, interests, personality traits, and skills. Your age, gender, or ethnicity may also play a role.

Once you personalize your vision of career success, you can set specific goals for self-improvement. The goal of your self-improvement plan should be to close any gaps between your qualifications and employers' expectations. Applying effective career decision-making skills will help keep you on track to reach your goals and achieve success. In this chapter, you will develop your own definition of career success, practice goal setting for self-improvement, and learn a process for making career decisions that you can practice with each career topic in this book now and throughout your career.

CASE STUDY

Derek was always interested in learning more about how Websites are developed and how they have emerged as such a powerful source of communication, education, and promotion throughout the world. While enrolled in a degree program for Web development, Derek spent his free time organizing events and programs to help educate low-income families about how to manage their personal finances. He enjoyed his community service work and often thought about establishing his own nonprofit organization to help educate more communities about how to become more self-sufficient. Derek grew up thinking that he would be a teacher, following in the footsteps of many members of his family.

When he was close to graduation, he interviewed with several companies interested in graduates with his technological background and experience. Before interviewing, Derek decided to speak to a career counselor at his school about how to weigh his strong sense of service with his interest in Web development in his career decision.

His career counselor advised him to take a self-assessment test that might help him find out more about career choices that best fit his values, interests, and personality. Derek scored high in areas that matched a career in the technology field, though he also scored fairly high in some social service career areas. Derek's counselor explained that no career assessment can tell you all the careers for which you are best suited. She also explained that there is not a perfect occupation for everyone and that Derek's first career decision was not a career choice for life. In fact, she explained that most people change jobs five to seven times throughout their lives. Career assessment is a continuous process that does not stop with the first job.

After thinking through his options, he decided to start his career as a Web developer with a Fortune 500 company that offered a competitive salary and an opportunity for Derek to continue his education when he was ready. Part of the company's core values was service to the community. Employees were able to volunteer on behalf of the company, one day per month, with an organization of their choice. Derek decided that his short-term decision made the most sense. He was doing work he loved and was in an environment where he could learn and continue to develop his skills. He knew that by taking this route, he would one day have the financial resources to open his own business if he still wanted to and have enough financial security for his retirement down the road.

Discussion Questions

1. How did Derek's view of success influence his career choice?
2. Do you think Derek made the right choice? Why or why not?
3. Can you describe the career decision making skills Derek applied?

3.1 YOUR DEFINITION OF CAREER SUCCESS

Your career plan will be built on your personal definition of career success. Now that you have thought about your own values, interests, personality traits, and skills, you can better describe what career success means to you.

Over the years, your view of career success changes. Talk with some successful people, and ask them what their definition of career success was when they first started their careers. They might say something like:

"I'd like to be earning six figures at age 40."
"I'd prefer to work independently, owning my own business."
"I'd want to be able to afford a second home to enjoy more leisure time."
"I'd like to be published in my field."

Then ask if that definition of success has changed over the years. In almost all cases, the answer will be yes. People who are more established in their careers will probably give some very different answers. Some examples are:

"I'd like to balance my time with family, friends, and my career."
"I'd like to be challenged in my work."
"I am concerned about the legacy I will leave once I retire."
"I'd enjoy mentoring others to reach their career goals."
"I'd like to be debt free."

The first group of responses tends to focus on achievement, status, and financial success. The second group of responses tends to focus on lifestyle, interesting work, and developing others. To get started, thinking about your own definition of success, think about some factors that influence individual definitions of success. For example, some research has shown that your age, gender, or ethnic background may influence your thinking.

CAREER SUCCESS AND AGE

Different age groups traditionally have varying viewpoints on career success. A look at how different generations think about success might help you develop your own definition of career success now and in the future. Review the basic profiles of four generations and then think about how each differs in their thinking about their career success.

NOTES	Four Generations in Today's Workforce
Millennials/Gen Y	Born after 1980
	Emphasis on family and personal time over career ambition
Gen X	Born between 1965 and 1980
	More concerned about work-life balance
Baby boomers	Born between 1946 and 1964
	Heavy emphasis on work and climbing the corporate ladder
Veterans	Born before 1946
	Work and family never meet

Veterans The career environment for these older workers was characterized by

1. Respect for authority
2. Discipline
3. Laddered career paths
4. Company loyalty

Career success for many in this generation was driven by achievement, status, financial comfort, and climbing the corporate ladder.

Baby Boomers The career environment for this generation is characterized by

1. "Workaholics"
2. Flexibility
3. Achievement
4. Focus on individual priorities

Career success for many baby boomers is driven by work as one's identity, broader interests beyond work, achievement, and choice to climb the corporate ladder or lateral career advancement.

Gen Xers The career environment for this generation is characterized by

1. More work-life balance
2. Less formal work environments
3. Stronger relationships with coworkers
4. Workplace learning

Career success for this generation is driven by quality of life, valuing others, and learning new skills.

Gen Yers   The career environment for this generation is characterized by

1. Autonomy
2. Flexibility
3. Stronger relationships at multiple levels at work
4. Customized career paths

Career success for this generation is driven by work-life balance, contributing to community, specialization, and entrepreneurship. Gen Yers rank their top work priorities as (1) the ability to realize their full potential, (2) working for an ethical organization, (3) performing interesting work, (4) making money, and (5) having good colleagues.

ACTIVITY 3.1

Career Success and Age

> Write down three or four ways you think your age might influence your definition of career success now and in the future.
>
> _____
> _____
> _____
> _____

CAREER SUCCESS AND GENDER

Some men and women think differently about career success. Different priorities about personal values and lifestyle goals seem to be the biggest influences on how men and women might think differently about career success. One study revealed that mid-aged men tend to value achievement and material success higher than life balance or relationships.[1]

One of their major priorities was to live without financial burden. Women valued life balance and relationships more than material success. In fact, only 3 in 20 women mentioned money as part of how they define success for themselves. Some women saw group achievement as more important than individual achievement, and most valued being recognized for what they accomplish at work very highly.[2]

Some of this is changing as more Gen X and Y women care more about income levels and opportunities for career advancement than those in previous generations.

ACTIVITY 3.2

Career Success and Gender

> Write down three to four ways you think your gender might influence your definition of career success now and in the future.
>
> _____
> _____
> _____
> _____

---

[1] L. Dyke and A. Murphy. (September 1, 2006). "How we define success: A qualitative study of what matters most to women and men." Retrieved August 31, 2009, from www.accessmylibrary.com/article-1G1-157839547/we-define-success-qualitative.html.

[2] Ibid.

CAREER SUCCESS AND ETHNICITY

Some studies show that there is a difference between how people with different ethnic backgrounds think about career success. Your ethnic background and experiences can shape how you develop your career goals and envision personal and professional success.[3]

Two main influences are socioeconomic background and your comfort level with seeking help with setting and attaining your goals. For example, some ethnic groups have a greater frequency of individuals with higher socioeconomic backgrounds. This provides those groups the opportunity not to solely focus on the financial aspect of their career and choose work that interests them over work that simply pays more. Financial concerns are not the only factor that influences how different ethnic groups think about career success. Seeking help in setting and achieving career goals is important to career success. Some ethnic groups tend to initiate a request for help from a career counselor or mentor more often than others.

Write down three to four ways you think your ethnic background might influence your definition of career success now and in the future.

_____

_____

_____

_____

ACTIVITY 3.3

Career Success and Ethnicity

CAREER SUCCESS AND CAREER CHOICE

As you decide on the career you will pursue, think about how well it will allow you to meet your individual definition of success. For example, will it provide you the level of financial stability you are looking for? Will promotion eventually require a higher level of education than you are currently pursuing? Will it enable you to satisfactorily maintain your relationships with family and friends? Ultimately, you need to ask yourself if your career choice will allow you to have the overall lifestyle you want. A successful career helps you lead a successful life.

QUALITIES OF SUCCESSFUL PEOPLE

Some qualities of successful people include goal-orientation, positive attitude, risk-taking, enthusiasm, and self-motivation. Successful people share many characteristics. By having goals, they are able to take small successes and use them to build bigger successes in the future. Successful people make the most of their intelligence by drawing on the knowledge they have to solve problems, create and market products, and manage people and systems.

---

[3] K. M. Perrone, W. E. Sedlacek, and C. M. Alexander. (December 2001). "Gender and ethnic differences in goal attainment." *Career Development Quarterly.* Retrieved from http://jobfunctions.bnet.com/?tag=nav; bizLib.

They have and use common sense. They are willing to explore new avenues of information. They are interested and interesting because they read extensively, listen well, and observe what is happening around them. They have ways of preventing disappointments and obstacles from becoming setbacks. Along with a positive attitude comes their ability to trust and believe in oneself and others. Successful people are good risk takers and are willing to accept failure as a learning experience.

Successful attitudes are built on enthusiasm and passion. Enthusiasm is the demonstration of a strong interest in something. It comes from within and has a strong effect on other people. Enthusiasm lends credibility to what you do and results in your own satisfaction. It builds spirit around an idea and is a great foundation for creativity. A fantastic idea that is presented with little enthusiasm can be rejected in favor of another idea that is delivered more enthusiastically.

Successful people are usually highly motivated. Motivation is an inner drive that makes you act on something. Motivation makes you productive and allows you to work well independently. If you are motivated, you have a healthy interest in yourself. Motivation goes hand in hand with a love for what you do. All these qualities of success must come from within. They are in your control. They are not something anyone else can instill in you better than you can instill them in yourself. Above all, success is an attitude. It is your choice to respond to problems as opportunities and to see alternate routes to your goals when others see only a path with a dead end.

Your career plan should include your action plan for developing qualities of successful people.

Real Life Stories

Sonia Sotomayor

President Barack Obama nominated Sonia Sotomayor to the U.S. Supreme Court. She was born of Puerto Rican descent in the Bronx. Sotomayor was raised by her mother after her father died when she was only nine years old. Her father had a third grade education and did not speak English. After her father died, Justice Sotomayor became fluent in English. She was a good student with an excellent attendance record and also worked to support her own education. Justice Sotomayor worked at a retail store and then a hospital. Even though she was accepted to Princeton University, she struggled with her writing and vocabulary skills. She asked for help and worked with a teacher over the summer to improve her skills. This helped her increase her self-confidence.

When she attended law school, Justice Sotomayor was co-chair of a group for Latin, Asian, and Native American students. After law school, she held a variety of positions to build her credentials. Justice Sotomayor often talks about times throughout her career when she was challenged by what she considered to be stereotyping. Some expressed concern about her ability to render objective decisions without the influence of her ethnic background and experiences. She worked to overcome their objections openly by addressing these concerns directly in many of her presentations, ensuring her commitment to bring an objective viewpoint to her work. Justice Sotomayor successfully addressed this question one more time during her confirmation hearings. In 2009, she went on to become the first Hispanic and the third woman to serve as a Supreme Court Justice.

Source: Accessed September 10, 2009 from http://www.whitehouse.gov/the_press_office/Background-on-Judge-Sonia-Sotomayor/.

ACTIVITY 3.4

Your Career Success Statement

Now that you are able to consider how age, gender, ethnicity, and qualities of successful people, may influence your own definition of career success, practice writing your personal career success statement. Because your definition of career success may still be developing and you may not be able to express your thoughts in a single statement, start by practicing two or three different statements that best express your thoughts at this time.

_____

_____

_____

 ## 3.2 SETTING AND WRITING GOALS FOR SELF-IMPROVEMENT

Throughout this self-assessment process, you have identified your own values, interests, personality traits, skills, and ideas of success. You have also reviewed those qualifications that employers prefer when deciding to hire a candidate.

CHARACTERISTICS OF A GOAL

Before setting your goals for self-improvement, you should be aware of the basic characteristics of successful goals. Well-set goals provide the motivation, or drive, to produce top performance on a daily basis. This drive can come from having a clear direction toward something you are passionate about. As you achieve certain milestones, be sure to acknowledge your progress and reevaluate your goals. You will probably find that you are able to set new goals beyond what you originally thought was attainable once you see the results.

Goals are motivational. The way you express your goals can have a lot do with how you feel about them. When goals are expressed by the positive outcome we are anticipating, we are better motivated to work toward the goal. The following example demonstrates how to express your goals with a vision of what the future will look like without emphasizing a current problem.

Desired Outcome	**Emphasis on the Problem**
Having my bills paid every month	Getting out of debt
Building a healthy body	Losing weight

Goals are based on desire and passion. Successful people are passionate about their career goals. To make your goals real to you, you should try to imagine the successful outcome of your work or actions.

A successful chef imagines how the dish being created will look and taste before it is prepared.

A successful athlete imagines winning the game before the game begins.

A successful Web developer imagines the look and functionality of a Website before it is developed.

Imagining success creates an emotional attachment to your goal. Desire and passion are important because they are just what you need to motivate you when you are having difficulty sticking to your goal.

Goals are specific. Your goals should be focused and clearly understood.

Goals are challenging. You should be able to grow, learn, and improve in achieving your goals.

Goals are realistic. Believing your goal is achievable builds commitment to achievement.

Goals are action-driven. Demonstrate specific examples that show how you plan to achieve your goals.

Goals are measurable. Create a plan for measuring your progress along the way.

Goals have milestones. Committing to a time frame for your goals to be accomplished is important to envisioning success.

It is important to know how to write effective goal statements. Writing effective goal statements will help you stay focused on achieving your goals because you will have a more specific road outlined for achieving your goal. Writing effective goal statements is also important when communicating your career goals to prospective employers.

The best way to learn to write effective career goals is to practice writing some using the SMART approach. The SMART approach to writing goals incorporates goals that are specific, measurable, achievable, realistic, and timely.

Before you practice how to write effective goal statements using the SMART approach, it might be useful to review some good goal statements compared to the vague statements that are commonly used.

NOTES | Sample Goal Statements

Vague Goal Statements	SMART Goal Statements
1. I want to save my money.	1. I will save 10 percent of my income to pay for my professional certification test to be taken next spring.
2. I want to be happy with my job.	2. By January, I will have my resume updated with the eight transferable skills from my current job with the goal of having a new job by April.
3. I want to work for a progressive company.	3. I want to work for a company that has customized career paths that will allow me to move to a senior financial analyst's position in five years.
4. I want to find an internship in my field.	4. I want a teaching internship to earn the 13.5 credits I need to qualify me for my student teaching by September.
5. I want to improve my skills.	5. I have registered for a six-week course in public speaking to learn how to present at my first management meeting in 8 weeks.
6. I want a raise.	6. I will ask for an 8 percent increase during my performance review based on the 10 percent increase in sales I led over the last six months.

7. I want to start my own company.

7. My first financial services business will open in January and by June we will have $200,000 in profits.

8. I want work-life balance.

8. My wife and I will dine at home four nights per week and I will play basketball one night a week with my son.

9. I want a job using my education and experience.

9. I only apply for jobs that require an Associates Degree in Health Services and hospital volunteer experience.

10. I want to improve my appearance for my next job interview.

10. I will lose 5 pounds in the next 6 weeks to be better prepared to present a professional appearance during my five interviews scheduled at Career Conference.

Review each of the following general goals. For each of these goals, create a SMART goal statement.

1. I will find a part-time job.

_____

2. I will stick to my budget.

_____

3. I will join a club.

_____

4. I will learn a new language.

_____

5. I will study harder.

_____

6. I will learn to swim.

_____

7. I will win my next race.

_____

8. I will do volunteer work.

_____

9. I will work with my career counselor.

_____

10. I will graduate.

_____

NOTES | **SMART Goals Worksheet**

Goal _____

Today's Date _____ Target Date _____ Start Date _____

Date Achieved _____

*S*pecific: Are your goals focused and clearly understood?

*M*easurable: How will you know when you have reached your goal?

*A*chievable: Is achieving this goal realistic?

Will it take much effort?

Will it take extraordinary commitment?

Do you have the resources to achieve the goal?

If not, how will you get them?

Realistic: Why is this goal important to you?

Timely: When will it be achieved?

ACTIVITY 3.6

Write Three Goals

Using the SMART approach to writing goal statements, practice writing three goals important to you now and three future goals.

Choose from the gaps you identified in values, interests, personality traits, skills, education, or experience and set goals for self-improvement. When you use the SMART method, you will include actionable steps and timetables that describe how you intend to reach your goal. Write three goals important to you now.

1. _____
2. _____
3. _____

Write three future goals.

1. _____
2. _____
3. _____

Making progress toward your goals is an ongoing process. When you think you are getting stuck, take time to evaluate what you perceive as obstacles that could stop you from reaching your goal. There are many reasons why people don't reach their goals. By being aware of some, you can plan not to let any setbacks stop your progress. Some ways to stay on track include the following:

- Break larger goals into manageable chunks.
- Take the first step, and then plan the next step.
- Believe that your goals are nonnegotiable.
- Create a daily routine that you can stick to.
- Fit new goals into your current lifestyle; don't try to change everything.
- Have patience with yourself.
- Don't try to do too much too soon.
- Have a plan to get back on track when setbacks happen.
- Keep your goals at the top of your mind.
- Reassess your goals.

Progress Check Questions

1. How often do you set and review your goals?

2. Can you give an example of when you overcame an obstacle to achieving a goal to use as a future reference when an important goal is difficult to achieve?

3.3 CAREER DECISION-MAKING SKILLS

Developing good career decision-making skills is important because when you take the time to think through your career decisions carefully, you have a greater chance of being more successful and satisfied with your career. By learning the process of making good career decisions you will be able to apply it many times in your career.

Start by better understanding the basics of the decision-making process and then applying that process to decisions about your career. Decision making is the result of a mental process leading to the selection of a course of action among a number of alternatives or choices. The alternatives you choose will be based on your values and preferences. When you follow a good decision-making process, you are better able to decide which alternatives have the greatest probability of success and best fit your goals, values, and lifestyle. It is important to realize that very few, if any, decisions are certain. But a good decision-making process will minimize most uncertainty.

The following discusses two different approaches to consider as good decision-making processes.

APPROACH 1 TO DECISION MAKING

1. Set a goal or reason for the decision.
2. Get the facts.
3. Establish criteria.
4. Develop alternatives.
5. Make the decision.

Prior to beginning any decision-making process, you should review, in your own mind, why the decision you are making is important to you. Most major decisions can have long-term consequences, so you want to make sure that the decision you make is purposeful in your life. For example, the reason for making an important financial decision may be to ensure that you will have enough funds to support yourself in your retirement.

It is important to get as many facts as possible that are important to your decision. You need to take into consideration that the decision-making environment may be such that you don't have all the information you want available to you at the time of your decision. This is when you need to weigh the risk of making the decision with the information you have. For example, if you want to save your money for retirement in a particular type of savings account or investment fund, you probably will not know what the actual value of your money will be over time because you cannot precisely predict the ups and downs of the financial market over the years. You can, however, obtain expert advice on expected trends and make a reasonable decision knowing there will be some uncertainty in the outcome. In this case, you use information to minimize the risk of the outcome of your decision.

It is important to identify any criteria you have for the decision you are making. The criteria are the characteristics or requirements that each alternative must possess to some degree in your opinion. An example of a criteria in your job search might be salary. Some job offers may meet your salary requirement, but not your choice of location or position. Location and position can impact your salary. If you have selected salary as a criteria for your decision on a job offer, then you are deciding to be more flexible with location and the type of position. It does not mean that it is not possible to have all three preferences available to you at the time of your job offer, but it does mean that if all three preferences are not available to you at the time, you will be prepared to base your decision on the salary.

Once you have set your goal and established your criteria, you will be able to explore alternatives that you are willing to consider as you make your decision. The alternatives that you choose should be those that have the greatest possibility for success and best fit your goals, lifestyle, and values. Each alternative will probably have advantages and disadvantages.

Once you think through the possible outcomes of each of your alternatives, you should feel better prepared to make a good decision. Going through this type of decision-making process will increase your confidence in the decisions you make and increase your chances of your decision leading to a successful outcome.

APPROACH 2 TO DECISION MAKING

Another way to approach making your decisions is to ask yourself a series of questions about the decision you are making. By doing so, you create a plan for making the most informed decision you can.

1. What am I trying to decide?

   Example: "I want to decide between applying for a position as a teacher or as a training assistant with a company."

2. What do I need to know?

   Example: "I need to know several things about both positions before I am able to decide including:

   > *Current job market*
   > *Typical level of education required*
   > *How my skills match the job requirements"*

3. Why do I need to know it?

   Example: "I need to know if the job market is better for one job so that I can position myself for a successful outcome of my job search."

4. How will it help me make a more informed decision?

   Example: "By knowing the preferred education for different levels of these positions, I will know whether or not I will need to further my education or need additional training."

5. Why do I need to know it now?

   Example: "I need to know if my skills match those required by the positions now, so that I will know if these are jobs that I qualify for now or will qualify for in the future once I have gained more experience or furthered my education."

6. How can I obtain what I need to know?

   People

   Example: "Are there people that I can observe, interview, or network with to obtain the information I am looking for?"

   Experience

   Example: "Will my internship, community service experience, or part-time job help me learn more about how my education and skills match the job requirements?"

   Research

   Example: "What Websites, trade journals, or professional associations are available to me to find more information?"

7. Who are my best resources for the information I need?

   Example: "Is my teacher, coworker, spouse, parent, career counselor, or current employer the best resource for me right now to discuss the information I need?"

8. Why do I think they are the right resources?

   Example: "My teacher and career counselor can advise me on the best match for my skills and education required. My employer can provide detailed information on career paths for training assistants."

....

Progress Check Questions

1. What do you think is the best career decision you have made to date?

2. What is the next career decision you think you will need to make?

....

Because self-assessment and career planning are continuous processes, you have learned the importance of knowing how to make good career decisions and set career goals periodically. By practicing career decision-making skills you can apply the process over and over again as you need to at any point in your career. You will also find that you write and rewrite your goals as often as you make new career decisions.

You have learned the 21st century skills that employers have identified as important to go beyond the traditional technical and transferable skills to include important life skills such as managing your health and wellness. In Chapter 4, you will explore how to manage these important life skills that are important to both your personal life and your career. For example, you will learn time and stress management skills. You will further build your career profile to include a review of your education and training and your experiences.

GOAL SETTING AND CAREER DECISION MAKING

Based on what you learned about the career decision-making process in this chapter, choose a career decision you are currently trying to make and practice the decision-making process by answering each of the following questions:

1. What am I trying to decide?

_____

_____

2. What do I need to know?

_____

_____

3. Why do I need to know it?

_____

_____

4. How will it help me make a more informed decision?

_____

_____

5. Why do I need to know it now?

_____

_____

6. How can I obtain what I need to know?

_____

_____

People _____

Experience _____

Research _____

7. Who are the best resources for the information I need?

_____

_____

8. Why do I think they are my best resources?

_____

_____

Personal Development

After completing this chapter, you will:

1   **Understand** the importance of good communication skills

2   **Develop** time and stress management techniques

3   **Identify** the importance of personal care and personal appearance

4   **Recognize** the importance of managing your personal finances

This chapter focuses on four areas of development that have a major impact on both your personal and professional success. These include learning to better manage your communication skills and your time, reduce stress, present a professional image, and manage your personal finances. In Chapters 1 and 2, you learned that employers listed these among the critical workplace skills and emerging content areas that they identified in the Partnership for 21st Century Skills report. Of all the applied and transferable skills, good communication skills may be your greatest asset as you develop your career in almost any field you choose. Good time and stress management skills are evidence of effective self-management skills.

Your appearance and overall image tells a lot about you to a prospective employer. Good grooming and appropriate interview and workplace dress are two essential components of your overall image. Knowing what to wear on an interview and how workplace dress may vary by type of industry or geographic region can help you dress appropriately for different situations. Good management of personal finances is important to your career, as well as personal success. Having a personal financial plan helps you evaluate job offers. The financial reputation of job candidates has become increasingly more important to employers who look for evidence of personal responsibility before agreeing to give individuals roles involving authority and decision making within their companies.

All of these self-management skills are the first step to demonstrating a positive image and establishing a good reputation as someone who is reliable, dependable, mature, professional, and serious about their career.

CASE STUDY

Cameron made it a point to be active in extracurricular activities while studying for her degree in criminal justice. She volunteered two days a week at a local agency, worked 25 to 30 hours a week at the mall to earn extra money, and was vice-president of one of the national student organizations on campus. She felt she was on a good path to building experiences that would help her compete for the job she wanted at graduation as a case manager with the local courts.

For the most part her high-energy personality and eagerness to be involved in meaningful work and activities were an asset to her. Cameron believed that the more she did, the better qualified she would be. Although Cameron really was passionate about everything she did, she found that she had difficulty getting things done. Her grades were very good. The one habit Cameron had was to put her studies before her work and other activities. She frequently volunteered for projects at the local agency and with her student organization on campus. Cameron was promoted to assistant store manager, which required her to stay through to the store closing four nights a week.

She began running late for her early morning classes once her work scheduled changed. She had to cut corners on the volunteer and organization projects she was committed to.

Her roommate, Michelle, was also involved in several activities on and off campus, but seemed to get major projects done on time, keep up her grades, and even have a small amount of free time every week for herself. Two nights a week, Michelle had a routine of keeping two hours open in her schedule.

Although she was involved in a lot of things, she spent those four hours a week working on her business plan for her entrepreneurship class. Michelle planned on opening her own catering business after graduation and was using this class project as her actual business plan with the help of her current boss and her teacher. A major part of her project was building a financial plan that would provide her the opportunity to start to make small, regularly scheduled, investments in a retirement account for herself. Michelle's grandparents advised her to do this after retiring and realizing that it was possible that they could outlive their retirement money. While Michelle kept a pretty busy schedule, she decided to hold back from making any extra commitments of her time until she was finished with her business plan.

Discussion Questions

1. How were Cameron and Michelle different from each other?
2. What could Cameron do to better manage her time and still accomplish her work?
3. Was Michelle's business plan realistic? Why or why not?

 ## 4.1 COMMUNICATION SKILLS

Communication skills are at the top of the list of most employer surveys conducted by professional associations each year. Employers require good communication skills because they are the foundation for most levels of job functions. Good communication skills are necessary for positions dealing with the public. You need good communication skills to work in teams and to mentor and lead others. In the workplace, you will be judged by the impression you make with how you communicate. Demonstrating that you are polished, professional, and knowledgeable in your communication builds credibility in you and in your company. Developing good communication skills is an ongoing process that includes formal learning in the classroom and practice through work and life experiences.

In addition, there are some basic steps you can follow to improve various aspects of your verbal and nonverbal communication skills.

VERBAL SKILLS

Verbal skills include speaking skills you use in one-on-one or group conversations, presentation skills, and phone skills.

FIGURE 4.1
Communication Skills

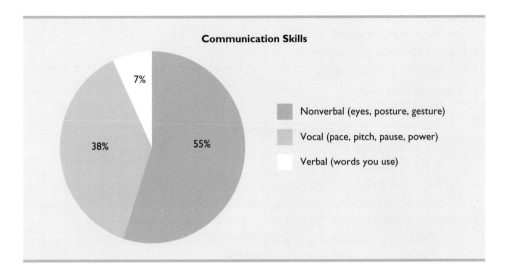

Communication Skills

7%

38%   55%

Nonverbal (eyes, posture, gesture)

Vocal (pace, pitch, pause, power)

Verbal (words you use)

Speaking Skills   The spoken word is a powerful tool for your success in school, at work, and in your personal life. The words you choose and how you sound shape how your message will be received. Try to practice thinking before you speak so that you can be sure of what you want to say and how you want to say it. By pausing to do this first, you will be more confident when you speak and more likely to deliver the message you intend. Being more aware of what you say and how you sound can help you know how you are coming across during a job interview, an oral presentation, or in a one-on-one or group discussion. Factors that may influence how your message is received include how fast you speak (rate), how high or low your voice is (pitch), how positive you sound (tone), and how clear your speech is (articulation). All of these dimensions of speech are learned over time, usually through one or more speech classes or lessons outside the classroom.

They take time to develop. In addition to any formal training, you may find the following basic tips to be helpful when preparing to speak one-on-one, speak in a group, or make a presentation. You can refer back to these speaking skill tips when you learn more about preparing for a successful job interview in Chapter 12.

When speaking, know your audience. Determining the level of formality you should speak with is largely dependent on the makeup of your audience. You may need to be more formal when speaking with those in positions that are senior to yours at work or with people you are meeting for the first time. While you might be less formal with colleagues you have known for some time, and with family and friends, practicing good speaking habits with them will help you develop and maintain effective speaking skills. The following are speaking skills that will help you effectively communicate with others:

- Think before you speak.
- Practice if you are unsure of how you will come across.
- Establish and maintain eye contact.
- Pronounce your words clearly.
- Keep a positive and professional or friendly tone depending on the situation.
- Use proper diction, which means correct and effective choice of words.
- Use proper grammar.
- Expand your vocabulary.
- Speak slowly.

- Avoid using jargon, which is terminology that relates to a specific profession, group, or activity. Examples of jargon related to some groups and professions or activity include:

  Text messaging jargon:

  > BKA = better known as
  >
  > CYM = check your e-mail
  >
  > NMP = not my problem

  Film/television jargon:

  > Talking heads = individuals speaking to the camera instead of each other
  >
  > Two-shot = shot of two people together

  Computer/Internet jargon:

  > FAQ = frequently asked questions
  >
  > MOTD = message of the day

- Do not use other informal language, including slang words or expressions. Examples of common statements using slang words or expressions:

  > "I did not get *good vibes* about the interview."
  >
  > "I was *bent out of shape* when I heard the news."
  >
  > "It was a *no brainer.*"

- Try not to repeat yourself.
- Avoid biased or judgmental statements.

Remember that while you might feel more comfortable using informal language with friends and family, these tips are to help you know how to communicate appropriately in more formal or professional situations at school, work, or other situations requiring knowledge of appropriate speaking skills, such as a job interview.

Progress Check Questions

1. Can you give five examples of situations when you need to be professional in the way you speak with others?

2. If you need to change how you speak in some of these situations to be more professional, what things do you need to change about how you speak now?

ACTIVITY 4.1

Set a SMART Goal to Improve a Speaking Skill

> Think about the preceding list of tips for developing good speaking skills. List two things you think you currently do well.
>
> **Example**
>
> Thinking before you speak
>
> Using a positive and friendly tone
>
> _____
>
> _____
>
> Identify two areas for improvement.
>
> **Example**
>
> Repeating yourself less
>
> Improving your vocabulary
>
> _____
>
> _____

Using the SMART method for writing goals that you learned in Chapter 3, write a goal for one of the two areas you think you need to improve.

Goal: _____

Write how your goal is:

*S*pecific

_____

*M*easurable

_____

*A*chievable

_____

*R*ealistic

_____

*T*imely

_____

Conversation Skills   Good conversation skills are important for many reasons. In the workplace, good conversation skills help you build a rapport with others and demonstrate your knowledge and interests about and beyond your work. Building rapport with others and being a broad thinker makes you a more interesting person for others to be around and can contribute much to your career growth. For example, a nurse with good conversation skills is able to make patients more comfortable if they are stressed. A financial planner may talk with you about the news or encourage you to talk about your interests.

This helps the planner to know more about your values and priorities in an informal way, which will influence the advice given to you and also helps to establish a level of trust that is important for your work together to be successful. Even at informal events at work, company dinners, or sporting events, your ability to converse well with others will help you be noticed.

NOTES | Awareness of the World Around You

Sources of Information

Economic trends	Internet
Job trends	*Wall Street Journal*
Major political events	*USA Today*
Cultural issues in your community	Community groups and organizations
Health-related issues	Professional associations
Bills being voted on that may affect you	Local and national political representative
Cost-of-living trends	Trade journals
Sports-related news	Television
Cultural activities	Social network (movies, plays, events)

To develop good conversation skills you might want to consider the following tips:

- Find out what the other person's interests are.
- Remember something you learned about the person if you have met that person before.
- Give your total attention to the other person you are talking with.
- Let the other person do much of the talking.

- Try not to interrupt or argue with the other person.
- Ask questions.
- Be tactful.
- Be open to different opinions.
- Listen to the news to stay current on current events.
- End conversations on a positive note.

Progress Check Questions

1. Can you think about a recent conversation that you really enjoyed?
2. What did the other person do to make the conversation stand out in your mind?

Telephone Skills   Telephone skills are an important part of business communications because much of your time in your job search, and even in a temporary or part-time job, will be spent on the telephone. Although you are not seen while speaking on the telephone, you are heard and judged by how you handle the call.

Here are some guidelines for making telephone calls:

- Before placing a telephone call, know the name of the person you are calling, his or her title, and the department he or she works in.
- First, identify yourself by giving your name and the reason for your call; then ask to be connected to the party you are calling.
- Always refer to the person you are calling by Mr., Ms., or Mrs. and the last name. If you know that the person has a specific title, such as Dr. or Professor, use it.
- Learn the proper pronunciation of the person's name before calling.
- If you reach your party, greet him or her by the proper name and title, introduce yourself, and state the purpose of your call.

- If you cannot reach your party because he or she is unavailable, leave a message that you called and indicate that you will return the call.
- Ask when would be a good time to do so, and then call back when you said you would.
- Always remain pleasant and professional, even when your frustration level is high. You don't want the message to read that you were rude.

Here are some rules for receiving telephone calls:

- No one should ever be left on hold for more than one minute. The first call always has priority.
- Transferring a call within a company requires thorough knowledge of the organization, of the various divisions' duties and responsibilities, and of the names of key people who will handle the call properly.
- If you are not sure where to transfer the call, put the caller on hold briefly, explaining that you are trying to find the proper source to serve the caller's needs; then find out where the call should go. When you are sure you can make the proper transfer, do so.

- If it's your job to screen calls, remember to do so in a professional manner.

- If you are a secretary, you may help an executive return calls by keeping a neat list of calls at your desk and asking the executive if you can place the return call.

- If you must take a message, politely explain that the party being called is unavailable and that you will be sure that the person gets the message.

It is important to remember that the way you handle yourself on the telephone says a lot about you and reflects an image of the company you represent.

Finally, be aware that taking a good message is an art. The following are elements of a good message:

- Name of the caller (correctly spelled)

- Telephone number, including area code if needed, and extension

- Name of caller's company

- Date and hour of the call

- Your name or initials

- A request to call back immediately, if the call is urgent

- The message

Voice Mail and E-Mail   Today's technology changes the art of message taking to one of message processing through the use of voice mail and e-mail (electronic mail). There are pros and cons for the use of these automated systems for leaving messages. The advantages are that the message sender can be sure the message is delivered exactly the way he or she wants. In both voice mail and e-mail, the recipient gets the sender's actual message rather than an abbreviated version that may come when a secretary or receptionist takes the message over the phone. Also, with voice mail and e-mail, messages can be sent any time of day, without the need to reach someone physically in the office.

The disadvantages are that not everyone is as fervent about reading e-mail as most people are about checking their message slips, especially those who work in an environment that is not technologically advanced. Also, taking down messages on slips usually brings both parties together verbally at some point. With voice mail and e-mail, the two parties may never communicate with each other verbally. This could lead to a feeling of depersonalization in the communication process. Finally, more people may hear or see the message left on voice mail or e-mail, causing the need for the sender to be conscious of the language in and the content of the messages sent.

In all, the benefits of voice mail and e-mail are tremendous. But to ensure their effectiveness, we should adhere to quick response times and professionalism in the way we communicate with either voice mail or e-mail.

More and more employers are monitoring Web and e-mail use among their employees. Many employers are using special software to monitor incoming and outgoing employee e-mails. According to the American Management Association, 60 percent of the 840 businesses it surveyed this year used software to monitor outgoing and incoming e-mail and 27 percent monitored e-mail between employees. One-fourth of the firms terminated employees for violating e-mail policies.

Although electronic modes of communication are becoming popular, they will not replace the human factor completely, nor do they diminish the need for or power of effective telephone skills in the workplace.

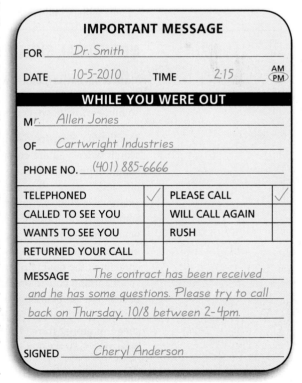

FIGURE 4.2

Sample Telephone Message

Cell Phones and Text Messaging   More people today use mobile phones than PCs for personal and professional business, especially college-age job seekers. How you use your cell phone to communicate during your job search and in other business situations can either help or harm the impression you make on others. For example, using text messaging with an iPhone or Blackberry as part of your job search can be helpful if you know their best use and avoid situations that can detract an employer from you. Asking a network contact for additional names of people that can help you in your job search through text messaging can be an efficient way to build a strong list of network contacts. It is not effective to use text messaging on your phone to actually ask for a networking meeting or interview.

Cell phone etiquette is much different for business than the rules you may or may not use for your personal use. Here are some simple, but important tips for managing the use of your cell phone for business use:

- Your personal greeting should be clear, concise, and professional.
- Be careful not to have music or noise in the background when recording your message.
- When you record your message, don't use a nickname or the same fun and casual message you might leave for personal callers. You may want to consider having two cell phones, one for business and one for personal use, if you can.
- Turn your cell phone off during interviews and meetings. You should also turn it off during meetings at restaurants. Those you are meeting with should feel that they have your uninterrupted attention.
- Use discretion when having cell phone conversations about business or personal topics in public areas. You do not want to provide access to confidential or sensitive information or discussion to any casual listeners.
- Know the state law about cell phone use while driving in different states. Many states ban cell phone use when you are driving.
- Return cell phone calls promptly.

NONVERBAL SKILLS

Nonverbal skills include writing, listening, and your body language. You might consider Internet communications as part of developing your written communication skills since so much of what we communicate is done through the Internet.

Writing Skills   Writing effectively can help you gain a competitive edge in your job search when you are composing letters or resumes or completing a job application. You should think about practice writing samples that you can use during interviews. Throughout your career, almost any job will require you to produce written documents. Some examples include writing meeting minutes, PowerPoint presentations, proposals, executive summaries, performance reviews, business correspondence, training materials, and product or process manuals. People form an impression about you through your writing. Well-organized thoughts and good grammar, spelling, and punctuation show the reader that you care about the quality of your work.

Learning how to produce a wide range of writing requires formal instruction and practice. If you are planning to write for business situations or for your job search, you should focus on producing a professional document that has content that is well organized and stated in proper form. The following tips and examples might be useful as review before preparing your written documents.

Tips for Writing Skills   Plan your content to deliver your message. To get started jot down some words or phrases that begin to define your message. *Ask yourself what you are trying to say.* For example, you might want to tell someone that you are prepared for a new job and for the interview. To get started, you might jot down some of the key thoughts:

- "I am prepared."
- "I have experience from my internship."
- "I have expertise in graphic design."
- "I have a degree qualification."
- "I have proof of what I can do."

Sequence your information by listing key points in order.

- "I studied graphic design, completed a practice project on my internship, and presented a sample of my work on my job interview."

Look to see if there is a flow to the thought process you are using and be sure there are no gaps. Choose a style of writing that suits your personality and the degree of formality needed for the audience.

- *"Dear Mr. Alonso . . . I will bring the same competitive spirit to the ad agency as I do to my weekly basketball game."*

When writing is required as part of your job search, be sure to let your individuality come through. You can be original and still be professional. Stand out with detail.

- Factual: *"I have all the necessary qualifications to work at your company."*
- Professional: *"My education, coupled with my work experience, makes me a well-qualified candidate for the job."*
- Distinctive: *"The leadership award I won in my community service class and the A I received in my communications class make me an excellent choice for your program director's position."*

Practice writing your main ideas and then build the detail.

- *"I had a great experience at your store . . . this is the second time that Kristen knew the exact songs I would want for my iPod and had them preloaded before I arrived at the store."*

Be concise.

- *"I completed my degree in massage therapy in June."*
                    versus
- *"When I started school I was unsure about what degree I would finally decide upon. I decided to study massage therapy and graduated in June with my degree."*

Use proper grammar, spelling, and punctuation. Proofread your work or have someone proofread it for you; use spell check.

- *"I took his advice and the effect was positive."*
                    versus
- *"I had taken his advise and the affect was positive"*

Avoid informal language.

- *"I didn't understand his point."*
                versus
- *"I didn't get it."*

Being conscious of how you can improve the impact of what you write and how you write it is the first step. By practicing the tips in the preceding list each time you are preparing an important document, these steps will become a habit and your writing skills can improve.

E-mails   Just as e-mail is a daily part of your personal life, you use e-mail daily to communicate with your boss, colleagues, clients, or prospective employers. It is important to get off to the right start with good e-mail habits to ensure you portray a professional image and are efficient with your and others' time. Some of the advice you reviewed previously for effective writing applies to e-mail writing as well.

Tips for Business E-mails

- Be clear and concise.
- Start by writing a clear subject. The subject sets the tone for the purpose and content of the e-mail.
- Keep the e-mail short. You can do this by managing the length of the content, using short sentences, and deleting old messages that are part of the e-mail stream if they are no longer important to the current message.
- Use correct spelling and grammar and avoid the use of jargon or slang.
- Limit your e-mails to professional use in the workplace.
- Don't use all-capital letters in the body.
- Proofread before sending.
- Know how to retrieve your e-mail in case you press the send button before your e-mail is ready to go.
- Use a professional tone.
- Address the recipient properly as you would in a formal paper document. Start with Dear Mr., Ms., Mrs., Dr., etc., followed by the name.
- Use a professional e-mail name yourself.
- If you want a fun or unusual e-mail name, set up a separate e-mail account for personal use, if you can.
- Try to avoid using e-mail to deliver bad news.
- Mark e-mails as urgent only in extreme circumstances and not as a routine.
- Use e-mail as one source for communication for important issues backed up with other forms of messaging to ensure important information reaches the recipient.
- You will learn more about e-mail as part of your job correspondence in Chapter 11.

Blogs   Blogs are a useful way to publish and share text on the Web. Blogging is a commonly used form of written communication on the Internet. Blogging requires a specific style of writing. Even though it is a different style, the same rules apply for avoiding the use of slang or jargon to maintain a professional tone.

Blogging is a great tool for communicating in many classroom, workplace, and social situations. You may have been part of a class that used blogging as a tool for journalizing. In this case, a class would be required to complete an assignment by making entries into an online journal. The teacher might have viewing rights and an online response feature so that instructor feedback could be provided along with feedback from classmates.

Blogs in the workplace take many forms. They can be used to post positions, provide training information, and provide company news updates. They are often used as a tool for employees in similar work groups to talk with each other about their work experiences. Blog groups might be organized by those with similar job responsibilities, cultural backgrounds, interests or hobbies or other types of common experiences and interests.

Some company executives have started to use blogs as a way to welcome communication directly from employees. When you research companies as part of your job search, you will find some company information available on blogs in addition to other resources. As with any form of communication, you should use caution when using blogs and not write anything that will create a negative impression about you or your company.

The information you post is made public for anyone to see, even those for whom it is not intended.

There are Websites that provide information on how to write a blog. Some are suggested in the on-line learning center resources for this chapter. Once you begin practicing you should be accustomed to the process within a few weeks.

Think about the above writing skills tips.
List two things you think you currently do well.

Example

Concise writing

Proper use of grammar, punctuation, vocabulary

_____

_____

Identify two areas for improvement.

Example

Less informal language in e-mails

Proofreading

_____

_____

Using the SMART method for writing goals that you learned in Chapter 3, write a goal for one of the two things you need to improve.

Goal: _____

Write how your goal is

Specific _____

Measurable _____

Achievable _____

Realistic _____

Timely _____

Progress Check Questions

1. Can you think of examples of how you might apply writing skills in the career field you are interested in?

2. Are you building samples of your writing skills that you can present to an employer if asked on an interview?

Listening Skills Listening is an important communication skill that is often overlooked. Listening is paying attention to and understanding what someone is saying. A good listener hears the message being conveyed and evaluates the meaning. Good listening is a form of learning because it reveals a knowledge of others. Hearing what is being said but not concentrating on what it means is called passive listening. In contrast, active listening means hearing what is being said and interpreting its meaning as well. Active listening makes you a more effective communicator because you are able to react to what you have heard.

As you are planning your career, you will find active listening to be helpful in many ways. Listening to business and personal acquaintances may lead you to a new contact. Listening to how someone talks about a company can tell you a lot about how the company is run and the morale of the employees.

Good listening includes being able to distinguish important from unimportant information, detect inconsistencies in information, and understand the main points of the message. When parts of a message are unclear, the best thing to do is to take

notes, jot down your questions, and wait until the entire presentation or discussion is finished before asking questions. It may also be appropriate to provide comments about what was presented or to provide feedback on what was said and how it was said. Remember that many times we have difficulty listening to what is being said because we are distracted by things that are bothering us or by things happening in our environment. Another distraction can be our own emotions about what is being presented or about the speaker.

The key to overcoming these distractions is concentration. By developing effective speaking and listening skills, you will become more confident in yourself and more effective in your interaction with others. To develop good listening skills you might want to practice the following tips:

- Make eye contact.
- Listen for the main idea.
- Ask questions.
- Take notes.
- Try to repeat back what you heard to confirm you understood.
- Watch the speaker's body language.
- Appear and be interested.
- Don't interrupt.
- Be open and nonjudgmental.
- Plan your response while the other person is concluding.
- Feel comfortable with silent space.

ACTIVITY 4.3
Active Listening

To understand the importance of active listening, sit across from a partner and, facing each other, prepare to engage in a brief conversation. Decide who will be person A, the listener, and person B, the storyteller. The storyteller should tell a three to four minute story about personal interests, family background, and career plans. The listener will repeat the storyteller's story, including as much detail as possible. To determine how accurate person A's listening skills are, you will both assess how effectively person A listened. Place a check (insert a checkmark) in the boxes that describe the listener's behavior while hearing the story.

LISTENING SKILLS CHECKLIST

The Listener's Self-Evaluation	The Storyteller's Evaluation of the Listener
If you were the listener, check the appropriate boxes below.	If you were the storyteller, check the appropriate boxes below.
I Think I	**I Think Person A**
❑ maintained eye contact	❑ maintained eye contact
❑ was attentive	❑ was attentive
❑ did not interrupt	❑ did not interrupt
❑ nodded to show agreement	❑ showed positive acknowledgment
❑ took appropriate notes	❑ took appropriate notes

When you communicate with others, it is important that they perceive you as a good listener. Very often you may think you have appeared to listen, only to find the speaker has a different perception of how well you listened.

PERCEPTIONS OF ACTIVE LISTENING

After each of you has completed your listening skills checklist, discuss how similar or different your responses were. Discuss with each other the behaviors you agreed on and those you did not agree on. By discussing those you did not agree on, person A can gain a better understanding of how well he or she is perceived to be an active listener.

ASSESSING ACTIVE LISTENING

Even though it is important to appear to be an active listener, the true measure of active listening is how well you can recall and interpret what you heard. Discuss how accurate the listener was in relaying the storyteller's story. Were any key points missing? How much detail was repeated? Did the listener provide any interpretation of observations of body language, facial expressions, gestures, or tone of voice?

Real Life Stories

President Clinton

Bill Clinton, the 41st President of the United States, is well known for his exceptional ability to connect with individuals and audiences through his strong communication skills. His active-listening skills are one of his prominent leadership traits. While there are many examples of his listening skills in his interactions with world leaders, there are also examples of his ability to demonstrate his active-listening skills with reporters.

During a press conference, following the 2006 Leaders in London Conference, a reporter tried to ask President Clinton a question. She could not speak English well and took too much time trying to explain her question. It was obvious that others in the room were frustrated and, because they did not understand her right away, they prejudged her question as unimportant. The conference moderator moved on to the next question. At the end of the press conference, President Clinton asked for the opportunity to respond to her. As it turns out, her question was about families in the developing world and no one, except President Clinton, understood that. The topic was very pertinent to his earlier remarks. Although not apparent at the time, Clinton was concentrating on her question and remained poised during the confusion. By later insisting that he address her individually, he demonstrated to the group that he had a genuine interest in what she said and was able to make her feel that her question was important. His actions provided a leadership example of how active listening can turn a difficult communication into a productive exchange.

Source: Accessed September 4, 2009, from www.easy-strategy.com/art-of-listening.html.

Body Language Body language is a form of nonverbal communication conveyed by certain body movements and expressions. Body language includes your facial expression, poise, posture, and mannerisms. When someone looks at you, certain clues can be detected through your body language as to how you feel or what you may be thinking. Facial expressions can show a variety of emotions. The following are just a few simple illustrations of how you communicate with your face, before any words are spoken.

Poise is your ability to act with ease and grace. When you are poised, you appear self-assured and composed in almost every situation. A poised person appears to be in control of most actions and reactions. Posture is one indicator of poise. Standing or sitting straight or still, without appearing tense or uncomfortable, creates an impression that

Facial Expression	Message to Others
Smile	Acceptance or approval
Frown	Anger, confusion, or disappointment
Wide-open eyes	Interest and confidence
Raised brows	Surprise
Wandering eyes	Boredom or distraction

you are confident about the situation you are in. Think about people you know who are noticeable when entering a room just by the way they hold their body. The way a person carries himself or herself indicates that person's level of self-confidence. Poised people can create energy just by walking into a room.

Each of us has certain mannerisms that either add to or detract from our image. Mannerisms are part of our body language and are formed by habits we have developed. They include using your hands a lot when you speak, tapping your foot while you wait or are in a hurry, or rocking back and forth or pacing when standing in front of an audience waiting to make a presentation. While certain mannerisms may have a positive effect, mannerisms like the ones just mentioned may not.

To build body language that makes a positive impression about you, consider the following tips:

- Maintain good posture.
- Maintain good eye contact.
- Nod to show agreement or understanding.
- Use facial expressions to show how you are feeling (smiling, serious, interested, excited).
- Appear to have and take time to listen.
- Appear confident.
- Control nervous habits such as tapping your fingers.
- Be calm.
- Be in control.

Progress Check Questions

1. Can you think of someone you know who takes control of a room as soon as they enter? What does their body language say that makes such a powerful impression?

2. What do you think others would say about your body language in most situations? What does that say about you?

4.2 TIME AND STRESS MANAGEMENT

Demonstrating effective self-management skills is an important first step to building a positive image and a good reputation as someone who is reliable, dependable, mature, professional, and serious about their career.

Time and stress management skills are two examples of important self-management skills. When you manage your time better, you reduce your stress. There are many benefits to learning time and stress management skills, including the ability to be more focused and think clearly, demonstrate that you are able to assume responsibility for yourself and others, and establish work-life balance. Another important benefit is increased productivity.

TIME MANAGEMENT

The first thing most of us think about when we set out to improve our time management skills is starting a plan of actionable items. Most miss the two most important steps: mental and physical preparation. Many people fail to achieve their goal to consistently manage their time because when they become overwhelmed they lose the energy and the motivation to sustain their plan.

ACTIVITY 4.4
Managing Your Time

Look over the following list of activities for the month of May:

At School	On the Job
Term paper	Performance review
Final exams	Proposal deadline
Counseling session	Monthly statements
Oral report	Attending a company function
Graduation	Training for a new job

Either of these scenarios may be familiar to you. If both of them are, chances are you have already had challenges with managing your time. Read each list carefully. Think about how you would accomplish these activities successfully. List a few of the decisions you need to make.

For School	For the Job
Example: Give up one night out a week to work on your Saturday morning assignments.	*Example:* Work to get caught up.

_____   _____

_____   _____

_____   _____

_____   _____

If it were April, what action would you take, knowing your schedule in May?

For School	For the Job
Example: Start term paper research now.	*Example:* Start a list of things to discuss during your performance review

_____   _____

_____   _____

_____   _____

_____   _____

Did these decisions come easily to you? Many people don't practice a decision process to prioritize their tasks; they simply follow a "do whatever comes next" approach. That approach may have worked for you up to now, but what will happen when you receive another important school assignment that must be completed by April 15? When you get sick the second week of May? When your car breaks down on Saturday morning? *Will you still meet your deadlines efficiently?*

Good time management planning is a process that helps you organize your priorities and create an action plan with allocated time for each task, including planned free time so there is still time to complete tasks that become off schedule due to unforeseen circumstances. The following are some tips for developing three techniques for effective time management: develop the right mindset, maintain good physical condition, and create actionable items as part of your plan. You will find the Urgent versus Important Tasks chart (at the end of this subsection) to be a useful tool for making decisions about how to prioritize your tasks based on when they need to be done and how important they are.

Change Your Mindset
- Start with your goal
- Believe you are in control
- Visualize success
- Set priorities
- Build confidence
- Stay focused
  Handle interruptions
  Be proactive
  Be flexible
- Build coping skills
- Make choices
- Be patient
- Celebrate milestones

Stay in Good Physical Condition
- Stay fit
- Sleep
- Eat breakfast
- Take 10 minute breaks
- Know your daily energy patterns
- Do more difficult things at your peak energy time
- Do the things you dislike first

Create Actionable Items
Plan.
- Take a day just to plan
- Plan in manageable chunks
- Evaluate your time—keep a daily time journal, actual vs. planned time to complete
- Prioritize daily, weekly, monthly
- Plan time out each day
- Plan to be early

Organize.
- Handling daily e-mails
  Sort
  Read now
  Handle now
  Handle later
  Read your e-mails at the same time each day
- Clean up your space daily

Create systems.
- Create a to-do list
    Organize your to-do list
    Keep one, not multiple, to-do lists
- Create a calendar
    Organize your outlook calendar
    Keep one, not multiple, calendars
- Create electronic or paper files
    Use a digital assist
- Make choices and decisions
    Say no
    Don't overextend yourself
    Delegate
    Ask for help

The following chart may help you visualize a way to make choices and decisions about the tasks you want to prioritize as part of your time management planning.

Urgent versus Important Tasks

	Important	Not Important
Urgent	1	2
Not Urgent	3	4

Urgent = Urgent tasks are deadline-based without a relation to importance. Here deadlines are often driven by others. Important = How important the task is determines how much time you want to spend on it. Here the quality of the result and the time needed are driven by you.

STRESS MANAGEMENT

Stress is a physical, psychological, or performance-related reaction to internal or external events. Examples of stressful events may include change, health issues, financial debt, or unemployment. Challenges that seem overwhelming to us are a cause of stress. Challenges can range in intensity from school work issues to overcoming a handicap to dealing with the sickness or death of someone close to you.

Financial concerns are one of the major sources of stress for many. Determining ways to afford your education is often first on your mind as a student. Poor health habits can create stress. Lack of proper exercise or diet does not provide proper physical energy or mental alertness needed to resist stress.

Overinvolvement in activities that you cannot handle all at once, even if you enjoy them, can leave you frustrated by your inability to do any of them well. Leaving home to go to college or start a new job are changes that are often stressful. Not connecting with new friends or coworkers can leave you feeling isolated and anxious. The wrong friend can apply pressure for you to be "like everyone else," leaving you the feeling that you won't belong unless you give in to that pressure. When you feel pressured to be someone you are not, you feel stressed. A lack of goals can leave you unsure of where you are headed and anxious about your future. A lack of confidence or personal problems can cause you to withdraw or internalize feelings, creating anxiety or tension. These are some of the potential causes of stress in your daily life.

Symptoms of stress include procrastinating, rushing or skipping meals, having difficulty listening or sleeping, misplacing things, being forgetful, lacking energy, lacking social time, frequently being late, or experiencing stifled creativity.

The results of prolonged stress may include a lack of productivity, depression, sickness, burnout, chronic tiredness, obesity, headaches, and a general lack of enjoyment or enthusiasm.

Being aware of some of the symptoms of stress will help you determine a plan to reduce your stress. Talk with friends, family members, and teachers, as well as counselors and other professionals trained to help you work through the issues causing you stress. Once you have determined the source of your stress, you can take positive steps to help yourself. The following are some tips for taking control of your stress:

- Develop the right mindset
  - Believe you are in control of your stress
  - Be aware of what stresses you have
  - Keeping a daily journal might help you become more aware of what overwhelms you and how you react
- Practice positive self-talk and maintain a positive attitude
- Develop a support system with family, friends, or coworkers
- Take time to relax your mind each day. Reading is a great way to decompress
- Stay in good physical condition
  - Exercise
  - Join a fitness club
  - Develop a walking routine with someone else
  - Participate in your favorite sport
  - Step out of your comfort zone; join a yoga or kick-boxing class
- Healthy eating
  - Eat meals at home more than you eat out
  - When you do eat out, make healthy choices
- Create actionable items
  - Develop a daily schedule
  - Get a part-time job if your financial situation is causing you stress
  - Limit involvement in outside activities to what you can manage
  - Complete one thing at a time
  - Make a list of your support resources and use them when you need to
  - Ask for help when you need
  - Don't quit
  - Don't take yourself too seriously; laugh at yourself more and take more time for fun

Complete one or both of the following two exercises

ACTIVITY 4.5
Stress Awareness

Check your major sources of stress:

❑ Schoolwork

❑ Personal problems

❑ Finances

❑ Lack of goals

❑ Poor health habits

❑ Involvement in too many activities

❑ Lack of friends

❑ Family problems

❑ Others:

_____

_____

_____

List the strategies you will take to reduce each of the stressors you identified:

_____

_____

_____

_____

Your Action Plan

Goal: _____

Start date: _____

Completion date: _____

When your action is complete, you will be able to manage stress previously caused by _____

_____

_____

_____

Think about the preceding tips for improving your time and stress management skills. List two things that you think you currently do well.

Example

Create systems.

Stay fit.

_____

_____

Identify two areas for improvement.

Example

Make choices and decisions.

Celebrate milestones.

_____

_____

Using the SMART method for setting goals you learned in Chapter 3, write a goal statement for one of the two areas in which you think you need to improve.

Goal: _____

Write how your goal is:

Specific _____

Measurable _____

Achievable _____

Realistic _____

Timely _____

ACTIVITY 4.6

Set a SMART Goal to Improve a Time and Stress Management Skill

---

Progress Check Questions

1. How will managing your time be an advantage to you in your career?
2. How will managing your stress be an advantage to you in your career?

4.3   PERSONAL CARE AND PERSONAL APPEARANCE

Your appearance plays a critical role in the impression you make on an employer during your interview. Good grooming and appropriate dress are the keys to a winning appearance on a job interview. Personal grooming, wellness, and professional dress all help you portray your best professional image.

GROOMING

A professional appearance is a statement of confidence. People are more apt to listen to you if you look like you take your job seriously. In general, basic grooming habits are important to your professional credibility no matter what career field you enter. Many employers follow grooming standards set for their industry.

The health care and food service industries are two good examples. These grooming codes exist not only for you to portray a professional image with the public, but also to meet required sanitation and health codes. A winning appearance begins with good grooming.

NOTES | Good Grooming Tips for Interviews

- Hair should be neatly cut and styled; avoid extreme styles or colors (green or orange). Be sure hair color or highlights are subtle.
- Wear light fragrances, if any at all.
- Nails are best kept short to medium length. Use neutral polish and save elaborate nail art for more social and casual occasions.
- Makeup should be worn lightly so that it accentuates your features instead of changing your looks.
- Body art (tattoos) should be covered.
- Body piercings should be limited to one earring per ear. Cover any other body pierces.

An important part of good grooming is paying extra attention to your personal hygiene. The confident smile that you want to show begins with good daily dental care, including freshly brushed teeth and fresh breath. When you shower, fresh, clean fragrances are better than strong fragrances that can be overpowering. There are different opinions about whether beards or mustaches are acceptable for interviews. The answer can vary by industry and company. The general rule is to be clean shaven and remove your facial hair. Women should also take care to be clean shaven to ensure a crisp appearance.

These efforts to create a well-groomed look are all critical to your credibility with a prospective employer. Too many times, job applicants fail to build a well-groomed image by addressing only one area rather than concentrating on the total look. For example, time after time, students have arrived for interviews with a new, well-fitted suit and old or casual shoes or long hair that is not properly maintained. Unless you commit to your whole look, employers may not view you seriously as a professional.

WELLNESS

Proper exercise and diet can help you look and feel brighter, more alert, and more energetic. Diet and exercise are often neglected because of constantly changing work or school schedules. Here are some guidelines for building healthy habits:

- Control total fat and salt intake. It is recommended that total fat intake not exceed 30 percent of caloric intake. Reading food labels can help you be aware of how much fat and salt are in the foods you eat.
- Avoid substance abuse that can result in overuse or misuse of alcoholic beverages, drugs, or tobacco. Overindulgence in any of these substances can seriously impair your health.
- Drink plenty of water. Drinking eight glasses of water per day helps keep the body in balance. If you find eight glasses excessive for you, be sure to incorporate at least five to six glasses of water in your diet per day.
- When dining in a restaurant, you can follow these same healthy guidelines if you choose the right items on the menu. Most restaurants offer a variety of leaner foods

(pasta, chicken, fish, and salads) and a choice of how food is prepared (baked, broiled, poached, steamed, or grilled).

- If you can, exercise moderately every day. You may decide to join a fitness center or a health spa, or you may prefer to develop your own routine, such as walking briskly for 20 minutes per day.

ACTIVITY 4.7

Self-Image Checklist

Whatever you decide needs to be done to make you look or sound better, do it now! Check off what you need to do:

- ❑ Exercise
- ❑ Lose weight
- ❑ Buy a new wardrobe
- ❑ Sit up straight
- ❑ Practice facial expressions in the mirror

- ❑ Smile
- ❑ Walk with more confidence
- ❑ Make more direct eye contact
- ❑ Hear yourself as others do

- ❑ Listen to your voice samples
- ❑ Practice out loud and listen to your progress
- ❑ Change your language (choice of words, organization, and support of your ideas)

STRATEGIES

- ❑ Do it yourself
- ❑ Hire an expert
- ❑ Work with a group

Which strategy will you choose?

_____

INTERVIEW AND WORKPLACE DRESS

Dressing appropriately for an interview and for work today can mean lots of different things. The type of work you do and the work setting define your work dress policies. Most jobs require a professional look appropriate to the job setting. Projecting a good image, no matter what work you do or with whom you interview tells others that you know what is appropriate and have pride in yourself.

NOTES | Choose a Professional Look

"While you should be aware of typical workplace dress in different industries, when you interview, you should go for the professional look. Once you get the job, you can adjust your style to the norm of the company."

NOTES | Workplace Dress by Industry Examples

This is just a sample of how workplace dress may vary by industry:

Uniforms	Health care, food service, hospitality, airline, law enforcement, cosmetology
Casual and Artistic and Business Casual	Outdoor work such as recreation and leisure, tourism, technology, advertising, acting, teaching, retail
Professional	Accounting, financial services, law firms, banking, insurance companies

While you should be aware of typical workplace dress in different industries, when you interview, you should go for the professional look. Once you get the job, you can adjust your style to the norm of the company.

The type of work you do and your work setting define your work situation. Different work situations require different styles of dress. For example, some jobs require uniforms. Most jobs require a professional look appropriate to the job setting—for example, an office, a store, a bank, or a restaurant. Projecting a good image in off-the-job situations is also important.

Uniforms Jobs in many fields of work require uniforms, especially in the health care, technical, food service, and hospitality industries. If your profession requires you to wear a uniform, don't assume that you can be lazy about your professional attire. When uniforms are required for work or the classroom, treat them as you would any other good clothing you would buy. Keep them clean, pressed, and new-looking at all times.

Uniforms should not be an excuse not to have to worry about dressing for work every day. Buy a good number of uniforms to be sure you always have a clean one available. Wear only uniforms that look crisp and clean. Replace a uniform when the fabric or color begins to wear. Wear shoes that are appropriate for the uniform. Do not over-accessorize a uniform with scarves, jewelry, and so on.

Professional Dress You should always strive for a professional look when dressing for an interview. If your profession requires you to wear a uniform or casual clothing, there may be situations when you would dress that way on your interview, but you should do that only if you have information in advance of your interview that this will be acceptable.

Carefully choosing the right clothes for your interview can make you feel more self-confident and tells the employer you care about the image you project for yourself and the company. To help you understand what a professional look is, here are some basic dress rules to follow that seem to be universal for both men and women:

- Choose well-coordinated outfits. This means mixing and matching colors and styles tastefully. For example, if you wear a blazer, wear tailored trousers or a skirt to go with it. You wouldn't wear a casual flared skirt or capri pants with a blazer.
- Suits and dresses are usually worn to conduct business. Don't assume you can dress casually. Even if you are interviewing for a job where you think you will be behind the scenes, you should show an employer you know how to present yourself properly. In fact, by taking that extra step, you may find the employer seeing you as a possible candidate for different jobs than the one you are applying for. If you find out that you don't need to wear a suit on the interview, it is best for women to wear a skirt or dress slacks and for men to wear a sport coat.
- Wear long- or short-sleeved blouses or shirts. Avoid sleeveless tops, unless you intend to keep a jacket over them. Do not wear a tank top.
- Accessorize tastefully with ties, scarves, or jewelry that is not too gaudy or trendy. For example, even though some men may wear earrings, this is not appropriate at an interview. A studded belt that looks really great with your denim jeans is not fitting on an interview.
- Wear closed-toe shoes that are new-looking and well polished.

Sound simple? It's easy to begin a business wardrobe with these basic guidelines. Having a few outfits that will give you a well-put-together, conservative look is essential for everyone. Activity 4.8 lists basic wardrobe items that are important to building your professional look. Determine which items you have or need, and develop an approximate budget to make any purchases.

There may be some jobs, such as a recreation coordinator, in which very casual attire is common because of comfort, safety, or convenience. However, most research shows that the professional look described here is the accepted and most often expected look. When considering your work situation and how you will dress, keep in mind that you should also use good judgment when dressing for company social events—formal or casual. If you are invited to attend a sporting event or a picnic, choose nice, casual clothing. Try to avoid jeans; wear casual slacks instead. Don't wear T-shirts that have writing or pictures on them; wear polo shirts or short-sleeved shirts or blouses instead. You want to portray a neat yet stylish image and avoid any clothing that might make you look cheap or sloppy. When attending more formal social events, such as a holiday party or awards dinner, avoid wearing low-cut or sheer outfits, or any type of dress that may be better suited for a school dance.

All these different work situations require your good judgment when it comes to dress. If you are not sure what is appropriate, observe what other people are wearing or ask ahead of time if there is a preferred dress style for the situation.

Business Casual Some companies have a "casual day" each week or month on which employees are allowed to dress casually. Many employers have adopted a business casual dress as standard policy. High-tech firms, retail stores, social service agencies, and school systems are good examples. While the purpose of business casual dress is to create a more relaxed work environment, guidelines should still be followed. If you know that the company you are interviewing with has a business casual dress code, this does not mean that wearing jeans, sneakers, flip-flops, shorts, old T-shirts, or athletic wear is acceptable. Avoid tight-fitting or extremely short skirts. It is best to wear nice casual slacks or skirts and tops or shirts that are casual but crisp and neat looking. Remember that you are still likely to attend meetings or greet visitors or customers coming into your work area, and it is important for you to maintain a positive image of yourself and the company in these situations.

Grooming and Dress on a Budget Not everyone can spend a lot of money on expensive hair stylists or clothes when preparing for a job interview. You don't have to spend a lot to pull together a great look. Here are some tips:

* Buy discount clothing. There are great outlet stores in most locations or discount stores that sell clothing styles you need for your interviews at affordable prices.
* Check out reputable clothing resale shops.
* Buy one or two outfits. You need one for a first interview and a second one for a second interview. You can wear these outfits, if properly laundered, from interview to interview.

Some cosmetology schools invite the public in for free hair appointments from time to time. If you can take advantage of this kind of opportunity, just be sure to tell the stylist that you need a conservative look for a job interview.

ACTIVITY 4.8
Wardrobe Inventory

Complete the following wardrobe inventory to determine what pieces of business attire you have and what pieces you need, indicating the approximate cost for each. This will help you plan to buy only what you need and budget properly for each purchase.

BASIC WARDROBE CHART

	Women		
	Have	**Need**	**Approximate Cost**
Suits			
Blazers			
Blouses			
Sweaters			

	Have	Need	Approximate Cost
Skirts			
Dresses			
Slacks			
Coats			
Shoes			
Boots			
Handbags			
Belts			
Scarves			
Gloves			
Total			

Men			
	Have	**Need**	**Approximate Cost**
Suits			
Blazers			
Dress Shirts			
Sweaters			
Vests			
Slacks			
Pants			
Coats			
Shoes			
Boots			
Hats			
Belts			
Ties			
Scarves			
Gloves			
Total			

Regional Differences   In different parts of the country, professional dress may vary according to a region's culture or climate. The North and Northeast are generally the most conservative in business dress, reflecting the overall conservative attitude in these areas. The colder climate also influences the selection of colors and fabrics. Colors tend to be darker and fabrics heavier (wool, gabardine, polyester blends). The South is not as conservative but is somewhat more formal in its attitude toward dress. In this warmer climate, colors and fabrics tend to be lighter (cotton, linen, silks).

The hotter climates of the West and Southwest tend to dictate less formal attire and, certainly, lighter fabrics and colors. However, it is important to note some things about this region. Even though the hot climate may be suitable for lighter-weight clothes, it does not give you license to wear low-cut, sheer, or see-through (voile, lace) clothing. These are simply not appropriate at any time in any business setting.

Accessories You can enhance your look by dressing according to your personality and body type. Choose clothes because they complement your figure and not just because they are the latest style. Remember that dark (black, brown, gray) and cool (blue, green) colors minimize size, while light (white, pink, peach) and warm (red, purple, yellow) colors maximize size. Vertical lines in clothes can help you look taller, while horizontal lines can make you look fuller.

Colors and styles can also reflect your personality. Bold colors (red) or combinations of colors (black and white) often depict an outgoing personality. Cooler colors (beige, light blue) might reflect a calmer or quieter personality or mood. Finally, business accessories can enhance your professional style.

Luggage. Discard your outdated and worn bags, and invest in some good luggage.

Briefcase. Regardless of the position you hold, using a briefcase is the best way to transport your paperwork to and from the office. Briefcases are not limited to use by executives; they are a useful and efficient way for almost anyone to keep important information organized.

Leather-bound notebook. These are used for holding notepads, handouts, or calendars when attending meetings, conferences, and workshops, and for keeping daily to-do lists. They look better than a notepad or loose-leaf paper and provide a convenient way to keep papers together.

Calendar. Keep a calendar on your desk, one at home, and one in your pocket or handbag. There will be many times you will not be in your work area when you are asked if you are available, and it is very frustrating not to be able to check your schedule immediately. Keeping a calendar at home that records your business schedule is extremely helpful when starting a new week or day.

Watch. Wear a watch so you can be on time. Punctuality is an important habit to develop.

Personalized stationery. Two types of personalized stationery can suit your needs—one for personal correspondence and a different one for business. When you use either kind, your correspondence is more professional.

Subscriptions to trade journals. Useful information about current trends in your career field can be found in trade journals. Make a habit of reading at least one regularly.

These are just a few examples of items that indirectly add to your professional image. These items also make up a terrific gift list for graduation, holiday giving, birthdays, or the start of your first job.

Dress can help you present a positive image of yourself if you choose clothing that is appropriate to your job, the area you live in, and your body type. Dress is a great form of self-expression and can reflect your individuality. How you dress for work can tell a lot about you and help you project confidence and pride in yourself.

 ## 4.4 PERSONAL FINANCES

Your ability to manage your personal finances tells a lot about your priorities, values, self-discipline, and overall ability to manage yourself. While good financial management skills are important to ensuring you have adequate personal financial resources for your lifestyle, they also impact your reputation and your ability to be hired by some companies.

SAVINGS

Having a plan to save money for your future is one of the most important habits you can develop. Establish an automatic deposit from each payroll check to a savings account.

Even small amounts are worth it because it will build over time. You should have a goal not to depend on your savings account for your monthly living expenses if you can.

BUDGETING

People make purchasing decisions they can't afford everyday. Determining how much you can afford to spend once your monthly financial obligations are met is the first step to managing your money well. Include your monthly savings in the calculation as an obligation to yourself. You are probably familiar with the phrase "live within your means." Simply put, don't spend more than you earn and don't rely on credit as the extra money that you don't have. Make choices. Decide what things you can do without. If you really need or want something you can't afford right now, save for it as opposed to buying it on credit. When you learn these basic principles early and practice them regularly, you will become a good manager of your money. Everyone's actual budget dollars vary according to current income levels and the exact amount of your take-home pay. Similarly, everyone's expense dollars are not exactly the same. So as you think about preparing your budget you can individualize it according to your situation.

The following sample budget worksheet is one example of how to approach your personal budgeting:

Type of Expense

- Household: a mortgage, lease or rent, taxes, and insurance
- Transportation: car loans, gas, insurance, maintenance, parking or tolls, commuter passes, and rail cards
- Debt: credit cards, student loans, and other types of loans
- Food: Grocery items including toiletries and other items used daily; restaurant or take-out food
- Household: energy, phone, and cable bills
- Savings: for something short term, like a vacation, or something long term, like retirement
- All others: clothing, charities, child or elder care, routine medical expenses, and miscellaneous monthly expenses

ACTIVITY 4.9

Your Budget Worksheet

To calculate the dollar amount of your expenses each pay period, enter in the amount of your total take-home pay per pay period and multiply it by the recommended percent allocated to each major expense item.

Your Total Take-Home Pay per Pay Period = $_____	% × Your Total Take-Home Pay per Pay Period	Total Dollars per Pay Period
Housing	30% × $ _____ =	
Transportation	18% × $ _____ =	
Debt	10% × $ _____ =	
Food	14% × $ _____ =	

Household	7% × $ _____	=
Savings	10% × $ _____	=
All other	11% × $ _____	=

Now, write in and calculate your approximate monthly and annual itemized expenses.

	Monthly Total	**Annual Total**
Housing		
Mortgage, lease, or rent		
Taxes		
Insurance		
Transportation		
Car loan		
Gas		
Car insurance		
Maintenance		
Parking/tolls		
Commuter pass		
Rail card		
Debt		
Credit card		
School loans		
Food and groceries		
Household		
Phone		
Cable		
Energy		
Savings		
Vacation		
Purchases		
Retirement		
Everything else Clothing		
Charity		
Child or elder care		
Miscellaneous monthly expenses		

DEBT MANAGEMENT

Most debt can and should be avoided. There is such a thing as good and bad debt. For example, your student loans are an example of good debt because when you graduate there is a return on your investment. We saw in Chapter 1 the incremental increases in life-time earnings related to degree attainment. Because your earning potential is significantly

enhanced by earning your degree, your choice to borrow money to fund your education is a good, long-term investment. Credit card debt, if not managed properly, is an example of bad debt.[1]

CREDIT SCORES

There is a double risk to you associated with credit card debt. The first is the financial threat posed to you if the debt is maintained over a long period of time. The second is your reputation. Your credit rating is a publicly held record that can be accessed by anyone who might be loaning you money. A poor credit rating can impact many aspects of your life. It can stop you from receiving education loans, a home mortgage, a cell phone account, or a car loan. More importantly, it damages your reputation for a long time.

Employers often conduct background checks, which include inquiries about a candidate's credit rating. Employers check credit scores for a variety of reasons. The way you manage your credit can be an indicator of your honesty and character. For example, banks and investment firms and other companies that require handling large sums of money view poor credit as a risk for theft. How you manage your personal finances tells what type of person you are. Because your credit profile also contains your employment history, employers may use it as a way to verify your previous employment. On the other hand a good credit score can work in your favor.

There are simple steps you can take to manage your debt. Maintain a checking account and try to pay everything you can from that account on a monthly basis. If you need to have a credit card, have only one. It is so easy to be tempted to apply for more cards because there are always great promotions to tempt you to open a new card. Better

FIGURE 4.3

Types of Debt by Generation

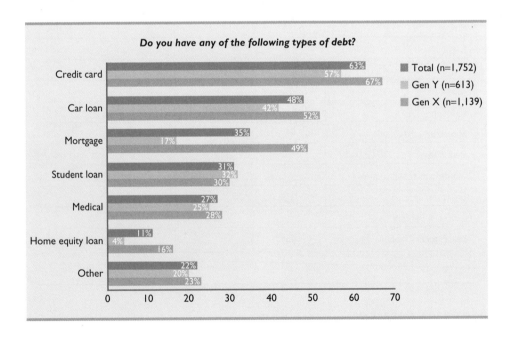

Do you have any of the following types of debt?

Total (n=1,752)
Gen Y (n=613)
Gen X (n=1,139)

Type	Total	Gen Y	Gen X
Credit card	63%	57%	67%
Car loan	48%	42%	52%
Mortgage	35%	17%	49%
Student loan	31%	32%	30%
Medical	27%	25%	28%
Home equity loan	11%	4%	16%
Other	22%	20%	23%

[1] American Savings Education Council and AARP. (March 2008). Preparing for Their Future: A Look at the Financial State of Gen X and Gen Y. Retrieved September 1, 2009, from www.choosetosave.org/pdf/preparing.pdf.

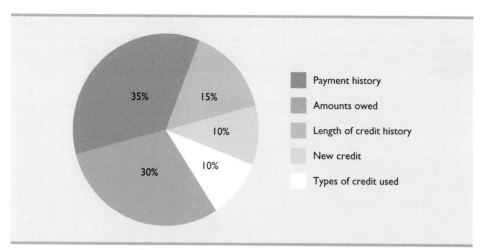

FIGURE 4.4

How Your FICO Credit Score Is Calculated

than a credit card is a debit card. The debit card enables you to draw money or to have the cost of a purchase charged directly to your bank account. It is used as an alternative method to paying cash. Using a debit card is the safest way to manage your spending as long as you are able to limit your spending to the amount available to you. Credit and debit cards and checking accounts are not a threat to your financial reputation if you use them properly.

Your Credit Score   The following chart explains what makes up your credit score. You need to be aware of the areas that can impact your score negatively or positively to be able to manage them. The myFICO.com Website is a comprehensive Website that provides useful information about credit scores and related credit management topics.[2]

Planning for Your Future   It is not a surprise that interest in retirement savings grows with your age. It's hard to think about yourself being in your sixties when you are in your twenties or thirties and even your forties.

But while you are in the process of committing to good personal budget practice, you should really become more aware of the benefits of retirement savings, even if you save only small amounts.

Some people avoid getting started because the need just seems too far in the future or because the process seems complicated. As you get started, be aware that there are three common sources of income for retirement.

- Private savings or investments, which include individual retirement accounts (IRAs).
- Employer-sponsored retirement plans, which include pension plans and 401(k)s.
- Social Security benefits.

Here is an example of how to go about thinking about what you should save for retirement. If you are in your twenties and plan to retire in your mid to late sixties, you should think about preparing a retirement plan that will cover at least 20 years. Once you make the decision to save for retirement, you should consider saving about 10 percent of your pay annually. You should plan on roughly 80 percent of your annual working pay during your retirement.

[2] MyFICO.com. (2009). Retrieved August 31, 2009, from www.myfico.com/Default.aspx.

It's important to just get started if you haven't already. You can always adjust your plan if your circumstances change. Once you get into the habit of saving your money, you will get used to living without it now and you will surely be pleased to have it available when you need it.

ACTIVITY 4.10

Set a SMART goal for Improving Personal Finance Skills

Think about the preceding personal finance skills.
List two things you think you currently do well.

Example

Savings

Budgeting

_____

_____

Identify a personal finance goal.

Example

Debt management

Retirement planning

_____

_____

Goal:_____

Write how your goal is:

Specific _____

Measurable _____

Achievable _____

Realistic _____

Timely _____

CHAPTER SUMMARY

Throughout your life and your career, you will continue to develop many important self-management skills. Some you may develop through further education in the classroom. You will also have the opportunity to improve self-management skills by participating in workshops or seminars. Perhaps the most effective way to ensure your continuous development of these important skills is by practicing them in your daily home, work, and social life. It takes repetition to form habits that can result in the behavioral changes you want to make.

This chapter focused on the importance of self-improvement in communication, time and stress management, presenting a professional image, and managing personal finances through the use of goal setting. By applying the goal-setting method you learned in Chapter 3, you gained practice in how to set self-improvement goals. You should now be aware of more aspects of both verbal and nonverbal communication, and what particular skills in each area you think you need to work on. Managing time and stress are critical to success in your career and your life. Not enough people really take the time to develop a plan that they can stick with to overcome problems with managing their time and their stress. Not having these two areas under your control can be damaging to your career and your health. Time and stress management are closely connected. When you are successfully managing your time, you will probably be less stressed. When you are stressed, it can interfere with your ability to stay focused on your time management plan. Keeping physically fit can help a great deal in both of these areas. Many of the same techniques for managing your time also apply to managing your stress.

Presenting a good image by practicing good grooming habits and dressing appropriately for job search and workplace situations will ensure you make a positive impression with employers and may help them see you as a serious job candidate.

While managing personal finances has always been a critical life and career skill, its importance has been made more prominent in recent years in light of an unstable economy that impacts personal finances. Knowing how to manage your personal finances is important to many aspects of your life. Being financially responsible for your personal money reflects positively on your reputation and sets the stage for you to better manage your future financial needs as you get older. A big key to managing your personal finances well is staying out of debt. Debt can burden you for a long time and negatively impact many aspects of your life and your well being. The next key is to plan for the future. If you are young, you may think that planning for your retirement can wait. It can, but the longer you wait to start, the less chance you will have to catch up on those missed savings that could diminish your financial potential later in life.

You will probably find these three areas to be a focus of some of your interview questions when you apply for a job. As employers told us in the Partnership for 21st Century Skills report, these are among the critical self-management skills necessary for career success. Taking control of these areas and managing them well should be your goal.

. . . .

PERSONAL DEVELOPMENT AND CAREER DECISION MAKING

Using the decision-making process you learned in Chapter 3, complete the following questions to better understand how communication skills, time and stress management skills, good grooming and dress skills, and personal finance skills might be connected to your career decisions.
What am I trying to decide?

Example: I am trying to decide how to better balance my time at work, home, and school.

Example: I am trying to decide whether or not I can afford a mortgage or if renting is a better
option for me right now.

_____

_____

_____

What do I need to know?

Example: I need to know how I am currently spending my time, what amount of time I consider to
be appropriate, and what distracts me from managing my time.

Example: I need to know what my monthly expenses are compared to my income.

_____

_____

_____

Why do I need to know it?

Example: I need to know where I am having specific problems with my time to know what actions
to take.

Example: I need to know which option is better so that I can avoid overextending myself
financially.

_____

_____

_____

REFLECTION EXERCISE

How will it help me make a more informed career decision?

Example: By better managing my time I can choose jobs that match the amount of time I can or want to dedicate to my career.

Example: I can consider whether the current salary I am earning now supports my decision or whether I need to consider a higher-paying job in the future.

_____

_____

_____

Why do I need to know it now?

Example: As I prepare to explore career paths and set career goals, this will be one of the criteria I will consider.

Example: I need to make my decision based on what I can afford now, as opposed to what I may be able to afford in the future. My goal is to not to spend more than I can afford or get into debt that I cannot manage.

_____

_____

_____

How can I obtain what I need to know?

People

Example: My teachers, the training coordinator at my company, a friend, a family member.

Example: My math or finance teacher, a customer service person at my bank, my parents or spouse, a financial advisor.

_____

_____

_____

Experience

Example: A workshop on time management can help me improve my time management skills.

Example: Calculating my current budget and the budget I need to afford a mortgage will tell me if I can meet all of my financial obligations if I am responsible for a mortgage.

_____

_____

_____

Research

Example: I can explore online resources that provide useful advice on time management.

Example: I can explore online resources that provide useful information on budgeting for and financing a mortgage.

_____

_____

_____

Who are my best resources for the information I need?

Example: My teachers and my training coordinator at work.

Example: The customer service person at my bank would be the best resource or one of my math or finance teachers.

_____

_____

_____

Why do you think they are the right resource?

Example: My training coordinator might be able to recommend a Time Management Workshop or adjust my work schedule.

Example: A professional advisor can help me develop a financial plan and friends and family can help me commit to it.

_____

_____

_____

Now that you have practiced reflecting on what you learned in Chapter 4 and seeing how to apply it in your career decision-making process, using examples, you will be able to repeat this process on your own in future chapters. You are on your way to further developing how to apply career decision-making skills, which are transferable skills that you will apply throughout your career.

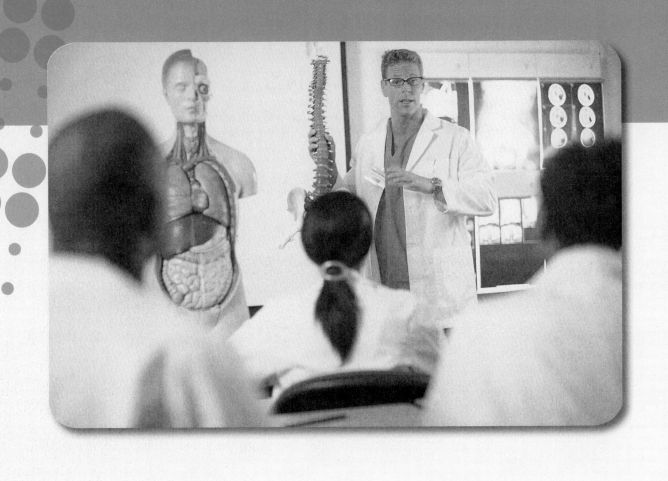

Career Paths Overview

After completing this chapter, you will:

1   **Explain** the difference between a job and a career

2   **Explore** career trends and growing career fields

3   **Describe** types of career paths

4   **Prepare** a career path inventory

5   **Recognize** the different sectors where you can find jobs

Being aware of different types of jobs and careers is an important first step to considering your own career options. The career path you select to start your career isn't necessarily one you will follow for the rest of your life. You may discover new career interests and opportunities as you gain experience in a particular job or industry. When you choose your career path, you will see how you will put your education to work and better understand what jobs and other experiences will help you reach your goal. Establishing your career path allows you to see your career as a progression of many different career experiences. A career path is a way of identifying both your ultimate career goal and the set of jobs you may need to succeed in before reaching that goal. It is important to have realistic expectations about the level of job you start with. When you have a career direction, it helps you value your early experiences more because you can see how they fit into the larger picture of your overall career plan.

In this chapter you will learn how to plan steps in your career by looking at differences between a job and a career; types of career paths; and growing career fields including employment opportunities in private, public, and international sectors. You will explore career paths that will help you write career goals that will guide your job search and career planning.

CASE STUDY

Mikayla graduated from the local cosmetology academy and began working right after graduation as a nail technician. She left her job as a promotions coordinator at the nearby civic center to pursue the career she was really interested in. She worked at a full-service salon with opportunities to provide other services including massage therapy, hair styling, and skin care treatments. When she was in school, she did so well with her program that her teachers recommended that she join the teaching staff some day after getting some work experience. Mikayla took pride in providing a personal service for others that was satisfying to her clients and rewarding to her. She thought about becoming an instructor. She was also curious about what it would be like to manage her own salon. After talking with some of her teachers and her salon manager, she decided the first thing she should do was get more experience in different jobs within the cosmetology profession. Mikayla began to rotate her work at the salon. She increased her experience in hair styling and skin treatments. She also became a licensed massage therapist. Three days a week, she opened and closed the salon for her manager who was ready to go on maternity leave. She worked with sales representatives, managed the staff schedule, and did the weekly banking. When her manager went on maternity leave, she acted as the assistant manager for six weeks. When Mikayla went back to providing services to her clients, she decided to study for a cosmetology instructor's license. She still didn't know if she wanted to teach or manage a salon operation, but through her experience and training, Mikayla had created options to pursue whichever career path she chose. After a few years, she went on to work for a chain of salons, starting as a trainer, and eventually became the director of the chain. Mikayla's career path was not always clear to her. By weaving her way through many different experiences within her field, she created more opportunities for herself than she might have had if she pursued a straight path to teaching or management. Her job was a perfect fit for Mikayla because she was able to advance her career by applying her technical and management skills in a profession that she really loved.

Discussion Questions

1. What resources did Mikayla use to help her make her various career decisions?
2. Do you think Mikayla made the right choice to pursue a management career path instead of teaching? Why or why not?
3. Can you think of any other career options for Mikayla using her skills and experience?

 5.1 JOB VERSUS CAREER

Many people have difficulty understanding the difference between a job and a career. Since it is an important part of making good career decisions, you should take some time to review your own thoughts about the relationship between jobs and careers and what it means to you.

Generally, a job can be a distinct period of employment, not necessarily related to a previous or future job. A career is made up of a path of jobs that are usually related. A career is a planned, logical progression of jobs within one or more professions that can span the majority of your working life. Your jobs might either take you to a desired, long-term goal or help you build experiences that help modify your original goal. In most cases, a career is a lifelong process that can take you to planned or unexpected experiences that help you fulfill a passion, make a positive contribution to your community, and ensure a comfortable living.

While you are planning your job search, think about what is important to you. While it helps to have a clear goal established, you may still be unsure of the exact career path you would like to pursue. Your job choice can help you "test run" your career preferences and help you decide what is right for you. Whether you prefer to pursue a career or a job is a personal decision that you make. Your choice really depends on what your view of work is for yourself. One is not more valid than the other. Initially, you might accept a job to gain needed financial income or experience. Over the long term, you should maximize the value of your education by identifying a career path that will challenge you and help you grow over your years of work. For many, work and personal life become closely intertwined as shown in figure 5.1. The following activity may help you better understand your own views on what a job or career might mean to you.

ACTIVITY 5.1

**The Difference Between
Jobs and Careers**

Using the following information, discuss your current views on what work means to you.

Job	versus	Career
Income for financial goals		Focus on passion and interests
Talents and skills not always aligned with job		Closely matches talents and skills
Little or no planning		Requires routine planning
Educational requirements not always needed		Applies education
Experience not always needed		Applies experience
Routine		Flexibility
Stability		Risk
Security		Opportunity
Work-to-live philosophy		Live-to-work philosophy
Need to do		Want to do
Less satisfying over time		Satisfaction is key
Little long-term attachment		Long-term attachment
Lifestyle defines work environment choices		Work and lifestyle intertwined
		Work as part of life

This activity can be a helpful tool to get you started thinking about how you feel about your own work philosophy. Being aware of this is important to decisions you make about your choice of jobs or careers. If you are interested in exploring more about this topic and how it relates to your career decisions, scheduling an appointment with someone in your career services center or an outside service that specializes in career counseling might be helpful.

Progress Check Questions

1. Do you think your current views of work might change in the future? Why or why not?
2. Do you think a job or a career best describes your current thoughts about what work means to you? Why or why not?

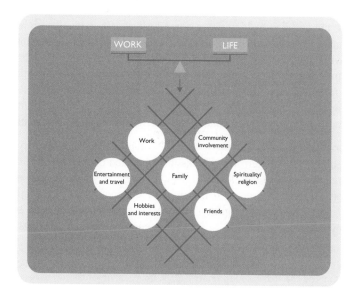

FIGURE 5.1

Work as Part of Life

5.2 CAREER TRENDS

The Bureau of Labor Statistics' *Occupational Outlook Handbook* provides information to help you understand career trends, including the fastest-growing career areas for job growth. Service-producing industries are expected to account for 15.7 million new wages and salary jobs generated through the year 2016.

NOTES | **Growing Industries Through 2016**

- Among all occupations in the economy, computer and health care occupations are expected to grow the fastest.
- Personal care services, which include home health care, will be among the fastest-growing industries, with growth expected at 51 percent.
- The information sector is expected to grow by 6.9 percent, with a gain of almost 212,000 new jobs:
  - Software publishing employment will grow by 32 percent.
  - Internet publishing and broadcasting employment will grow by 41.1 percent.
  - Wireless publishing and broadcasting employment will grow by 40.9 percent.
- Computer systems design and related services will increase by 38.3 percent.
- Health care and social assistance will grow by 24.5 percent.
- Accountants, auditors, and management analysts will constitute more than 381,000 new jobs combined, expecting to grow by 17.7 percent.
- Financial services employment is projected to grow by 14.4 percent.
- Leisure and hospitality careers will grow by 14.3 percent.
- Accommodations and food services will grow by 11.4 percent.
- Private and public educational services will grow by 10 percent and add 1 million new jobs.
- Office and administrative support positions will grow by 7.2 percent.
- Government employment is expected to grow by 4.8 percent.
- Retail jobs will increase 4.5 percent to between 15 million and 16 million new jobs.
- Sales and related professional positions will grow by 1.2 million new jobs, or by 7.6 percent.
- Trade, transportation, and utilities will grow by 6 percent.[1]

GROWING CAREER FIELDS

Accounting Career opportunities in accounting usually remain high regardless of the state of the economy. The advice that accountants provide is often the most important information for the decision-making process in a business. Individuals also rely on the best financial assistance to make well-informed decisions regarding their investments. The fastest-growing jobs within the accounting field include consultants and credit specialists. Consulting services are aimed at assisting companies in applying the factual information they have about their finances to an effective business decision. The need for credit specialists is growing because of the problems plaguing the credit and loan industry. Public accountants, management accountants, government accountants, and internal auditors are always in demand.

Computer Security Specialists Potential threats to security in the United States remain high since the terrorist attacks that occurred on September 11, 2001. These attacks renewed the cyberterror fear around the globe. Cyberterrorism is the convergence of terrorism and cyberspace. It is generally understood to mean unlawful attacks and threats of attacks against computers, networks, and the information stored therein. Examples of cyberterrorism include breaking into computer games, stealing personal data

---

[1] U.S. Department of Labor, Bureau of Labor Statistics. (May 13, 2009). Tomorrow's Jobs. *The Occupation Outlook Handbook, 2008–2009 edition.* Retrieved September 1, 2009, from http://www.bls.gov/oco/oco2003.htm.

or trade secrets, vandalizing Websites, disrupting services, sabotaging data and systems, launching company viruses and worms, conducting fraudulent transactions, and harassing individuals and companies.

These acts are facilitated with easy-to-use software offered for free from thousands of Websites on the Internet. Businesses and government continue to invest in cybersecurity, protecting vital computer networks and electronic infrastructure from attack. The result is a steady growth in the number of computer network security jobs.

Customer Service   The customer service representative's job can take on various functions, ranging from resolving customer complaints, to generating new business through new sales, or servicing existing customer accounts. Customer service representatives are key to providing important customer feedback that can help drive business planning.

Education   Rising student enrollments at all levels of education are increasing the demand for a wide variety of educational services. The number of preschool and child care center or program educational administrators will grow the fastest. When the unemployment rate is high, many people return to school to retool their qualifications for new jobs. More people are opting for new professions in growing fields, showing interest in higher degrees, and seeking certifications and further training in different industries.

Employment Services   Among the fastest-growing industries in the United States, employment services will provide the most new jobs. More and more major corporations are choosing to outsource their recruitment functions to employment services. Increasingly complex labor laws are making firms more vulnerable to potential labor disputes. Outsourcing employment services can substantially reduce a company's recruitment cost and overall human resource management overhead. Employment services will continue to be almost two-thirds of all new jobs in administrative and support remediation services.

Entrepreneurship   As many large corporations continue to downsize and restructure, and more small to medium-sized firms emerge, the opportunities for entrepreneurs continue to multiply. Most entrepreneurs own businesses involved in delivering services or creating and manufacturing products. Entrepreneurs must be resourceful to bring the right combination of talent to their businesses.

Financial Services   The need for financial planners continues to grow as the aging population and younger professionals seek advice to maximize their financial resources. The continued growth of finance careers is a result of globalization of the securities market and the number of tax-favorable retirement plans. Employment in credit intermediation-related services (banks) will add about one-half of all new finance jobs.

Food Service   Many factors are influencing the continued growth in food service careers. Educated consumers are choosing healthier menu options for their families. Social trends, ranging from increased obesity and other health-related issues in children, to increased needs for managed food services for the elderly, are influencing nutrition trends in the food service industry.

Celebrity chefs continue to grow in popularity, elevating the appeal of media food service careers in television, radio, the Internet, and publishing. Advances in food technology are creating new career opportunities for food technologists and for professionals in food research and in product and concept development.

Health Care   Health care practitioners include everyone from doctors and nurses to emergency medical technicians, medical assistants, dental assistants, physical therapists, and health care administrators. The demand for health care professionals to provide services to private hospitals, nursing and residential care facilities, and individuals and families will grow.

Employment opportunities are plentiful because the population is growing older and has longer life expectations. The biggest impact on the health care industry is the managed care approach to health services. The emergence of health maintenance programs (HMOs) is providing a wide range of related career opportunities in the areas of HMO administration, finance, health services, human resources, public relations, management information, and marketing. This means that the number of jobs in related services, such as membership services coordinators, claims adjusters, compliance officers, human resources coordinators, and network administrators will grow.

Hospitality Careers in hotel management continue to grow. A wider range of leisure industry careers spans opportunities in sports, entertainment and event management, recreation and travel, spa management, golf management, and careers in the gaming industry. Careers in management of life care facilities will continue to grow in response to lifestyle needs of the older population.

Information Management The fastest-growing information services careers are in computer-related industries and include software and Internet publishing, broadcasting, Internet service providers, Web search portals, and data processing services. Increased demand for residential and business landline and wireless services, cable services, high-speed Internet connections, and software will create consistent job growth in these industries.

Marketing Businesses must depend on creative marketing strategies to differentiate themselves to customers. Advertising, marketing, promotions, public relations, and sales managers are needed to coordinate market research, marketing strategy, sales, advertising, promotion, pricing, product development, and public relations activities. Brand management has been an emerging marketing career. It focuses on identifying the brand essence of a business, mapping out competitors in the brand's category, creating marketing strategies, and communicating the unique benefits of that product or service. Career growth in marketing is a result of domestic and global competition in products and services offered to consumers.

Office and Administrative Support The demand for administrative services managers, responsible for performing a broad range of duties in virtually every sector of the economy, will increase. Administrative service managers coordinate and direct support services to organizations as diverse as insurance companies, computer manufacturers, and government agencies.

Personal Care Services Increased interest in health, including ways to better manage stress, is increasing the demand for personal care services, including fitness trainers, nutrition coaches, private or personal chefs, spa services, home care workers, and financial advisors.

Retail Retail remains one of the largest and most demanding markets. The faster-growing segments of the retail career field include e-commerce, catalog sales, and Internet and television sales. Consumer spending on retail goods accounts for a major portion of the nation's gross domestic product. No change in the number of jobs is predicted for retail buyers through 2016.

Security The emergence of the Department of Homeland Security in the United States is creating unprecedented job growth. There is a greater demand for developing surveillance software, assistance in integrating the agencies brought together to make the Department of Homeland Security, and analyzing foreign intelligence data. Identity theft is another emerging security issue contributing to growth in security careers. Identity theft and theft fraud are terms used to refer to all types of crime in which someone wrongfully obtains and/or uses another person's personal data in some way that involves fraud or deception, typically for economic gain.

Social security numbers, bank account numbers, credit card numbers, telephone calling card numbers, and other valuable identifying data can be used by others to personally profit at your expense. The FBI and the National Security Agency project consistent growth in entry-level careers with their agency because of these trends.[2]

---

[2] Ibid.

● 5.3 CAREER PATHS

Understanding career paths can play a significant role in your career decision making. For example, being well informed on the types of jobs that fit into a variety of career paths can help you better understand how roles compare across a company and where you fit in. Your knowledge of career paths and how they work in different companies makes it easier for you to explore and create diverse career options and develop realistic career goals. The information that follows will help you understand how career paths can be different from one another. You can apply what you learn by writing two sample types of career paths and defining your own career path inventory that can guide you once you begin your job search.

TYPES OF CAREER PATHS

One way to think about types of career paths is to visualize a ladder or steps moving in an upward direction. Another way is to visualize a web or the pattern of a chain-link fence where the design zigzags up, down, and across. There are many ways to get to different points, and no way is necessarily right or wrong. Career ladders are usually depicted as linear jobs that move from the bottom up, with increased responsibilities through each phase. While this traditional type of career path is still common today, many companies have developed more flexible and personalized career paths, which are frequently referred to as career lattices. Figure 5.2 summarizes some of the differences between laddered and latticed career paths.

Laddered Career Paths In an organization that promotes career ladders, you might expect more predictable career moves from an entry level to senior role over a period of time. There are defined experiences that are spelled out that are critical steps to moving up the "corporate ladder." This type of environment works well for you if you have a clearly defined

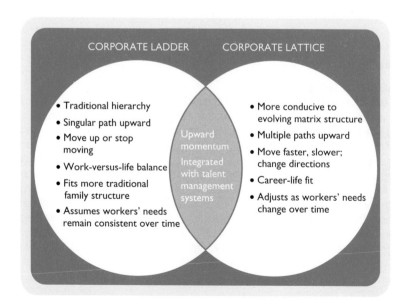

FIGURE 5.2

Ladder versus Lattice

FIGURE 5.3

Sample Laddered Hospitality Career Path

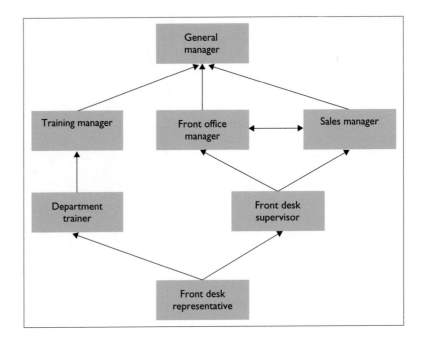

career goal in a specialized area and are fairly certain that you would like to advance upward to a top position in your field. In an entry-level phase of your career, you will probably be more of a generalist, being trained in and being exposed to a wide range of roles and responsibilities. The purpose is to acquaint you with an overall picture of your job and how it fits into the company. The first phase is meant to provide you with work experience that prepares you for the next job level over a period of time that may last anywhere from six months to a few years.

The second phase of your career will be characterized by jobs that are more specialized. You can expect to spend a few years in mid-management and/or specialized jobs. Specialists play a significant role in the company because senior management relies so heavily on the expertise and specific knowledge of individuals in specialized roles. A rewarding career can result in maintaining jobs within this area because they are highly interesting, make use of your special skills, and have a tremendous impact on keeping the company current enough to maintain a competitive edge.

The third phase of your career would likely be management, which moves you back to a more generalist position with significant responsibility and authority. Each job prepares you for the next, more advanced, better-paying job. The example in Figure 5.3 represents a career path that is more laddered than latticed.

Real Life Stories

Hospitality Career Ladder

In high school, Juan worked at a local hotel during his summer vacations. He worked in a number of seasonal positions to earn some extra money to help pay for his tuition. He liked working with people and enjoyed the energy and fast pace of the hotel environment. He spent most of his time near the reception area since he rotated between working as a bellman and parking attendant. He observed the day-to-day interaction that the front desk staff had with the guests and began to realize what an important role they played with ensuring that the guests were satisfied with their stay. Juan enrolled in a Hospitality Management program at the college where many of the hotel staff had graduated from. He continued to work part-time at the hotel through college and completed two internships to have some meaningful work experience when he was ready to apply for a full-time position at graduation.

He completed a front desk internship and an internship in the rooms division. When he graduated, he was hired as a sales assistant. He really liked the hotel company, which had hundreds of properties throughout the United States. To Juan, this meant that there would likely be many career experiences at different types of hotels within the same company. His next job was sales manager at one of the smaller economy hotels. He wanted to vary his experience and applied for a sales manager's position at a larger convention hotel that did three times the amount of annual sales as the smaller property he started at. He was hired and soon became responsible for event booking at 15 hotel properties. Juan wanted to add one more experience to his resume.

He moved on to a small luxury hotel property as a senior sales manager. By now, Juan had created a variety of career options for himself. He could continue in a sales role at any one of the hotels within the company. He could also plan a next step to a general manager's position at any of the three types of hotel properties. Juan decided to take that next step and was promoted to a general manager's position at one of the convention properties, an area where Juan saw a lot of challenge, a work environment that he favored, and much room for further career growth.

Latticed Career Paths Companies are now moving toward more flexible models of career advancement to be more responsive to the changing needs of both the company and individuals over time. This has become a key strategy to attracting and retaining Generation Y talent who look for more career customization or opportunities to build individual career plans. In latticed career paths, the employer and the employee work together in partnership to develop an individualized career plan. As a result, more career-long options can be developed for individuals creating a stronger connection to the employer. This helps to build more company loyalty and the tendency for individuals to stay longer with their employer. The new latticed model is flexible and involves career-long learning and relearning in the workplace. The TJX Companies, Inc.; Deloitte & Touche USA, LLP; and Ogilvy and Mather, the world's largest marketing communications organization, are examples of companies committed to building latticed career pathing for their employees. The latticed model also works very well in smaller businesses. The nursing and teaching professions use the career latticed approach to career development to provide accomplished teachers and nurses with opportunities for career growth where they do not have to move out of a classroom or nursing practice.

The flexibility in latticed career paths makes it easier to adjust career decisions to better match your personal priorities as they change throughout different phases of your life. The example in Figure 5.4 represents a career path that is more latticed than laddered.

Real Life Stories

Information Technology Career Lattice

Sarosh was enrolled in a technology program but was not yet sure what he wanted to do. He liked his part-time jobs as a repair technician in a computer store and at the computer lab help desk at school. He always had a curious mind and enjoyed troubleshooting to resolve problems with systems or processes. When Sarosh was an information technology (IT) intern at a bank, part of his assignment was to interview two people to learn about their IT career paths. He decided to interview Adam, the IT manager, and Shabri, the database administrator. He asked them to describe their career paths.

Adam started as a computer support specialist and soon moved on to become a computer programmer. His next jobs were in network systems starting as an analyst and then moving into an administrator role, which he enjoyed and found challenging. It allowed him to use many transferable skills, in addition to his technical skills. He enjoyed mentoring team members and leading the annual planning and budgeting process with the team. He became known as a leader with excellent communication and decision-making skills. His next role was IT consultant, which led him to his current position as the IT manager.

Shabri's career path was very different. She also started as a computer support specialist and, like Adam, moved on to a computer programmer's position. She really enjoyed the detail of her project work and wanted to further develop her technical skills. She spent time as a network systems and data communications analyst, until she assumed the role of database administrator. Shabri preferred her lead role in a specialized area to the management track that Adam took. She was easily frustrated with difficult to manage staff members and did not have the patience to work with the staff through planning and budgeting exercises. As database manager, she had a small staff and her interaction with them was mostly helping them resolve technical issues and find new ways to upgrade systems and processes. Both Adam and Shabri were satisfied with the different paths they chose. The contrast in interests and their experiences demonstrated to Sarosh that successful career progression did not always mean working up the corporate ladder but that lateral moves can be just as satisfying.

FIGURE 5.4

Sample Latticed Information Technology Career Path

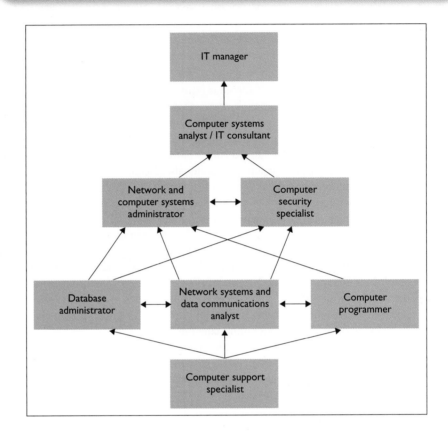

ACTIVITY 5.2

Identifying Types of Career Paths

Write an example of a career ladder and lattice for long-term health care either using the diagram (Figure 5.5) or researching more long-term health care career paths in the *Career Directions Handbook.*

1. Review the sample career path in Figure 5.5 for long-term health care. If you are not familiar with any of the terms in the job titles, look up their definitions on the Internet. Write down two or more jobs in the diagram in Figure 5.5 that move from bottom to top to form a long-term health care career ladder. Write down two or more jobs that move across in the diagram in Figure 5.5 to form a long-term health care career lattice.

2. Refer to the health care career paths in the *Career Directions Handbook.* To identify a career ladder in this field, choose one career area within the health care career paths and write down a list of jobs that move from bottom to top to represent a career ladder within that single career area. To identify a career lattice in this field, choose two or more career areas within the health care career paths and write down a list of two or more jobs across these areas that might represent a latticed career path within a few different areas.

HEALTH CARE

Sample Career Ladder (Jobs move from bottom to top in one career area)	**Sample Career Lattice** (Jobs move across from one career area to another)

```
_____|_____
_____|_____
_____|_____
_____|_____
_____|_____
```

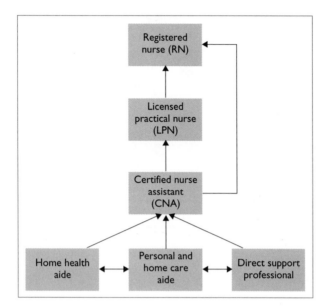

FIGURE 5.5

Sample Career Path: Long-Term Health Care

ACTIVITY 5.3

Identifying Types of Career Paths

Write an example of a career ladder and lattice for retail services either using Figure 5.6 or researching more retail career paths in the *Career Directions Handbook*.

1. Review the sample retail services career path in Figure 5.6. Write down two or more jobs in the diagram in Figure 5.6 that move from the bottom up to form a retail career ladder. Write down two or more jobs that move across in the diagram in Figure 5.6 to form a career lattice.

2. Refer to the retail career paths in the *Career Directions Handbook*. To identify a career ladder in this field, choose one career area within the retail career paths and write down a list of jobs that move from *bottom to top* to represent a career ladder within that single career area. To identify a career lattice in this field, choose one or more career areas within the retail career paths and write down a list of two or more jobs *across* these retail career areas that might represent a latticed career path across a few different retail career areas.

RETAIL SERVICES

Sample Career Ladder (Jobs move from bottom to top in one career area)	**Sample Career Lattice** (Jobs move across from one career area to another)

FIGURE 5.6

**Sample Career Path:
Retail Services**

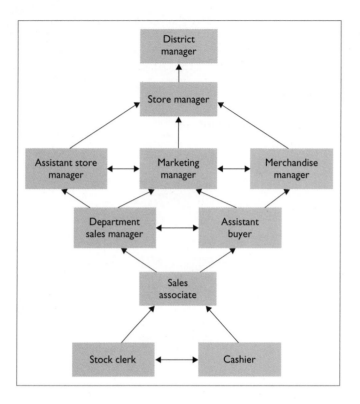

5.4 RESEARCHING YOUR CAREER PATH INVENTORY

You need to define and research the information required to help you determine whether a career path is right for you. Once you have done this, you can evaluate how well prepared you are for the career path you are considering.

The following are some of the key areas to consider in your research.

- Work environment
- Values and interests match
- Education and training
- Skills
- Choice of academic major
- Types of positions
- Employment outlook
- Salaries

The Career Voyages Website (www.careervoyages.gov/), put together through a partnership with the U.S. Department of Labor and the U.S. Department of Education, is a useful resource for obtaining current information on a wide range of careers. Figure 5.7 shows the type of information available on the Career Voyages Web site.

ACTIVITY 5.4

Career Path Inventory

This inventory has been designed as a guide to help you learn how to explore your own potential career paths. As you gather facts about one career, be on the lookout for related career areas that could provide other career alternatives. Refer to the *Career Directions Handbook* and the Career Voyages Website for information that can help you answer some of the following questions.

INTRODUCTION

Write down the career area you think you would like to pursue.

_____

Describe the career you chose and how you feel about it. State clearly what a person in this occupation does (e.g., a career counselor helps students consider career alternatives, arranges for on-campus interviews, and conducts career workshops).

_____

_____

_____

How would you describe the working environment? _____

_____

What do you especially like about this career? _____

_____

What are some things you might not like about this career (e.g., work inside or outside, work schedule, salary potential)? _____

_____

VALUES AND INTERESTS

How might your values and interests be satisfied with this career?

_____

EDUCATION OR TRAINING REQUIRED

Check the amount of education the career requires:

❑ Vocational training beyond high school
❑ Two-year degree
❑ Four-year degree
❑ Master's or doctoral degree
　Other _____

What particular skills are required for this career? _____

_____

What academic majors lead to this career? _____

_____

Is your major one of these? _____

_____

CAREER ENTRY AND ADVANCEMENT

Where might you obtain your first position? Name the types of employers likely to hire you.

_____

_____

CAREER ADVANCEMENT

As you look beyond the entry-level position in this career, consider the following questions:

To what positions in this career might you advance?

_____

_____

What other careers related to the one you chose might you also qualify for?

_____

_____

EMPLOYMENT OUTLOOK

List the national projections for employment in this field.

_____

_____

Do you have a preference for a particular geographic region? If so, what is the employment outlook in that region? _____

_____

SALARIES

	National	Geographic Area of Interest
Entry salary ranges		
Average salary ranges		
Advanced salary ranges		

SOURCES OF INFORMATION

List the names and addresses of major professional associations from which you may get helpful information.

_____

_____

SUMMARY

Review the notes you made in response to these questions. If you had to decide today whether or not to pursue this career path, what would decide and why?

_____

_____

FIGURE 5.7

Top 10 In-Demand Occupations

RELATED OCCUPATIONS AND THEIR PROJECTED 10-YEAR GROWTH

Occupation Title	Projected Need for Employees (2006–2016)	Projected Growth	2006 Hourly Wage Range			Education & Training		
			Bottom 10%	Median	Top 10%	High school or less	Some college	College degree or higher
Registered nurses	1,001,000	18–26%	$20	$29	$42	1%	43%	56%
General and operations managers	441,000	0–8%	$21	$43	>70	20%	33%	47%
Physicians and surgeons	204,000	9–17%	$23	>70	>70	0%	0%	100%
Elementary school teachers, except special education	545,000	9–17%	Annual wages: $31,480 (bottom) $47,330 (median) $74,670 (top)			0%	5%	95%
Accountants and auditors	450,000	18–26%	$17	$27	$47	4%	17%	79%
Computer software engineers, applications	300,000	27+%	$25	$40	$60	2%	13%	85%
Lawyers	228,000	9–17%	$25	$51	>70	0%	1%	99%
Sales representatives, wholesale and manufacturing, except technical and scientific products	476,000	0–8%	$13	$24	$50	21%	28%	51%
Computer systems analysts	280,000	27+%	$21	$35	$55	7%	25%	68%
Management analysts	264,000	18–26%	$20	$34	$63	7%	16%	77%

Source: Accessed September 1, 2009, from www.careervoyages.gov/top50occupations-popup.cfm?language=.

5.5 WHERE THE JOBS ARE

Employment opportunities exist in many different areas. Understanding the options available will help you make more educated decisions about your career path. The three main avenues for employment are the private sector, the public sector, and the foreign sector. Within the private sector, career opportunities exist with individuals, corporations, and institutions. The public sector deals with government employment, and the foreign sector with business or government agencies conducting business overseas. The private and public sectors make up our national economy. Foreign sectors comprise the economy outside the United States.

PRIVATE SECTOR

Small businesses, large corporations, franchises, entrepreneurial enterprises, and non-profit corporations are examples of where jobs are in the private sector. Although there are increased employment opportunities with smaller firms, large corporations still employ the majority of American workers.

Franchise opportunities are always expanding. A franchise is developed when one company assigns to another the right to supply its product. Starbucks and McDonalds are examples of successful franchise operations. Individual franchises are required to put up the capital, with the franchisor providing training, technical assistance, specialized equipment, and advertising and promotion. Entrepreneurs bring together their product knowledge and business expertise to start their own business and make a profit. They take on the risk associated with the new venture and are responsible for successfully managing the company.

Nonprofit corporations are developed to provide a service, usually aimed at helping the human services, supporting environmental projects, or doing other work related to improving the world we live in. Although nonprofit corporations are not established to make a profit, they are usually run like successful businesses and may generate a profit. When they do, the money goes back into the operations rather than to the individuals who own it.

PUBLIC SECTOR

Most opportunities in the public sector are careers with the government. Some federal agencies where employment opportunities exist include the following:

- U.S. Air Force
- U.S. Army
- U.S. Navy
- Department of Health and Human Services
- Department of Housing and Urban Development
- Department of the Interior
- Department of Homeland Security
- Department of Transportation
- Justice Department
- Treasury Department
- Legislative and judicial agencies

All these agencies offer opportunities with a wide variety of options for professional careers. There are some distinct advantages and disadvantages with working for the government. Some of the advantages include: challenging work, job locations throughout the country and around the world, considerable responsibility, diversity of career paths, and flexible hours. Some disadvantages may include: extensive paperwork and intricate processes and procedures associated with many jobs, lack of personalization because of vast size, and sometimes, poor working conditions. Many career opportunities also exist in state and local governments. Your state's Department of Human Resources can provide you with a list of job openings and the qualifications needed to fill them.

INTERNATIONAL SECTOR

International jobs are becoming more popular as communication and ease of travel among countries throughout the world have increased. When considering an international career, determine the reason you want the experience. Experience with other countries and their cultures can be personally and professionally rewarding because it broadens your perspective of the world. You may think about an international career in or outside the United States. Many foreign-based companies operate within the United States. Abroad, you will find opportunities with American-based companies and companies based within each individual country.

You may find the same variety of private-sector opportunities as available in the United States, as well as many opportunities in the public sector. For example, the Peace Corps is an independent agency of the federal government with paid as well as volunteer career opportunities both in and outside the United States.

TRANSFERABLE CAREERS

In addition to deciding which sector your career path will be in, you may want to think about some career options that exist in almost any field. These transferable careers can be developed as a result of having experience in a particular discipline. For example, consulting, teaching, writing, or owning or operating your own business are possible in almost any field. Usually, these career paths can be pursued after you have attained a high level of professional experience in your particular field.

If you are considering work abroad, keep in mind that transferable career areas can move with you wherever you go. Developing a transferable career is a wise choice for professionals who relocate frequently because of their own initiative or because a spouse has been transferred to a new job in a new country.

Progress Check Questions

1. Can you name some jobs in the private, public, or international sector that are within your career field?

2. Why is it important to know about how you might fit into a career path in these different sectors?

CHAPTER SUMMARY

By exploring the career paths overview in this chapter, you have had the opportunity to build a strong career planning foundation and establish direction for your job search.

Beginning with knowing the difference between a job and a career is important in two ways. First, it helps you decide which of the two is a better choice for you and why. And second, while you can change your course at any time in the future, it is best to have a direction so that you don't lose time with a series of unrelated jobs if you later decide you want to pursue a career.

Understanding how jobs relate to different career paths is key to successfully managing your career moves as you work your way along your career path. The number and types of career paths available to you will always be changing along with periods of growth and decline in the economy and the rate at which companies are able to create more or new job opportunities in response to changes in the market. Being knowledgeable about current trends in job growth or emerging career areas is important. It will ensure you know whether you have a strong future in your career field or need to think about a change moving forward. You might learn that some new jobs require different education or training than you currently have. Then you will need to decide whether to further your education or training or choose different jobs or a new career path. The more familiar you are with a wide variety of career paths, the more comfortable you may be with being open to new career opportunities.

Being flexible in considering different career options can help you advance your career more quickly and ensure that you have options during periods of recession and high unemployment. Another way to building career options for yourself is to think about what other industry sectors have jobs that you qualify for. For example, when there may be a decline in hiring training staff in private industries when unemployment is high, there may be opportunities with the federal government or in education to apply your training skills.

Your career path inventory will be a reminder of what you need to know to stay current on career trends. By having this tool and updating it regularly, you can evaluate whether you are moving along a career path with high growth potential. Having a good understanding of different career paths can help you remain flexible and better deal with changes in the job market.

CAREER PATHS AND CAREER DECISION MAKING

Based on what you have learned about career paths in this chapter, identify two potential career paths you think you would like to pursue:

_____

_____

To try to decide which career path might best suit you, answer the following questions.

What am I trying to decide between my two options?

_____

_____

What do I need to know?

_____

_____

Why do I need to know it?

_____

_____

How will it help me make a more informed decision?

_____

_____

Why do I need to know it now?

_____

_____

How can I obtain what I need to know?

People _____

Experience _____

Research_____

Who are my best resources for the information I need?

_____

_____

Why do I think they are the right resources?

_____

_____

REFLECTION EXERCISE

Your Career Portfolio

After completing this chapter, you will:

1 **Know** the employment skills you need to demonstrate to employers

2 **Plan** for your career portfolio by building your skills

3 **Collect** evidence of your employment skills

4 **Develop** a career portfolio

5 **Plan** a portfolio presentation

Your career portfolio is a tool you can use to present your unique employment skills to a potential employer on a job interview. Your career portfolio should contain samples of work and other documentation of your skills and credentials that employers in your career field are interested in. This will be an enhancement to using only a resume to present yourself professionally. While certain fields, such as advertising and public relations, have traditionally required job candidates to have portfolios, the use of portfolios is now more widespread as employers focus on finding job candidates with specific workplace skills.

Because usually you do not assemble your actual portfolio until just before a job interview, you might make the common mistake of not starting early enough to focus on developing and collecting evidence of your skills for a portfolio presentation. If so, your portfolio will be incomplete and a less effective tool for promoting yourself.

At the very beginning of your career education, you should develop your plan to build the skills employers value and collect evidence of those skills on an ongoing basis. Together, your plan and your collection of accomplishments and skills will help you demonstrate your unique qualifications to potential employers.

CASE STUDY

Kim started attending resume workshops in January to prepare for her job interviews in the Spring. Kim frequently went to her school's online career center and used the tutorials to practice writing resumes and job search letters.

At one of the workshops she learned that many graduates were also preparing portfolios for their interviews. Kim had saved some samples of her accomplishments from time to time, but never had a plan for developing and organizing a portfolio. She had many experiences listed on her resume that she thought would help her stand out during her interviews. She had completed two internships, traveled to Germany for a study abroad experience and had three months of community service experience. Kim was an honors student and had several merit certificates to prove it. She felt well prepared after practicing talking about her resume in mock interviews with her career advisor.

Leila remembered her high school guidance counselor stressing the importance of documenting your skills for prospective employers. Leila developed her first portfolio in her high school communications class. She used it when she interviewed for Admissions to her college and found that it really gave her a lot of confidence knowing she was able to show her skills and accomplishments through some original work. In her first year in college, she started planning her career portfolio. As she started to prepare for her interviews, Leila reviewed those portfolio entries that she felt best demonstrated skills that matched the jobs she was interviewing for. Leila had performance evaluations from the same two internships she did with Kim. She had a few writing samples from her communications classes, letters of recommendation, and a copy of the case study she completed with her team during her community service experience. Her grades were average, but she felt prepared for her interviews. Kim and Leila both received several different job offers. Kim was very excited to obtain an offer to join the Management Training program at her company of choice. Leila received an offer from the same company but was placed directly into a higher level position than Kim based on her proof that she had already developed many skills that would normally be learned in the company's training program. For both Kim and Leila, their hard work paid off. Leila's portfolio was a tool that helped her show that she had the skills needed for the job and gave her a competitive edge in her job search.

Discussion Questions

1. Do you think that Leila actually had better experience than Kim or was she just able to market herself better with her portfolio?
2. Based on her experiences, what type of documentation would have made Kim more competitive during her job interviews?
3. What are some of the specific things that Leila did in preparing and presenting her portfolio that really helped her stand out?

6.1 BUILD SKILLS EMPLOYERS VALUE

On your road to career success, you should know the paths you will follow to reach your goals. Employers provide you the map they think will be your best guide by identifying the skills you need for a successful career. Your school provides you the opportunities to build and collect evidence of your skills, helping you gain entry into the world of work.

To ensure that your plan to build skills is headed in the right direction, review the skills employers say they value most. In Chapter 2 we discussed the findings of the Partnership for 21st Skills report. It outlined the knowledge and applied skills and the emerging content areas that 401 employers cited as critical to success in the 21st century workplace.

NOTES	How Some 21st Century Skills Are Used on the Job
Applied/Transferable Skills	**Possible Applications on the job**
Critical thinking	Creating a timeline and necessary steps to complete a project on time
Problem solving	Identifying reasons for customer complaints
	Using customer feedback to create an improvement plan
	Devising a new process to do more with less cost
	Recommending solutions to an employee dispute
	Including conflicting viewpoints in decision making

Oral communications	Explaining product features to customers on a sales call
	Making presentations at a staff meeting
	Interviewing for a new job in your company
	Addressing an audience as a guest speaker
	Calling clients for a telemarketing campaign
Written communications	Writing proposals to justify resources or explain plans
	Preparing instructions for operating simple machines
	Developing a narrative to explain graphs or tables
	Writing company handbooks
	Writing letters and memos
Teamwork/collaboration	Including all team members in decision making
	Encouraging team members to present ideas
	Participating in brainstorming
	Working cooperatively with coworkers
	Pitching in when a person gets sick to get a job done
	Pitching in to complete deadlines
	Sharing information with others to achieve a common goal
Diversity	Making customers with different ethnic backgrounds feel comfortable working with you
	Relating the experience of older workers to a project
	Including different age and cultural groups in planning meetings to represent different perspectives
	Showing respect for those observing cultural holidays and traditions that are different than yours
	Providing help for an employee that is behind in training because of a language barrier
Information technology application	Using software and multiple types of computer files to develop an e-portfolio for a performance review
	Using the Internet for researching a project
	Using the Internet for translation or to learn a second language
	Using the Internet to research industry trends and forecast sales
	Mapping and updating a company Website
	Creating a customer profile using a statistical database
Leadership	Demonstrating confidence in coworkers
	Enlisting the support of coworkers
	Setting an example for your team
	Recognizing others' contributions
	Helping others learn by their mistakes
	Refusing to take individual credit for group results
	Fostering trust in others
	Providing feedback, including constructive criticism, to an employee who works for you
	Handling unanticipated problems confidently
Creativity/innovation	Developing an ad campaign to open a new restaurant
	Implementing brainstorming ideas
	Implementing a new, online site for catalog sales for an existing product
Lifelong learning/self-direction	Monitoring learning needs using performance reviews
	Identifying areas for improvement
	Participating in employee development programs at work
	Taking ownership of learning through use of the Internet, research, workshops, and seminars
	Finding time to return to further education
Professionalism/work ethic	Attending meetings on time
	Responding to e-mails in a timely and professional manner
	Dressing appropriately for the position you are in
	Refusing to criticize a coworker or others in public
	Regularly attending work on time
	Promptly notifying your supervisor if you are going to be absent or late

Ethics/social responsibility	Refusing to take shortcuts that could compromise your work
	Reporting an employee who reports more hours than actually worked
	Refusing to make a popular decision if you know it is wrong
	Writing truthful marketing messages
	Organizing or participating in company-sponsored cultural events
	Participating in company-sponsored community service
	Representing your company on committees with outside organizations

Emerging Content Areas	**Possible Applications on the Job**
Health and wellness choices	Creating a walking routine with coworkers
	Participating in an employee development program on stress management
	Maintaining routine medical appointments
	Making healthy food choices, when possible, at company events
	Participating in health education workshops to learn to manage your own health
	Meeting with your company's benefits coordinator to better understand your health insurance plan
Personal financial responsibility	Developing and implementing departmental budgets
	Handling financial transactions
	Advising clients on investments
	Balancing company checkbook(s)
	Paying company bills on time
	Reconciling differences between inventory and financial records
	Projecting revenue for your business
Entrepreneurial skills	Developing a business plan
	Recognizing new customer base for an existing product or service
	Modifying an existing product or service for a new customer base
	Recognizing opportunities for partnership
	Conducting workshops on proposal writing
Economic issues	Recognizing the impact of the economy on your company's financial success
	Recognizing the impact of the economy on your job or career
	Determining opportunities to save money in your department budget or spend resources in better ways
Globalization	Demonstrating awareness of differences in business etiquette between countries when arranging a meeting with managers from an international division
	Conducting a workshop on different meanings of body language in another country to prepare staff for international meeting
	Relating the way national and international decisions regarding airport security impact business travel
Informed citizenship	Recognizing each person in your work team as a full and equal member
	Monitoring citizenship status and eligibility to work for you or those you supervise
	Coordinating a green project in your department to help improve the workplace environment
	Recognizing opportunities to help others at work
	Recognizing that workplace events, problems, or decisions must be considered with the entire group in mind, and not limited to your personal situation
Importance of non-English language skills	Writing training materials in a different language
	Conducting interviews in more than one language
	Understanding customers who speak another language
	Conducting company tours and orientations in other languages
	Providing coaching or mentoring sessions with non-English speaking employees

Real Life Stories

TSA and Unisys

The Transportation Security Administration (TSA) was created by the U.S. government when better systems were needed to improve security at airports across the country. As a new agency, the TSA needed to build a computer network structure from scratch. One of the goals was to create an information technology system that would help the TSA's security screeners to provide a high level of passenger screening that would not create a poor customer service experience. After considering many companies for this job, Unisys was selected. Unisys worked with other partner companies to accomplish this goal. The TSA first needed to determine what passenger information was important to screen. Unisys then needed to map a process to capture and manage the data that would be collected to provide the most secure and reliable information source based on the TSA's requirements. Unisys and their partners provided information technology and telecommunications services to the TSA. These included hardware and software services, and help desk and network security operations. The result was the creation of a technology-based information system that the TSA uses to screen for people who might be potential threats to airline and airport security.[1]

Progress Check Questions

1. Which of the applied/transferable skills were applied in this situation?
2. Can you think about ways you have applied the same skill in your own life?

EMPLOYER EXPECTATIONS

In addition to workplace skills, employers also consider key experiences as important indicators of a candidate's readiness for the workplace. For example, work experiences obtained from part-time jobs, internships or cooperative education programs, community service, study abroad, and involvement in extracurricular activities, such as clubs and professional organizations, are all important. By looking at the total package of education and experiences, employers can make more informed hiring decisions.

What employers want most from candidates is to know how that person can add value to their company, that is, what they can contribute to the growth and development of the business. Examples of how you can add value to a company include your ability to increase profits, reduce employee turnover, or develop a new product line.

NOTES	Employer Expectations
1. Career planning	A clear career goal and a strategy for achieving it
2. Academic achievement	Ability to acquire the basic skills needed for employment
3. Technical skills	Ability to perform the technical skills for a job
4. Work experience skills	Real-world experience and realistic expectations
5. Leadership	Ability to lead, coordinate, and contribute
6. Community service	Commitment to contribute to society
7. Financial responsibility	Commitment demonstrated through financing your education; ability to manage your finances
8. Professionalism	Attendance, grooming, and dress; work ethic

---

[1] AllBusiness.com, Inc. (2009). TSA Awards Unisys Major Homeland Security Program. "Federal Computer Market Report." Retrieved September 1, 2009, from www.allbusiness.com/company-activities-management/contracts-bids/7944776-1.html.

9. Global perspective	International work, study, or living experience
10. Effective communication	Writing, speaking, listening skills
11. References	Proven success recognized by others
12. Job search skills	Ability to secure employment independently
13. Personal qualities	Ability to manage yourself and deal effectively with others
14. Role models and mentors	Learning from others
15. Special distinctions	Personal achievement, standing out from the competition
16. Career management	Making successful career moves
17. Added value	What value do you bring to your employer?

6.2 PLAN FOR YOUR CAREER PORTFOLIO

As you move through each experience of your education, you will acquire new workplace skills and obtain documentation that provides evidence of your skills. This documentation will help you create a personal career portfolio that can be used on your job interviews to prove your qualifications to a potential employer.

IDENTIFY OPPORTUNITIES TO BUILD SKILLS

The more employment skills you build in school, the more career opportunities you will have and the higher your earnings can be over your lifetime. We saw in Chapter 1 that earnings increase with increased levels of education and that unemployment rates are usually lower for college graduates than for the general population. Take advantage of every opportunity your education affords you to build employment skills. The following sections show you how to develop a plan to do just that.

Opportunities in the Classroom   Each course you complete as part of your progress of study is designed to help you develop employment skills. While some courses teach you technical skills, such as cost accounting, ice carving, or desktop publishing, others teach you life skills that are transferable from job to job, such as leadership, time management, or critical thinking. At the beginning of each course you take, identify, with your instructor, the employment skills you can develop throughout the course. When you complete the course, review and record the skills you have developed.

ACTIVITY 6.1

Applied/Transferable Skills Developed Through Course Work

For each course you complete, begin to record the employment skills you have developed.

Course Name	Skill Developed
1. English Composition	1. Writing a research paper
2. Communications	2. Delivering a presentation at a meeting
3. Intermediate Information Technology Application	3. Information technology application
4. Leadership for Business	4. Leadership
5. Business Ethics	5. Ethics

Course Name	Skill Developed
_____	_____
_____	_____
_____	_____
_____	_____
_____	_____
_____	_____
_____	_____

You will use this list to help you organize your resume, prepare for a job interview, and work with your career advisor to assemble your career portfolio. (You may need to develop your own or additional lists to record all the courses in your program of study.)

Opportunities Outside the Classroom Opportunities to develop employment skills outside the classroom include, but are not limited to, part-time and summer jobs and internships, externships, and cooperative education experiences. Beyond work experience, opportunities outside the classroom include volunteer work, involvement in clubs or professional associations, and sports activities. To take full advantage of the opportunities outside the classroom you need to know what they are. Complete Activity 6.2 to help you identify these opportunities and Activity 6.3 to help you choose those you wish to take advantage of.

Employment skills can be developed through your accomplishments in any of these areas. For example, if you are an accounting major, you may learn how to complete an income tax return in your tax accounting class, prepare computerized monthly budget reports on your part-time job, and teach high school students how to balance a checkbook through your volunteer work in the community. Developing a plan to select experiences that will build your career skills is the first step to developing your career portfolio. The more experiences you have, the more entries you can make in your portfolio.

While it is natural to refine your job target from time to time, it is important also to refine your plan for building proper credentials for your job if necessary.

Example

Original job target: Financial analyst for a firm in the United States

Refined job target: Financial analyst for a U.S. firm in Europe

The basic job target is the same in both situations, but to work in that same job overseas may require the addition of proficiency in a foreign language or a work or study abroad experience. Your job target is a constant reminder of why you are pursuing your education.

YOUR GRADUATION DATE

No matter how sophisticated your plan to reach your job target is, you cannot complete your plan unless you graduate. Although many experiences outside the classroom will be key to your career development, your classroom experiences will provide you with the strongest foundation to develop the critical skills you need for the workplace.

If you are less interested in or have more difficulty with some courses than others, don't get discouraged. Seek the help you need to keep you on track academically. You may not always have been able to see how your course work is preparing you for your job. When you can see this connection, you will probably become more motivated to succeed academically.

ACTIVITY 6.2

Opportunities to Develop Skills Outside the Classroom

Working with your instructor or a student service professional at your school, list all the opportunities available outside the classroom to help you build employment skills.

Opportunities Outside the Classroom	Possible Skill Development
1. National student organizations	1. Leadership
2. Community service	2. Social responsibility
3. Sports teams	3. Teamwork
4. Cross-cultural workshops and seminars	4. Diversity
5. Spanish lessons	5. Important non-English (Spanish) language skills

Opportunities Outside the Classroom   **Possible Skill Development**

_____   _____
_____   _____
_____   _____
_____   _____
_____   _____
_____   _____

(You may need to develop your own or additional lists to record all the opportunities available to you.)

ACTIVITY 6.3

Choose Your Opportunities

Review the list of opportunities available to you outside the classroom and the skills they can help you develop (Activity 6.2). On the basis of your knowledge of the job you want and the skills you need to qualify for the job, prepare a list of the opportunities outside the classroom you will choose to become involved with. For each opportunity you choose, indicate the skills you plan on developing.

EXAMPLE

Opportunities Outside the Classroom	Skill to Develop
Varsity sports	Teamwork

Opportunities Outside the Classroom   **Skill to Develop**

_____   _____
_____   _____
_____   _____
_____   _____
_____   _____

You will use this to help you organize your resume, prepare for a job interview, and work with your career advisor to assemble your portfolio. (You may need to develop your own or additional lists to record all the opportunities you choose.)

6.3 SAVE AND COLLECT CAREER PORTFOLIO MATERIALS

Begin with the end in mind. As you plan to start saving materials to include in your portfolio, try to visualize what forms of evidence you think will be most important to your career field. For example, if you are an art major, it is obvious that your prime portfolio entries will be the best of

---

NOTES | Portfolio Time Line

	Months/Weeks Prior to Interviews	
Planning Phases	**Hard-Copy Portfolios**	**e-Portfolios**
Phase 1: Plan your portfolio	6+ months	6+ months
Phase 2: Assess your inventory	6+ months	6+ months
Start saving materials	6+ months	6+ months
Phase 3: Save materials	2–4 months	2–4 months
Organize and assemble	2–4 months	2–4 months
Publish e-Portfolio online		2 months
Phase 4: Practice presenting	1 month	2 months
Final edits	2 weeks	1 month
Phase 5: Present your portfolio	Interview time	Interview time
Phase 6: Reflect, refine, edit	After interviews	After interviews
	Before next interviews	Before next interviews
	After interviews	After interviews
	Before next interviews	Before next interviews
Target dates:	Interview dates: _____	
Target date:	Graduation: _____	

---

your personal art work. If you are a marketing major, writing samples or business plans you might have written for a class or an internship might be important. A hospitality major may keep a customer service award earned at a part-time job or internship or a facilities plan completed for a facilities management class. Graduates from almost every major will benefit from keeping good writing samples or evidence of awards and recognition and copies of special licenses or certifications important to the industry you are about to enter.

FORMS OF EVIDENCE

Many forms of evidence can document your skills. Even though you may not use all the documentation you collect for every job search, you should still be sure to collect as much evidence as you can to demonstrate and verify your skills. The following are some examples of evidence you can collect and explanations of how each one can help you.

Resume A well-prepared resume is evidence of good career planning and job search skills. In particular, it demonstrates your ability to set and communicate your career goal. A good resume can convince an employer you have the best background for the job.

Photographs Photographs may include those of your work, of you receiving an award or recognition, of you in a professional publication, or of an event you planned. Try to collect photographs that are processed well and that portray your message professionally. As you collect your photographs, keep them stored in a plastic sleeve, album, or photo box to avoid damage or store your digital photos electronically.

Computer Discs Many employers prefer to receive resumes on disc so that candidates' qualifications can be sorted and stored for easy access in a databank. You may also use a computer disc to illustrate a facilities plan you designed, to provide evidence of the computer program you designed to create a new system or procedure at your job, or to show a computerized accounting procedure you can work with. These are only a few of the many skills you can demonstrate on a computer disc.

Writing Samples   Writing samples may include a term paper, an article for the school newspaper, an ad campaign written for your advertising class, business letters, or any other of your original writings. Use only writing samples that demonstrate the following: good grammar, proper spelling and punctuation, and clearly organized thoughts. Seek the advice of a faculty member when deciding what your best writing sample may be.

Audiotapes and Videotapes   Audiotapes can be used as evidence of your verbal communication skills. For example, a tape of a speech that you delivered particularly well is a strong indicator of your public speaking skills. Audiotapes can also be used as a means of walking the employer through the contents of your resume or portfolio, or to demonstrate foreign language or translation skills. Videotapes help demonstrate your body language and professional appearance as well as your verbal communication skills.

Letters of Reference   Your current and past employers are your best resource for reference letters. Most employers will be willing to write a reference letter for you if your employment with them has been a positive experience for the company as well as for you. Letters from past or current employers to prospective employers should prove your ability to perform in the workplace. Other sources of reference letters are professional associations, teachers, and in some cases, personal contacts.

Letters of Commendation   Any congratulatory letters you receive for winning an award or competition, receiving academic honors, or performing well on the job should be saved as evidence of your outstanding accomplishment. If you have customer contact, you should focus on letters received from customers praising the level of service you provided them. These can be used to demonstrate that you have good customer service skills, one of the skills most widely sought after by employers.

Employer Evaluations   When you successfully complete an internship, externship, or cooperative education assignment, you will probably have at least one written employer evaluation of your work performance. Employer evaluations from part-time, full-time, summer, or volunteer work are also worth keeping if they are good.

Performance Reviews   Like employer evaluations of your work, your performance reviews are worth keeping. Most often, employers share with an employee written copies of his or her review both as documentation of what occurred during the review and as a guide to help the employee target the areas of performance that need improvement.

News Articles   If a newspaper has published an article about one of your jobs, awards, honors, or other accomplishments, be sure to save a copy.

Blueprints   A sample set of blueprints you have designed is a great example of your computer-aided drafting and design (CADD) skills.

Menus   If you are in the food service profession and have designed some menus of your own or helped someone else design menus, copies of those menus should be kept to show to a prospective food service employer. Menus that illustrate meals you have actually prepared, even if someone else created the menu, are also great samples of the types of cuisine you can prepare.

Facilities Designs   If you have learned how to lay out the design for new office space, a new restaurant or hotel, or a new retail store, you have a skill a prospective employer should know about. If you have designed one or more spaces, keep copies of your work to show the variety of designs you have worked with.

Business Plans   Writing a business plan utilizes many skills employers will be interested in. In addition to demonstrating your business writing techniques, your business plan communicates your ability to conceptualize, plan, promote, and potentially operate a business.

Certificates of Completion   Certificates of completion are often given to you when you attend a professional workshop, conference, or seminar. Keeping these types of certificates is important because they confirm your participation in a program that has contributed to your professional growth and shows your commitment to continued education and lifelong learning.

Grades and Transcripts   It may be worthwhile to show employers that you have done well in the courses aimed at developing the particular skills they are looking for. If all your grades are good, then it can be a help to show your transcripts to an employer. If some of your grades are below average but you have done well in the courses that specifically trained you to do the job you are applying for, then it isn't a problem to show an employer your transcripts. If your academic performance is consistently below average, then you may want to focus more on skills gained from your volunteer work, work experience, or involvement in sports or clubs and organizations.

Attendance Record   Many college students do not think of attendance in school as a factor that can affect their employment prospects, but employers say good attendance in school is a potential indicator of good attendance on the job. Good attendance is evidence to an employer of your reliability, dependability, and work ethic—all of which are important to success on the job. Keep your record of attendance to demonstrate both your commitment to your education and your professionalism.

Manuals and Procedures Developed   A procedural manual you helped develop through one of your jobs, for a club or organization, or through your volunteer work is a great sample of the work you are capable of doing.

Honors and Certificates   The reason you are working toward developing a career portfolio is to show employers your special distinctions. Any honor or award you receive usually recognizes some type of accomplishment that gives you special distinction. Keep copies of letters or certificates you receive for doing something special. For example, a certificate of achievement for completing a leadership course or a certificate verifying you were the employee of the month at your part-time job would be good evidence of your special achievements.

Licenses   Certain professions require job candidates to have licenses for work in the field. Whether it is required or not, if you have a special license that attests that you can perform certain skills, keep it ready to show to an employer.

Now that you know the types of documentation that can be presented in your portfolio, you can set goals toward accomplishments that will help you collect evidence of your employment skills. In this process, it is very important to remember that although the items listed are only a few of the many possible items you can accumulate, you do not need all of them to prepare an effective portfolio. Also keep in mind that you should collect evidence mainly of your best work. If you have any of the listed items that do represent some of your best work, then be sure to save them. On the other hand, you may have improved significantly in a skill area and want to show an employer the progress you made because of your persistence and hard work. In this case, it may be helpful to keep samples of both your average work and your excellent work to show how much improvement you have made over time.

In any case, do not feel compelled to keep work that is not your best. Everyone is better at some things than at others. You should end up with a portfolio that focuses on your strengths, not your weaknesses. Remember, the purpose of creating a portfolio is to promote your unique talents and skills.

ACTIVITY 6.4

Your Documentation Record

As you collect evidence of some skills, keep a list of the documentation you have and the skill(s) you think it helps you demonstrate to a prospective employer. By maintaining this record, you will readily know the possible career portfolio items available to you when you prepare for your job interviews.

Record of Evidence and Documentation	What It Demonstrates
Attendance record	Professionalism, reliability, work ethic
Letter of recommendation	Validation of proven success
Writing sample	Writing skills
Team project	Teamwork

Progress Check Questions

1. What kinds of evidence do you need to build for your career portfolio?
2. What are the most important forms of evidence you have to date?

 6.4 ORGANIZE AND ASSEMBLE YOUR CAREER PORTFOLIO

At this point you have already collected much of the evidence to show you have industry credentials. When you are about to interview with potential employers, select the evidence that is most valued by each employer and plan to present that evidence effectively. You can organize and assemble your career portfolio in either a hard-copy or electronic format. Whichever you choose really depends on what you are comfortable with using as your presentation to employers. How comfortable you are with your computer skills also makes a difference, since creating an electronic portfolio requires application of different types of computer files and software products.

TYPES OF PORTFOLIOS

As you think about preparing a portfolio to showcase your employment credentials you will need to choose between preparing a hard-copy or an e-portfolio. e-Portfolios are more commonly used than hard-copy portfolios in almost all industries. In some industries a hard-copy portfolio may be more effective, but in today's electronic recruitment environment, you will be expected to be able to share your documents and other portfolio entries online. While the following information provides some of the basic information you need about these two types of portfolios, you should make use of the Websites listed in the online learning center. Look for the Weblinks in the Career Resources section for Chapter 6 to explore your options in greater detail.

Hard-Copy Portfolios   There are many types of portfolio products. The product you choose will depend largely on the career field you are interested in and the types of samples (photos, written material, etc.) you are likely to present.

Three-ring binders (8½″ × 11″) that hold acetate-covered pages or plastic sleeves are commonly used for portfolios. These are practical because the pages or sleeves can hold all types of written evidence as well as photographs. Special vinyl slide sheets, three-hole punched, can be added to hold slide samples if appropriate.

Large portfolio cases (17″ × 22″) are available in most art supply stores and are usually needed by writers, journalists, artists, photographers, or advertising majors. They provide enough space to display full-page ads and printed articles from all sizes of newspapers and magazines. Both types of hard-copy portfolios are excellent vehicles for saving and displaying your work samples and other credentials. Be sure to make copies of whatever you put into your portfolio in case an employer asks you to leave your portfolio behind. You should try not to leave any original pieces of your work. To respond to an employer's request to keep the content of your portfolio a little longer for others in the company to see, have copies of as many things as you can. Art supply stores and bookstores at colleges that offer a degree in art are two great places to purchase some of the materials necessary to assemble your portfolio.

e-Portfolios   Kelly Driscoll, president and founder of Digitation, an e-portfolio service, describes what e-portfolios are and how they can be an advantage to you in your job search. Driscoll explains, "An e-portfolio is a collection of work, published online to document achievements, ideas, progress, performance, and activities. It can also showcase, publish, and compile your work to expand on a personal vision or life goal and create an archive of experiences"[2]

E-portfolio's have several advantages. An electronic version of your credentials makes it possible to share them with a wider audience, regardless of location. They are more practical than the hard-copy versions, usually binders, because your work can be better protected online and there is no need to transport the materials with you to interviews.

When you develop an e-portfolio, you are applying your technology skills. You may prepare media presentations or use different software programs. Your e-portfolio can contain digital versions of your resume, references, work samples, program sheets, letters of recommendation, evidence of community service work, a performance review, or certificates, awards, and scholarship award letters. The specific materials you use for interviews will depend on the type of job you are applying for. In one survey about the use of e-portfolios in the hiring process, employers expressed their preferences for types of portfolio materials.

---

e-Portfolios

Top 5 Types of Information Employers Say Are Valuable

Information	Employer Rating (%)
Resumes/references	93%
Written work	39
Projects	37
Presentations	33
Lesson plans	23

Source: www.educause.edu/EDUCAUSE+Quarterly/EDUCAUSEQuarterlyMagazineVolum/EPortfoliosasaHiringToolDoEmpl/ 163439

---

[2] R. Zupek. (February 29, 2008). Stand Out with an E-Portfolio. Retrieved September 3, 2009, from http://msn .careerbuilder.com/Article/MSN-1486-Cover-Letters-Resumes-Stand-Out-With-an-E-portfolio/.

---

e-Portfolios

Examples of Electronic Files

Text	Presentations
Images	Hyperlinks
Audio files	JPG files
Video files	Tiff files

Of the employers surveyed, 95 percent said they preferred to access e-portfolios via a Web-based link. Employers did not favor the use of CDs and DVDs as highly.[3]

To collect and organize your work in an e-portfolio you should think about using multiple file types and decide on a type of software that will be easy for you to manage. File types may include word documents, spreadsheets, and photographs. In some cases you might enhance your presentation with a sound recording or video clip. The use of various file types demonstrates the diversity of your technology skills as well as different forms of learning you have experienced. Most important, they provide vivid examples of what you can do for a prospective employer.

There are many software options for developing your e-portfolio. The following are examples that range from easy-to-use to more advanced options.

---

e-Portfolios

Examples of Types of Software

Netscape Composer

Blackboard 6 ePortfolio environment

Macromedia Dreamweaver, Fireworks, and Flash (photo gallery and video clips)

Netscape Composer is an easy-to-use software for beginning to develop your portfolio online. Netscape Composer also has intermediate and advanced versions if these better meet your needs. Blackboard 6 ePortfolio environment is a more intermediate application of e-portfolio software but still very versatile and an effective tool for creating an e-portfolio.

Macromedia Dreamweaver, Fireworks, and Flash are advanced software applications that provide a wider range of features such as audio and visual capabilities for Websites.

These are only a few examples of file types and software that can be used to develop your e-portfolio. There are many more, and with continuous advances in technology, new tools are constantly becoming available. The Internet is the best source for keeping informed on the most current file and software options for e-portfolios.

Tips for e-Portfolio Users There are some things you should consider when using an e-portfolio.

Protect Your Privacy Manage the access to your information online. Be selective about who you give your password to. You can password protect your documents to ensure that only those you grant permission to can access your documents. This will reduce your risk of identity theft and ensure that only appropriate individuals can view it.

---

[3] C. Ward and C. Moser. (October–December, 2008). E-Portfolios as a Hiring Tool. Retrieved September 3, 2009, from www.educause.edu/EDUCAUSE+Quarterly/EDUCAUSEQuarterlyMagazineVolum/EPortfoliosasaHiring ToolDoEmpl/163439.

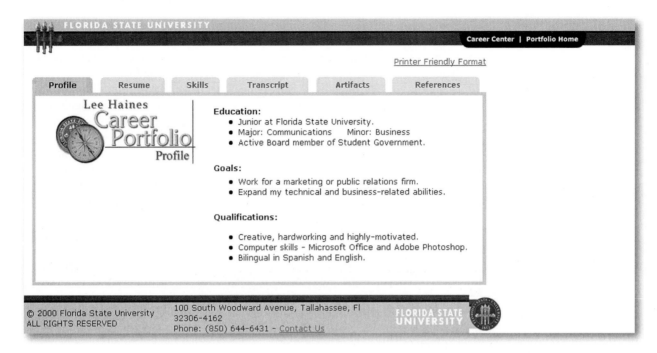

FIGURE 6.1

Sample e-Portfolio

Source: © Florida State University Career Center.

Manage a Variety of Content   Being able to use multiple file types will help you demonstrate your accomplishments in a variety of ways. For example, the sample portfolio above contains a wide range of content ranging from word documents (resume, transcript) to work samples that might take a variety of forms (artifacts). Using different methods to tell your story will help you stand out from others and will better engage those you are presenting your accomplishments to. If you need to learn different file types, ask a teacher for some help. You might also find some online resources easy to understand.

Prepare Off-line Access to Your e-Portfolio   Although you will probably create your e-portfolio as a Web-based link, you should know how to download it onto a USB driver, a CD, or other devices. There may be times when you will want to present your portfolio off-line, and you will want to be prepared to do so in advance.

Make Your e-Portfolio Searchable Online   In Chapter 1 you learned that employers frequently use online social and professional networks to screen job candidates. When employers are screening online, e-portfolios are also accessible to them. You can stand out as someone who is professional and serious about your job search with your e-portfolio. Use keywords throughout your e-portfolio to be sure employers can find you online. Examples of keywords for applied and transferable skills and keywords that are used in particular industries can be researched on the Internet. Some online resources are listed at the end of this chapter.

Promote Your e-Portfolio Web Address   It should be listed on your resume and the footer of your e-mail address for e-mails you send related to your job search.

Never include original work if you are leaving an off-line version of your e-portfolio with someone.

Progress Check Questions

1. Do you think a hard-copy portfolio or an e-portfolio is best for you? Why?
2. What types of computer files and software would you use to build your e-portfolio?

DECIDING ON CONTENT

Before you assemble your portfolio for presentation, determine how you will select the items to go into it. Up till now, you have collected as much evidence as possible to show an employer. When you are about to interview with a potential employer, you must select the evidence that is most valued by that employer. Do not show your entire collection to every employer. Not only will there be too much material for an employer to review, but much of it will not even be targeted to the specific job you are interviewing for.

Plan your selection of portfolio items by focusing on evidence of skills that are industry specific, employer specific, and job specific as shown in figure 6.2. For example, in the hospitality industry, excellent customer service is an industry-specific skill. A particular hotel chain may require candidates to have an international experience because new hotel construction in the Pacific Rim is producing more jobs there than in the United States; in this case, international experience is an employer-specific skill. A job-specific skill then might be the ability to speak Japanese for a reservationist's position in the hotel's Tokyo location. While evidence of good customer service skills is extremely important, this job probably cannot be filled by someone who does not speak Japanese. In this case, it is critical to build a portfolio around international experience including any evidence of experience with cultures in the Pacific Rim, in particular, Japanese culture.

For example, a nationally recognized food service employer in Rhode Island identifies work experience as the most valued credential an applicant can present. A worldwide beverage distributor, however, asks for prescreening of candidates by grade point average first. Although both these employers basically value candidates with appropriate industry training, each employer goes one step further in identifying a specific credential as being most important.

A candidate applying to both these companies for a job may, in fact, meet both these criteria for employment but should concentrate primarily on emphasizing the credential each employer is most interested in. As a result, the candidate may not show transcripts to the first employer but would be sure to highlight good transcripts to the other.

The real key to making your portfolio effective is knowing how to move it from being industry specific to being employer specific for a job interview. The more time you spend getting to know how employers may evaluate you, the more effective your portfolio can be during the interviewing process.

ARRANGING PORTFOLIO MATERIALS

FIGURE 6.2

Your Portfolio Materials Represent Your Specific Skills

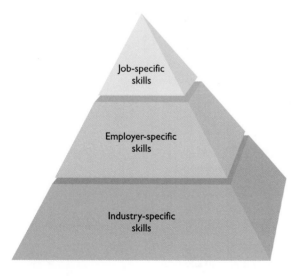

You should give some thought to the order in which you will present the materials in your portfolio to maximize the effect of your presentation to a prospective employer. To arrange a winning portfolio, go through all the materials you initially decided to include. Choose two pieces that are evidence of your best work as well as different from what you think other candidates will have. Place one of these pieces on the opening page of your portfolio and one on the last page. The first should pique the employer's interest to go on to see more of your credentials. The last should leave the employer with a positive impression of you and your abilities.

One way to think about arranging the pieces in the middle of your portfolio is by theme, for example, international experience or community service and volunteerism. Your theme should be chosen keeping in mind the experience the employer is looking for and your own strengths. In each case, focus most of the entries in your portfolio on evidence demonstrating one of the preceding (international or community service work experience) as your strength or specialty area. This approach gives you the opportunity to focus your presentation on promoting a strength you know the employer is looking for. If you do not have enough experience in one specialty area but do have lots of experience in many different areas, then show the diversity of your experiences as your strength. Think carefully about how you arrange your portfolio so that it can make a maximum impact on a prospective employer.

6.5 PRACTICE AND PRESENT YOUR CAREER PORTFOLIO

Your time with an employer on an interview is limited, so manage your portfolio presentation well. You may have to narrate to provide both flow to the presentation and a coherent picture of your credentials to the employer, but be prepared to have only one or two succinct comments about each page you show. Plan what you will say to complement your interview, not monopolize it.

It is important for you to tell the employer at the beginning of the interview that you have your portfolio with you and will speak about it later in the interview. This alerts the interviewer that you are well prepared. The initial stage of the interview is the time for general discussion about the company, your career interests, and the type of position available. Once these topics have been covered, the interviewer will get into more specific questions about your experience and your qualifications for the job. This is the time to bring your portfolio forward. Use it to illustrate how you have already applied the skills you say you have. For example, when you are asked about your experience and skills, answer by first describing your skills and experience and saying that you have some examples that demonstrate your accomplishments and abilities (see Activity 6.5).

Finally, make sure you have created a memorable impression of yourself. Take a "leave-behind" piece from your portfolio on your interview. Remember to make a copy of something you can actually give to the employer with your resume. And then, when you write a thank-you letter for the job interview, mail one more short sample of your work to continue to remind the employer of how qualified you are for the job.

ACTIVITY 6.5

Summarize Your Skills and Role-Play

Work with another person, who will play the role of an interviewer. Summarize the skills and accomplishments you want to highlight to an employer, and select the evidence you have to demonstrate to them. Have the "interviewer" ask you about your skills, and role-play your response to each question and the presentation of your portfolio.

It may take a few practice sessions to become familiar with promoting yourself this way, but it will be worth it when you convince a prospective employer you are a highly qualified candidate for the job.

EXAMPLE

Interviewer Asks: Can you give me an example of a situation in which you displayed leadership skills?

Sample Response 1: Yes. As an officer of Future Business Leaders of America, I was responsible for motivating the membership to initiate an annual fund-raiser for the homeless in our community. Let me show you some letters of appreciation from the mayor and the homeless shelter we worked with.

Sample Response 2: Yes. In my research and design class, I led our work group in presenting our marketing proposal to a local business firm. Here is a copy of our proposal, which was accepted and implemented.

Progress Check Questions

1. What parts of your career portfolio do you find easier to talk about?
2. What can you do to become more comfortable talking about the other areas?

 6.6 REFLECT, REFINE, AND EDIT

Your portfolio will evolve over time with each new professional experience you build. It is helpful to have your portfolio assessed from time to time to help you determine whether or not you are building the best credentials for your career goal. The best evaluators of a portfolio are employers. Arrange to have an employer in your career field critique your portfolio at least twice during your academic experience. Career counselors and faculty members are also good resources for helping you assess your portfolio. When you have your portfolio assessed, focus on finding out what additional experiences you need to become better qualified to attain your career goal. You may show a lot of work experience but little evidence of community involvement. An employer may recommend more community involvement for you to help you demonstrate more of a balance in your life. Or all your work experience may be in one industry segment, and an employer may recommend more work experience but in different aspects of your industry.

Another area of major importance to your portfolio assessment is consideration of what further training you need to become better qualified for a particular job. If you need further training, you will need to decide whether to obtain that training directly with an employer, on the job, or in school. An employer, career counselor, or faculty member can help you with this decision. Before you conduct any employment interviews, be able to tell an employer what further training you think you need to be effective and the plan you have for obtaining that further training.

Progress Check Questions

1. Can you identify the next major accomplishment that will prompt you to update your portfolio?

2. What is your plan for regularly assessing your portfolio?

The information studied in this chapter is your guide to planning, developing, and presenting your career portfolio. A career portfolio is an important tool for demonstrating your distinct qualifications to employers. Being aware of ways in which 21st Century Skills are applied at work helps you identify which skills you need to document in your career portfolio for your job interviews. Planning for your career portfolio should start early. The more time you plan for experiences that build your workplace skills, the more evidence you can build in your career portfolio. A strong career portfolio should make your resume come alive with vivid examples of what you can do.

You need to make several decisions about your career portfolio. For example, you need to determine whether a hard-copy or electronic version of your career portfolio is best for you. e-Portfolios can be an advantage because when they are Web-based, employers can search for profiles online that match certain skills required for jobs at their company. Having a searchable e-portfolio can be helpful to your job search.

Whether you choose a hard-copy portfolio or an e-portfolio, you should be sure to update it often so that it reflects your most current qualifications. Employers will expect you to convince them that you are better qualified for a position based on evidence in your career portfolio.

Having experience talking confidently about your qualifications will also prepare you for career networking opportunities during your job search and during different phases of your career. In Chapter 7 you will learn more about career networking and the important role it can play in your career if done well.

CAREER PORTFOLIOS AND CAREER DECISION MAKING

Based on what you learned about career portfolios in this chapter, think about what decisions you need to make about developing your career portfolio.

What am I trying to decide?

_____

_____

What do I need to know?

_____

_____

Why do I need to know it?

_____

_____

How will it help me make a more informed decision?

_____

_____

Why do I need to know it now?

_____

_____

How can I obtain the information I need?

People _____

Experience _____

Research _____

Who are the best resources for the information I need?

_____

_____

Why do I think they are the best resources?

_____

_____

Job Search Techniques

Career Networking

After completing this chapter, you will:

1 **Identify** types of career networking

2 **Document** lists of network contacts and career networking events

3 **Develop** your own career networking message

4 **Apply** career networking skills

5 **Recognize** the best use of online career networking

Career networking is the most widely used resource in successful job searches. According to a study conducted by the U.S. Department of Labor, 63.4 percent of people find their jobs through networking.[1]

Career networking helps you develop contact with people who can provide you with job leads or career advice. The most effective methods of career networking are person to person, networking events and social and professional networks online. In this chapter, you will identify types of networking, create your own career networking message, learn how to network, document a helpful list of contacts and career networking events and learn about various online networking tools.

CASE STUDY

Sarah wanted to learn more about different jobs in the criminal justice field. In her career development class, she learned about many different career paths. Her instructor told her that many of the jobs in criminal justice were not as easy to find as those in some other fields. There were jobs with the federal government that she applied for online, but Sarah knew that securing a job with the government involved a long process and felt that she was at a disadvantage because she did not know how she could personally contact any of the hiring managers directly. Sarah's instructor recommended that she put together a networking plan to get the word out that she was looking for a job in her field. Sarah remembered industry guest speakers she had met at the Criminal Justice Career Fair at her school and the recruiters she had met from some government agencies. She also made some contacts at a career fair sponsored by the local chamber

[1] Career Playbook. (2009). Job and Career Networking. Retrieved September 1, 2009, from www.careerplaybook.com/guide/networking.asp.

of commerce. When she was at her friend's house one day, she was talking about her job search. Her friend's father thought he could help and joined the conversation. He had been a policeman in their town for 10 years. Sarah talked about a job in loss prevention at a local department store that she had applied for online. She had not received any response. Her friend's father said he knew the manager of security at the company's home office which was located in a nearby state and offered to call the manager. This was a contact that Sarah needed but would probably never be able to make on her own. Because Sarah had already taken the initiative to apply for the job online, the manager knew she was seriously interested.

Sarah was interviewed and was offered the job. In the meantime, Sarah maintained her online profile and kept in touch with three of the contacts she had made at the career fairs. One of them asked if he could pass her information on to two colleagues he knew from a professional association he belonged to. A few weeks later, Sarah received a call for an interview for a position with a private security company. She did not get the job and decided to accept the loss prevention position at the department store. Sarah kept in touch with her other contacts and periodically learned of open positions she might be interested in. Sarah was grateful that her instructor had been honest with her about how difficult the job market could be and for encouraging her to develop and maintain a career network.

Discussion Questions

1. What things did Sarah do to build her career network?
2. Should Sarah have networked outside of her field? Why or why not?
3. Was it important for Sarah to maintain her contacts once she began her new job? Why or why not?

7.1 TYPES OF NETWORKING

The three commonly used types of networking are person to person, over the telephone, and online. To build a wide range of networking resources, you should try to use all three. Face-to-face, person-to-person networking has always been thought to be the most effective. Some of the personal connections made with this form of networking are thought to be the most lasting. Networking by phone may help you follow up on a lead, obtain valuable information about jobs or other contacts, or initiate a face-to-face meeting. If done professionally, online networking can be the most effective because it allows you to connect with a much broader audience at the same time and can be done anytime. Person-to-person and online social and professional networks can be valuable networking resources to you in your job search and throughout your career. Learning to build and manage them well is key to your success.

PERSON-TO-PERSON NETWORKING

Person-to-person networking involves direct contact with individuals either one on one or in a group situation. Taking the time to think about and record a list of all the career network contacts you already know and those you would like to develop is a great start to organizing your person-to-person networking. Some career network contacts might include the following types of people.

Instructors Your instructors at your school are excellent networking resources. Many schools require instructors to stay current in their field by developing and maintaining industry contacts. They may do this through one-on-one relationships with employers, faculty internships, or memberships in professional associations. One of the advantages of including some of your instructors as part of your network is the opportunity to stay connected to them after you graduate. Alumni usually stay connected to some former instructors after graduation and often seek career advice or connections to contacts that help them make a successful career move.

Alumni   Former graduates from your school are a great resource for making connections for you within their company or through professional and personal networks they have built. Successful alumni are usually happy to talk about their career path and refer you to others in your career field who can share useful information and contacts. Many alumni return to campus to speak in the classroom or participate in career fairs. You will sometimes be surprised to learn that the hiring manager at the company you are interested in is an alumnus of your school. You can probably check your online alumni center on your school's Website to find alumni in hiring or recruiting positions.

Counselors   Check to see if you have access to a career or academic counselor or advisor at your school. If you do, they might have industry contacts that could prove useful to you as you develop your career. Professional career counselors can also be a resource to you. Their client base may include people with career experience in your field that would be willing to share career information with you.

Coworkers   The people you work with can sometimes provide valuable insight into which individuals at your company are best to connect with for career advice.

Community Members   Within your local community, you may be a member of different groups, such as social or professional groups. You probably became a member because you share common interests with the group. The community members you interact with can be very good sources of information on business activity that may result in job leads or new networking opportunities. Staying connected with your community is one way to build important networking relationships.

Relatives and Friends   Sometimes we overlook our relatives and friends as possible networking resources for us. Even if none of your relatives or friends are working in the field or at a company you are interested in, they may know somebody that can help you. Don't forget to tell people that you interact with on a regular basis about your job search. People you meet at your church or other place of worship, the gym, the beauty salon, sporting events, and through volunteer work might be able to make a connection for you.

Names	Phone Numbers	E-mail Addresses

ACTIVITY 7.1

Create a List of Career Network Contacts

7.2 NETWORKING CONTACTS AND EVENTS

Networking events create other opportunities for you to connect one on one with individuals that can help you with your job search. Three of the more popular types of career networking events include career fairs, professional association meetings, and professional conferences and workshops.

CAREER FAIRS

Career fairs are excellent networking opportunities for finding job leads or learning more about your career field or careers with particular employers. Before attending a career fair you should do some homework. If the list of participating companies is published, do some research in advance so that you can determine which companies might best fit your career interests. It is helpful to jot down some notes about the company and to create a list of questions you might ask the company representative. This is important because if the event is heavily attended, employers will need to budget their time spent in conversation to ensure they can speak to as many interested participants as possible.

While you may be most familiar with career fairs held at your school, you should also consider career fairs held in your local community or on a regional or national level. The Internet lists some career fairs held in different states or major cities. For example, you can go to nationalcareerfairs.com and search for career fairs by region and career field.

PROFESSIONAL ASSOCIATION MEETINGS, CONFERENCES, AND WORKSHOPS

One-on-one contacts can be developed through members of professional associations you may join. Belonging to professional associations is an effective way to connect with influential people who are already in your career field. Through members you meet at conferences or workshops, you can explore job leads or career advice or obtain referrals to other helpful contacts in your field of interest. The *Career Directions Handbook* has lists of professional associations by career field for you to refer to as you try to decide which organizations might be the most useful career networking resources. Students can often get student rates for memberships and conference attendance. Be sure to ask about this when joining a new organization or preparing to attend a professional conference. In addition to contacting the organization to find out about student rates, ask your instructors. Many of them may know which organizations offer student rates or other opportunities for events, programs, and activities targeted specifically to students.

ACTIVITY 7.2

Create a Calendar of Career Networking Events

Date	Event	Location

7.3 YOUR CAREER NETWORKING MESSAGE

The first step to successful career networking is creating a message about yourself that clearly communicates why you are making the connection and briefly introduces you. For example, the reason you are making a connection might be to be hired for an internship or a full-time job, introduced to an employer, advised on the industry you are interested in, or advised on your job search and career planning.

NOTES | Networking Goals

Obtain an internship or full-time job.
Obtain an introduction to an employer.
Obtain industry information.
Obtain job search and career planning information.

Once you have established how you would like your networking to work for you, you will be better able to develop a strong written or verbal message. The following are some examples of mini-messages that might help you communicate who you are, your strengths, and what benefit you offer.

Example 1: Student Seeking an Internship

"My name is _____. I am a student at _____, majoring in accounting. I am interested in your accounting internship position. I hope to learn more about preparing income tax statements for nonprofit companies like yours. As a senior, I have completed three courses in taxes and have held a part-time job for two years at an accounting firm. My G.P.A. is _____. I am an honors student and was the team leader for my career capstone project. I am providing you my contact information so that you will know how to reach me after today's meeting."

Example 2: College Graduate Seeking Career Position

"My name is _____. I am graduating/graduated from _____ with a degree in _____. I am looking to obtain an interview for a marketing position. I have completed a three-month marketing internship at _____ bank. The customer service training manual I prepared as my project is now used to train new employees at the bank. I am vice president of the marketing association on campus. My concentration was in Internet marketing, and I have an example of an Internet marketing project in my portfolio. My career goal is _____. I am providing you my contact information so that you will know how to reach me after today's meeting."

Example 3: Student Seeking Career Information at a Career Fair

"My name is _____. I am seeking information on the types of positions that are available to me with my degree in _____. I am interested in working for a small company like yours and would like to compare how your career opportunities might be different from the larger corporations I spoke with today. I enjoyed my experience helping a nonprofit, start-up business organize their community outreach program. I am bilingual and looking for an opportunity to use my translation skills in my work. I am providing you my contact information so that you will know how to reach me after today's meeting."

Each of these examples starts with an introduction, gets right to the purpose of the connection, and provides information about the person, with a particular focus on the person's unique strengths, and ends with leaving contact information for future follow-up.

ACTIVITY 7.3

Create Your Career Network Card

Your career network card summarizes key points from your career network message and includes your contact information. You may want to use two sides of the card to ensure you provide all your contact information while keeping the print large enough to read easily.

Create your career network card:

Side One

Your name: _____
Objective: _____
Degree: _____
Major: _____
E-mail address: _____

Side Two

Your name: _____
Cell phone number: _____
Mailing address: _____
_____

Website address (if available): _____
Fax number (if available): _____
Print your career network card on a 3½ × 2 inch card.

7.4 HOW TO APPLY YOUR CAREER NETWORKING SKILLS

Knowing how to network, and practicing your networking skills often, will open many doors with people that can help you throughout your career. The following basic networking steps can be applied to most networking situations. Whether you plan to network person to person, through networking events, or online, you will need to show that you are prepared, can connect effectively, and can follow through with the contacts you make.

PLAN

Know what you want. Are you looking for advice, a better job, a change in career, an introduction to a contact, perhaps someone who is at a higher level than you that you can't get on your own?

- Be confident.
- Build a list of e-mail addresses.
- Plan your career networking message.
- Practice your presentation.

ESTABLISH RAPPORT

Ask questions that show you are interested in the person you are speaking with. Try to ask questions that are open ended. Open-ended questions invite the other person to take the lead in the conversation. You can ask open-ended questions that prompt the other person to talk about their personal interests, career, or the company they work for.

Here are examples of how to begin an open-ended question:

- "Tell me about . . ."
- "What do you think . . ."
- "What was your experience . . ."
- "What do you do . . ."

CONNECT

Call or write directly to the person you want to connect with. Even though your communication may be screened, there may be times that you will get right to the person you want to reach. Some people will be impressed with the personal effort you make to connect.

Attend the same professional and social events as the people you want to network with. Being seen regularly at these events provides an opportunity for you to get noticed and for you to establish and maintain ongoing contact.

Shake hands and introduce yourself. Take the lead.

Work the room when attending networking events. The following tips for working the room at a career fair explain how to use your time well at networking events and ensure you leave a positive, lasting impression.

ENGAGE

Engage the other person in a conversation about why you are interested in connecting with that person. There might not be a lot of time for small talk, and you want to be sure that you achieve your goal for networking with that person. Use your career network message to shift the focus of the conversation to why the other person should be interested in you.

FOLLOW UP

Make a list of the contacts you made that you think are the most important for you to stay connected to. Make a note in your calendar to connect with them two or three times within the next few months.

BUILD RELATIONSHIPS

Not all networking is a one-time activity. Some of the contacts you make will be important to grow and develop. Relationships are not built in a day. They take time and effort. Make a list of the people you want to develop and maintain long-term relationships with and create a schedule of activities that you initiate with them periodically. This might include calling or e-mailing them, inviting them to lunch, or planning to meet them at an upcoming social or professional event.

NETWORKING AT A CAREER FAIR

You can efficiently prepare for a career fair by following this step-by-step action plan:

1. *Know what you want.* Review your networking goals. Are you looking for an internship position or a full-time job? Are you interested in an introduction to an employer? Are you interested in obtaining industry, career, or company information? Do you need career planning or job search advice?

2. *Research participating companies.* Although you will use the career fair as an opportunity to find out more about the companies attending, you should research as many as you can before attending the career fair. Plan to use your time wisely and try not to waste your time speaking with companies that you already know don't match your career interests. Having some prior knowledge of the companies you are interested in

will make it easier for you to initiate your conversation with them.

3. *Prepare a list of questions.* Try to develop a list of questions that cover three areas: company/industry information, job leads and referral, and introduction to other contacts.

4. *Update and print your resume.* Have hard copies of your resume ready to leave behind. Some company representatives will tell you that their policy is not to accept hard copy resumes and that you need to apply online first before an interview can be arranged. In this case, save your hard copy and bring it with you should you end up qualifying for an interview.

5. *Prepare and print your career network cards.* You may want to use your cards as leave-behinds, especially with those companies that might not accept hard copy resumes at career fairs. It can be a reminder of your meeting and provide the company representative easy access to your contact information. The company representatives will also have something from you with your name on it that they can write brief notes on about some things they want to remember about your conversation at the career fair.

6. *Dress professionally.* Be sure to look your best. If you know that your career field generally has a less formal dress code, you can consider wearing business casual dress to the event. You might find that depending on the type of company you will be talking with, some of the company representatives are wearing company uniforms or branded clothing such as shirt with a company logo. Although situations vary according to industry and company culture, it is best for both men and women to wear a suit. This is probably your first introduction to these companies. You want to stand out as someone who knows what it means to look and conduct yourself in a professional manner. If it turns out that you can see more relaxed dress might be appropriate for follow-up meetings, then adjust your presentation accordingly. Review the information in Chapter 4 on interview and workplace dress as you prepare for participating in career networking events.

How to Work the Room at a Career Fair

1. Target the people you want to meet.
2. Introduce yourself.
3. Get information that pertains to you.
4. Get them interested in what you do and who you are.
5. Make friends—find common ground.
6. Take notes to remember what they told you.
7. Try to schedule a time for another appointment.
8. Offer to leave your resume.
9. Thank the person.
10. Move on to the next person.

Follow up after a Career Fair

1. Follow up within 24 hours or at the time you were asked to.

2. If you were referred to someone else in the company, follow up and introduce yourself to that person. Let the person who referred you know that you followed up.

3. Send a thank you note to the company representative you spoke with.

Progress Check Questions

1. Can you think of other ways to use your career networking message other than at a career fair?

2. What is the hardest part of career networking for you? What can you do to develop more confidence in that area?

 7.5 CAREER NETWORKING ONLINE

There are many different types of online career networking that can be helpful in your job search. These include both professional and social networking sites, virtual career fairs, career podcasts, webinars, and chat rooms. The use of online networking is important because so many professional contacts are now made online. For many, online networks can be an effective launching pad to person-to-person networking. You should balance your networking plan using online resources with person-to-person and networking events. In many industries, meeting people in person and making personal phone calls is still a more powerful way to connect and make a lasting impression.

PROFESSIONAL NETWORKING SITES

LinkedIn[2] is one of the leading professional networking sites used today. This is a business-oriented social networking site that allows you to build a network of industry experts in the career area you are interested in. The industry experts who participate can share career advice by answering questions you can ask directly.

Job leads are available on the site as well as access to current or former classmates or colleagues. Professional Associations online often offers opportunities for online networking about a variety of areas including career advice and job leads. You can use the *Career Directions Handbook* to access names of professional organizations to explore for possible professional networking opportunities in your field.

SOCIAL NETWORKING SITES

Many employers use online networking sites like MySpace and Facebook to advertise their company, network with potential candidates, or check profiles of potential hires. MySpace, Facebook, and Twitter[3] are probably the most often used social networking sites.

Before you start your job search review any online profiles you already have posted and update them. It is just as important to protect your reputation online as it is in other forms of communication during your job search. One way to do this is to use separate sites for personal and professional use. This helps keep your personal and professional life separate, but you would still need to maintain a professional look to your personal site because it is still

---

[2] Linkedin.com. (2009). Build your network. Retrieved September 1, 2009, from www.linkedin.com/.

[3] Myspace.com. (2009). Retrieved September 1, 2009, from www.myspace.com/; Facebook.com. (2009). Retrieved September 1, 2009, from www.facebook.com/; Twitter.com. (2009). Retrieved September 1, 2009, from http://twitter.com/.

searchable by potential employers. The best thing to do is to use the privacy control options provided by the specific sites. For example, Facebook has standardized privacy options that can help you tailor what information you share and who you share it with. Using privacy options helps you create a professional image on any social or professional networks that you join to ensure that you do not detract from yourself as a potential job candidate.

NOTES | Tips for Managing a Professional Profile

1. Use a conservative photo of yourself.
2. Your written profile should be brief and simple.
3. Focus the information you provide on your professional and career-related background.
4. Be careful what you say and how you say it. Avoid unprofessional or casual language, information, or comments.

Once you develop a positive profile, you can begin to career network with others and feel confident that you are an attractive candidate to an employer who might access your profile.

Real Life Stories

Tom's Career as a Chef

Tom was graduating in three months with a degree in culinary nutrition. His career goal was to work as a chef preparing creative, healthy choice, spa menus. His dream job was to eventually work in a test kitchen for a large international hotel chain that had two resort properties with spas and that featured spa dining in its marketing. Tom posted his profile on LinkedIn, Facebook, and MySpace. At first he received no responses. He was talking with his instructor who asked to see the profiles Tom had created. Tom was embarrassed to find that he had forgotten to update his profile on Facebook originally created for his family and friends to view. It included pictures of him on vacation and photos of him playing at a local club with the band he belonged to.

Music was his second passion. He had not intended that site to be viewed by professional contacts, but forgot to apply the managed access feature that would ensure only his family and friends could view that profile. After he replaced it with a professional profile, he was contacted from time to time for some very good positions in the culinary field, but had not yet received a response that fit his specific career interest. When he graduated, he accepted an entry-level position with a large food-service company that provided food service to hospitals and schools. Once a week, Tom spent 30 minutes online updating his contacts.

When Tom's sister was on vacation, she stayed at a spa hotel. Tom had asked her to make some inquiries while she was there to see if the hotel needed a spa chef. She introduced herself to one of the chef managers and told her about Tom's interest. There were no current openings, but the chef manager provided her e-mail address and asked that Tom send his resume to her online. When she received it, she obtained Tom's permission to forward it to two contacts she had made through an online resource created by a leading culinary professional association. Tom was grateful for her response and told her that he had recently posted his profile on that same site. She told Tom that he needed to target his posting on the advanced search feature of the site. Here his profile could be accessed by employers by zip code, position title, and his culinary specialization and specific skills. This allowed Tom to tailor his online networking to attract contacts interested in his culinary nutrition degree and experience and from the geographic area he was interested in. He modified his profile using the advanced search feature and was contacted by several chefs and hiring managers interested in his specific qualifications.

Progress Check Questions

1. Can you name any online career networking sites that are targeted to your career field?
2. Do you feel more comfortable with networking online or in person? Why?
. . . .

VIRTUAL CAREER FAIRS

You can build your career network online by participating in virtual career fairs that are now offered in a wide variety of career fields. It is not difficult to participate in a virtual career fair. The normal process would include your accessing registration information for students and employers, a hot links page for companies that have preregistered, a sample listing of companies that have preregistered, and examples of how the virtual booths might work. Booth information might contain job descriptions, company information, Web page links, and e-mail links. You can search the Internet for listings of virtual career fairs that pertain to your career interests.

PODCASTS

Podcasting is a form of audio broadcasting on the Internet, which allows you to listen or watch an audio or visual file. The word *podcast* is a combination of the words broadcasting and iPod. An iPod is a portable music player. The most popular format of a podcast is your MP3 player; however, Podcasts can also be accessed on your computer using certain software, such as Media Player. Many career-related podcasts exist and some have useful information about effective career networking.

WEBINARS

A webinar is a Web-based seminar that provides the ability to give, receive, and discuss career information. Webinars are often found on professional association Websites. Often conference presentations or workshops are recorded when being delivered and then made available online as a webinar. You should become familiar with Websites that pertain to professional associations related to your career interest and search those sites for webinars that are career related. The advantages of doing this are that they are current and available to you at no cost. Career webinars provide a convenient and interactive form of online career networking.

CHAT ROOMS

A chat room is an online interactive discussion in real time. Some career chat rooms might be found on your school's career center or alumni Website or on employer Website career centers. Some of the better sources for career networking podcasts, webinars, and chat rooms can be found on the major commercial career Websites such as Monster.com, CareerBuilder, and Vault.com.

Virtual career fairs

_____

_____

Podcasts

_____

_____

ACTIVITY 7.4

Create Your Own List of Online Career Networking Resources

Webinars

_____

_____

Chat rooms

_____

_____

CHAPTER SUMMARY

Effective career networking skills are among the most important job search skills you can develop. Setting networking goals is an important first step to a productive exchange with the people you will be in contact with. Carefully planning your career networking message will make a difference in the way people respond to you and can set the stage for a successful exchange. Maintaining a professional approach, even on your social online networks, is key to making your connections work in your favor. Knowing how to network is important. If you simply view networking as a one-time activity instead of an opportunity to build ongoing, valuable relationships, you may be disappointed with your results.

If you take the time to practice networking, you will become more confident with the process. You will probably find that well-developed career networking skills can be useful in areas of your life other than your career. You should use a combination of person-to-person and online career networking in your job search to ensure that you maximize your opportunities for developing a strong network of contacts. In Chapter 8, you will see that one of the ways you can use your networking skills is to research and find an internship position or other types of important resume building experiences. You will also learn to recognize how those experiences expose you to contacts that can become an important part of your career network.

REFLECTION EXERCISE

NETWORKING AND CAREER DECISION MAKING

Based on what you learned about career networking in this chapter, complete the following questions.

What am I trying to decide?

_____

_____

What do I need to know?

_____

_____

Why do I need to know it?

_____

_____

How will it help me make a more informed decision?

_____

_____

Why do I need to know it now?

_____

_____

How can I obtain what I need to know?

_____

_____

    People _____

    Experience _____

    Research _____

Who are my best resources for the information I need?

_____

_____

Why do I think they are the right resources?

_____

_____

Internships and Co-op Programs

After reading this chapter, you will:

1   **Recognize** the value of internship and co-op programs to career success

2   **Create** learning goals for an internship or co-op experience

3   **Evaluate** and research different types of internship and co-op programs

4   **Define** your role in the success of your program

As you prepare for your job search, you want to ensure that you have the strongest credentials to present to your prospective employer. This means being able to demonstrate on your resume and in your portfolio that you have acquired the skills and experiences that employers have said are most important to your career success. Employers want to know that you can apply the skills and knowledge you learn in the classroom through work experience. There are many forms of work experience ranging from part-time jobs and externships to internship and cooperative education (co-op) experiences. The two most commonly known types of formal work experience that employers look for are internships and co-ops. In this chapter, you will learn why internships and co-ops are important, and consider steps you can take to ensure that your internship or co-op experience is successful and becomes a valuable asset to your job search.

CASE STUDY

After enrolling in an interior design program at a local college, Liz learned about many career options in the interior design field. Not sure which path she really wanted to pursue, Liz took advantage of the school's co-op program. Liz completed two co-op experiences, one in retail and one in the commercial area.

Her retail co-op experience was with a home furnishings store. Unlike the sales work she did as her summer jobs, her co-op position was designed to be a learning experience for Liz and an opportunity to gain experience with the interior design function at the store. Much of her co-op experience was spent shadowing and assisting the store's interior designer.

Liz learned to coordinate colors and patterns. She used AutoCAD to practice designing floor plans using her knowledge of space planning. Liz scheduled home consultations and accompanied the interior designer on some visits. She learned to work with clients to make recommendations on color schemes, fabric selection, and furniture layout that fit the clients' lifestyles and budgets. Liz also worked with a visual merchandising project. She assisted the interior designer with conducting weekly "power walks" through a few of the branch stores and participated in providing feedback to the merchandising department regarding showroom layouts.

Her second co-op experience was working with an architectural firm on two projects. Liz assisted the architects with small-scale commercial projects including a local fitness center. Her second assignment was assisting clients to determine space configuration and layout for a commercial office space using systems furniture. She used AutoCAD and Photoshop to edit floor plans. When the project was completed, she assisted with coordinating photo shoots and organized an opening event to promote the architectural firm's work.

In the office, Liz was responsible for keeping the architects' workspace organized and updating contact lists. When she graduated, she had a job offer from both of her co-op employers. The architects watched for co-op students who would be a possible fit for a full-time position with the firm. The firm extended a job offer to Liz at a higher starting salary than other entry-level hires and placed her directly into field work bypassing entry-level training. Liz accepted the position and credited her co-op experiences with helping her decide the type of work she wanted to do and helping her gain a competitive edge over most graduates applying for the same job.

Discussion Questions

1. Can you make a list of some specific skills Liz gained from her co-op experiences?
2. Can you identify technical and transferable skills that Liz learned in the classroom and applied on the job?
3. How can the real-world skills gained from a co-op experience help with making career decisions?

8.1 THE VALUE OF INTERNSHIPS AND CO-OP PROGRAMS

Internship and co-op programs provide experience that many employers look for in college graduates. The National Association of Colleges and Employers conducted research to support how highly employers value this type of work experience. The results showed that more than three-fourths of employers say they would prefer to hire new college graduates who have relevant work experience gained through an internship or co-op.[1]

For you, this means that an internship or co-op can help you build self-confidence, acquire or enhance skills, broaden your knowledge, or even evaluate a company as a potential employer. You become better qualified for the first job you want, and you enhance your long-term career potential.

Internship and co-op programs can slightly vary across institutions, so it is best for you to meet with a faculty or career advisor to discuss how these programs work at your school.

Generally the following distinguishes internship and co-op programs:

Internship: Internships are typically one-time work experiences related to your program of study or career goal. Students work in a professional setting with on-site supervision.

Internships can be paid or unpaid and can grant academic credit or no credit.

Cooperative education (Co-op): Cooperative education generally describes multiple work experiences a student may have with one or more companies. The student alternates terms of work experience in his or her field of study, usually full-time, with classroom

---

[1] International Association of Employment Web Sites. (2009). "Work Experience Key for New College Grads Seeking Employment." Retrieved September 1, 2009, from www.employmentwebsites.org/work-experience-key-new-college-grads-seeking-employment.

study. Almost all co-op positions are paid and grant academic credit. Internship and co-op programs are not the only forms of learning in the workplace, but they are the most widely recognized.

Some important things to consider when looking for the right program for yourself include your learning goals, whether the position is paid or unpaid, whether it offers academic credit or no academic credit, and if the work experience is full or part time.

BENEFITS OF INTERNSHIP AND CO-OP EXPERIENCES

There are many benefits to participating in a co-op or internship program. For example, you can:

- Improve basic work skills.
- Develop an understanding of the professional demands and requirements within your particular field.
- Test theories you learned in the classroom.
- Sometimes gain financial assistance to help defray educational expenses.
- Obtain job experience without a permanent commitment to the company.
- Gain exposure to facilities, equipment, and situations not available in the classroom.
- Build opportunities for higher starting salaries.
- Develop potential contacts for employment after graduation.
- Build your ongoing career network.

8.2 CREATING LEARNING GOALS FOR YOUR EXPERIENCE

Deciding your learning goals before selecting an internship or co-op experience creates a foundation for an experience that is right for you. Many schools require students to have written learning agreements prior to program participation.

Work with your faculty or career advisor to determine the goals that best fit your interests and level of experience. Some things to consider when identifying your learning goals:

How will I apply what I learned in class?

Do I want to learn or enhance a skill?

Do I want to further my knowledge or awareness about a career field and the positions within it?

Do I want to explore my fit with a particular type of organization?

Do I want to explore my interest in working with this company full time after graduation?

Do I want to learn about networking opportunities in my field?

These are only a few examples. The point is that there are many different reasons for doing an internship or co-op, and you should determine what you hope to gain from your experience. You should meet with a faculty member to get help in forming your learning goals.

ACTIVITY 8.1

Writing Learning Goals

SAMPLE LEARNING GOALS

1. Expand my use of technology by learning two new Excel applications by January 15.
2. Learn the new online system for patient registration by June 10.
3. Learn two different career paths in my field and document them in my journal by March 1.

Using the SMART method for setting goals you learned in Chapter 3, write a learning goal statement for your co-op or internship experience.

Goal: _____

Write how your goal is:

Specific _____

Measurable _____

Achievable _____

Realistic _____

Timely _____

Write three other possible learning goals for a co-op or internship experience using the SMART method:

1. _____

   _____

2. _____

   _____

3. _____

   _____

8.3   EVALUATE AND RESEARCH THE RIGHT PROGRAM FOR YOU

You can learn about internship and co-op programs available to you from your instructors, Professional Association members, or career advisors; or at career fairs and information sessions or on the Internet.

It is best to start with your school's resources to tap into the opportunities available to you. In most cases, your school is working through established relationships with employers who understand the type of experiences that best fit your degree program and background. These ongoing relationships with industry often provide the opportunity for feedback between the employer and faculty that helps to improve these experiences for both you and your employer. Online resources are also helpful with researching available positions by industry, geographic location, company, or position and providing a wide range of information and advice about these programs.

PAID OR UNPAID EXPERIENCES

Most internship and co-op experiences are paid. There are industries in which it is not customary to pay students. When developing a pay structure, an employer may consider your year of study. Some calculate a percentage of the starting salary being offered to graduates that year to determine an hourly rate. It is up to the employer to decide whether the experience will be paid or not. In some cases, the decision is influenced by state labor laws pertaining to certain industries. While pay most certainly will be an important consideration in your choice of program, you should first consider the quality of the experience you will have, if you can. Some of the best learning experiences are unpaid.

Most employers do not offer benefits, but some may provide paid holidays or relocation assistance. Talk with your faculty or career advisor to evaluate options that are best for you.

ACADEMIC CREDIT OR NO CREDIT

Schools have different approaches to granting academic credit for work experience programs. In almost all cases, co-op positions have some form of academic credit attached to the experience. These are typically more structured experiences. Students may or may not receive academic credit for internships. Talk with your faculty or career advisor to evaluate whether or not academic credit is associated with your experience at your school.

FULL TIME OR PART TIME

You should consider whether it will be best for you to participate in an experience that is full time for a term or runs part time, in conjunction with your classroom work throughout the academic year.

Full-time opportunities can be available year-round, but many companies structure their programs to run during the summer. If you are interested in a full-time experience, you have the option of traveling to and living in another geographic location. If you choose to relocate for your experience, be sure to budget the cost of travel, housing, and living expenses to ensure you can afford the related expenses. Many students choose to stay local for their experience due to financial concerns with relocating, or family commitments. Some students who live on campus, choose to stay local not to lose the opportunity to stay connected to campus activities, such as clubs and organizations, career fairs, and on-campus recruiting. Part-time internships and co-ops allow you to continue taking other classes during your experience.

NOTES | A Day in the Life of Accounting Intern, Leah

CPA Firm

8:00 am–9:00 am	Observe staff meeting with partners.
9:00 am–11:00 am	Assist CPAs with work related to preparing tax returns.
11:00 am–12:00 noon	Call clients to obtain missing information needed to complete their tax return.
12:00 noon–1:00 pm	Lunch with intern advisor.
1:00 pm–2:00 pm	Present update on intern project and receive feedback from supervisor.
2:00 pm–3:00 pm	Organize and file client folders.
	Bring mail to the post office before closing.
3:00 pm–4:30 pm	Attend training on new computer system.

NOTES | A Day in the Life of an Ad Sales Associate Intern, Carla

Theme Park

9:00 am–10:00 am	Register sales associates for executive management meeting.
10:00 am–12:00 noon	Assist with media planning project.
12:00 noon–1:00 pm	Take calls at the reception desk.
1:00 pm–2:00 pm	Lunch with graphic designer.
2:00 pm–2:30 pm	Update client profiles in client database.
2:30 pm–4:00 pm	Summarize customer survey results for morning meeting.
4:00 pm–5:00 pm	Make copies.
	Shred confidential research reports.
	Clean up meeting room and organize for next day.

> ### NOTES | A Day in the Life of a Merchandising Co-op Student, Anthony
>
> **Discount Retail Store**
>
> | | |
> |---|---|
> | 7:30 am–9:00 am | Meet other co-op students and travel to home office. |
> | 9:00 am–11:00 am | Tour the distribution center. |
> | 11:00 am–12:30 pm | Participate in panel discussion: logistics team and co-op students. |
> | 12:30 pm–1:30 pm | Working lunch: orientation on mystery shopping assignment. |
> | 1:30 pm–3:30 pm | Mystery shopping at area competitors. |
> | 3:30 pm–5:00 pm | Write and turn in mystery shopping reports. |
> | 5:00 pm | Co-op students travel home. |

ACTIVITY 8.3

Internship and Co-op Research

Using the Internet, research sites that provide information on how and where to obtain a co-op or internship experience, including actual position postings. You can use information on Weblinks in the Career Resources section for this Chapter on the online learning center or explore other sites on your own. Write down the name of three companies and intern positions that you could possibly be interested in:

Company   **Position**

1. _____

2. _____

3. _____

Write down the reasons why you think these experiences can help you learn something new or acquire new skills.

1. _____

2. _____

3. _____

Real Life Stories

Rachel's Internship in Human Resources

Rachel obtained an internship in human resources at a leading financial company. The ad that she read on Twitter outlined the job description. It read that the intern would be involved in assisting the training coordinator with promoting the company's training programs to all department heads, conducting and analyzing surveys to evaluate the programs, and matching new trainees with mentors within their department. It also read that occasionally there would be opportunities to work on projects with the benefits coordinator. This sounded ideal to Rachel who wanted to know the ins and outs of human resources, which was her concentration in school.

During her first week on the job she met a number of people and became familiar with the training schedule and survey tool to be used. She noticed that some program sessions were filled and some still had many open slots. She immediately proposed some ideas of how to promote the sessions to increase enrollment. She was told not to worry about that, and that she was needed to help organize the sessions already scheduled. Her supervisor gave her a checklist of daily tasks. Rachel was disappointed to see that her work consisted of making copies, setting out refreshments for breaks, and ensuring that the audiovisual equipment was up and running properly each day. She could not observe the sessions because she had to answer the phones while the human resource assistant participated.

While she was in the office, she was given a pile of survey forms to sort by department and then turn over to someone else who would consolidate and analyze the data. She had a weekly appointment scheduled with the director of human resources to talk about career paths in human resources, discuss her progress, and provide feedback on her experience.

For the first three weeks the meetings were cancelled because of unexpected circumstances requiring the director's attention. Rachel didn't say anything to her instructors at school because she was afraid that she would lose the internship which was for academic credit and required for her graduation. She completed her 12 weeks there without doing much more than basic clerical work. At the end of the internship, Rachel switched her concentration, deciding that human resources was not the career path for her.

Progress Check Questions

1. What are some things Rachel could have done to try to get her experience on track?

2. What are some things Rachel could have done before making the decision to switch her major?

8.4 YOUR SUCCESS WITH YOUR PROGRAM

Once you have been selected for your internship or co-op position, there are some things you can do both during and after your assignment to gain the most from your experience.

DURING YOUR EXPERIENCE

Set Goals Your learning goals will keep you focused throughout your experience. Keep referring back to them.

Project Professional Image Maintain a professional look and communication style.

Immerse Yourself Spend time observing how people and positions relate to one another.

Take the Initiative Look for opportunities to volunteer to do more than you are assigned if you are able.

Be Willing to Learn Look for opportunities to ask others to show you how something, other than your work, is done and why it is important.

Be Willing to Work Hard Show that you will do what it takes to get the job done.

Locate a Mentor   If a mentor is not assigned to you, seek someone out that can help guide you through the company culture and provide career advice.

Monitor Your Progress   You will have formal performance reviews that will tell you how well you are performing. Take the extra step and ask your supervisor if you can complete a pre-performance self-appraisal in advance of your performance review meeting. This will provide the opportunity for you to initiate conversation with your supervisor about how you both feel about the progress you are making.

Obtain Feedback   Ask for input from your supervisors and peers along the way. Their feedback will help you know if you are on track and in what areas you could improve. It may also open opportunities for you to discover more challenging work sooner than planned.

Build Career Network Contacts   Some companies offer opportunities to build connections with students. These can include anything from having students observe weekly management meetings; "lunch and learn events"; presentations by key departments within the company; breakfast, lunch, or dinner meetings with key executives; executive speakers or any other exchange that connects students with the company at a business level. Keep a journal of people you are meeting that might be helpful to you long after your experience is over.

AFTER YOUR EXPERIENCE

Once you have completed your internship or co-op assignment you should take the time to reflect on your areas of improvement as a result of the experience. With your ideas well formulated, you should then set up a meeting with your faculty and/or career advisor to discuss the experience. This meeting is often referred to as an exit interview. Be sure to send a thank you letter to your site supervisor. Finally, be sure to update your resume and your portfolio to reflect your newest experience.

ACTIVITY 8.4

Reflect on Your Accomplishment

Answer the following questions:

What have I learned? _____

_____

Work-related skills _____

_____

Insight into my personality and work style

_____

_____

Insight into my strengths and weaknesses

_____

_____

Did I achieve my learning goals?

_____

_____

Did I enjoy the position/experience that I was exposed to?

_____

_____

Would I want to do this work full time?

_____

_____

Is this the industry or career field I want to be in?

_____

_____

Would I want to work for this employer again?

_____

_____

Would I recommend this experience to another student?

_____

_____

Has this experience confirmed, or caused me to rethink, my original career goal?

_____

_____

Debrief with Your Faculty and/or Career Advisor This is an opportunity to confirm how your experience helped you achieve your learning goals. This is important because if you have any areas of concern about the value of the experience or other issues pertaining to the employer you worked with, your feedback can help improve the experience for other students.

Send a Thank You Letter You should always send a thank you letter to your site supervisor. This is the person in the company who has committed the most time and energy with you and with whom you have likely developed the closest relationship. Even if the experience was not all that you expected, you should be courteous and acknowledge his or her work with you. This is particularly important if you think that you would like this person to serve as a reference for you or if you are considering the company for a full-time position. Figure 11.13 in Chapter 11 is an example of a Format for an Application Letter for an Internship or Co-op program.

Update Your Resume Update your resume to reflect, not just the work experience, but also new skills or knowledge you gained. Review your career objective on your resume. You may want to adjust your objective based on what you learned about your career goals during your internship or co-op.

Update Your Portfolio You may want to update your portfolio if you have new evidence of your skills from your work. You may have completed a project, developed a new procedure, implemented a new computer system, received a certificate of merit or recognition, or have other examples of work that will add value to your career portfolio.

Real Life Stories

Liam Stays Positive

Liam always wanted to work at a theme park as a tour manager. He felt he would be in an exciting environment, meet new people, and help to create a memorable guest experience while using the management skills he learned in school.

Liam obtained a summer internship at an internationally recognized theme park which he thought would provide him with the experience he needed to obtain a full-time position there after graduation. He was assigned to provide tours in one area of the park. He conducted the same tour at the same time every day. His guests were mostly families with small children. In many cases, he observed, the children were too young to enjoy the experience. The parents often requested special assistance to make touring with the children easier. He had the most fun with his tour when he saw a family really excited and curious about the attraction. He loved it when they asked lots of questions and didn't want to stop frequently in the gift shops. Within a month of his three-month assignment Liam became bored with the job. He understood at the beginning of his assignment that rotations were not possible, so he could not ask for another assignment. His supervisor noticed that his guest evaluations were very high and suspected that Liam wanted a change. Within the next six weeks, Liam was provided two other rotations that left him feeling that his co-op experience was very valuable. One included conducting tours at a section of the park frequently visited by international guests. At the end of his co-op experience, he told his co-op advisor that he no longer wanted to be a tour manager. He said that he discovered he really enjoyed working with international guests and he knew that his strengths included good communication and customer service skills. He also liked the satisfaction he received from seeing families enjoy their time together. He found a job in Madrid as an account representative for a US distributor operating in Europe. He enjoyed the international travel, had fun introducing new toy products, and was on a career path that could lead to management responsibilities at the home office.

Progress Check Questions

1. How did Liam turn what could have been a negative experience into a learning experience?

2. Should Liam have taken the lead to ask for a new assignment during his co-op experience? Why or why not?

While there are many different types of work experience that can contribute to your career success, internship and co-op programs can provide a more structured learning experience that clearly connects your classroom learning to workplace performance. Employers rate these experiences as very important when considering candidates at hiring time. You can improve your chances of obtaining a meaningful job in your career field at graduation by participating in work programs offered at your school. You need to be well prepared for your experience by knowing your goals and researching companies and positions that fit your qualifications and meet your career interests. You might talk with an instructor as you go through that process and inquire about availability of a co-op or internship advisor to help you make the most of your experience. Once you have been hired into a position, it is important for you to know how to take ownership of your experience. Finally, when you have completed your assignment, take time to reflect on how your experience may influence your current and future career decisions.

INTERNSHIP AND CO-OP PROGRAMS AND CAREER DECISION MAKING

Based on what you have learned about the value of Internship and co-ops programs to your career success, complete the following exercise.

What am I trying to decide?

_____

_____

What do I need to know?

_____

_____

Why do I need to know it?

_____

_____

How will it help me make a more informed decision?

_____

_____

Why do I need to know it now?

_____

_____

How can I obtain the information I need to know?

People _____

Experience _____

Research _____

Who are my best resources for the information I need?

_____

_____

Why do I think they are the right resources?

_____

_____

Sources of Jobs

After completing this chapter, you will:

1 **Recognize** the value of exploring different sources of job information

2 **Utilize** published resources, referral services, the direct approach, and networking to obtain information and interviews in the *visible job market*

3 **Utilize** published resources, referral services, the direct approach, and networking to obtain information and interviews in the *hidden job market*

learning outcomes

The workplace is global, and more small entrepreneurial firms have emerged. The job market is more fluid than ever. Every day, hundreds of new jobs become available through company start-ups, corporate reorganizations, mergers, joint ventures, and acquisitions. The economy is a fast-moving target, and if you are not prepared to move with it, many jobs will pass right by you without your ever knowing it. To put yourself in control of uncovering a variety of job options, you need to understand that while some jobs are advertised in traditional ways, other jobs may never come to your attention if you are not creative and persistent in your job search.

One of your challenges is keeping informed about jobs that are available in your field. You may not be familiar with all the sources of jobs available to you or with ways to promote your availability for employment in everyday situations. Even if your school makes interviews available to you, you will want to seek out some companies on your own. Learning how to secure your own interviews will also be important to you once you are established in your career but wish to move on to a new job.

CASE STUDY

Linda completed her nursing degree and wanted to gain some work experience before applying for a full-time nursing position. She was working full time as an office manager for an insurance company, a position she held for the last 10 years while raising her daughter and attending nursing school part time. Linda was open to working in a variety of settings. She searched the Internet for job postings in her area to keep informed about the various types of nursing jobs available. She knew from fellow adult students, also making a career change, that it was sometimes difficult to find a job in a new field without some work experience. Even though the job market was very good for nurses in the state she lived in, Linda decided to work for a temporary services agency that specialized in placing nurses and obtained a weekend job as a visiting nurse.

Linda had her profile posted on MySpace and LinkedIn. On LinkedIn, she connected with others in the nursing field and sometimes learned of open positions. One weekend, when Linda was obtaining her assignment from the temp service, her placement coordinator told her that another client just called with a job lead. Linda obtained the person's contact information, connected with him, and learned of an opening that was about to be advertised for a nurse at the children's hospital where he worked. The children's hospital encouraged its employees to refer qualified individuals to open positions through its employee referral program. Her contact explained that although Linda would still need to follow the company's policy to apply directly online, that she would probably obtain an interview since she was referred directly through the employee referral service. The hospital preferred to hire qualified people referred by someone it knew. In the meantime, Linda also received an e-mail from another insurance agency about an available position. The company had several hundred employees working at the home office which was located a few miles from where Linda lived. The e-mail described a position for a corporate nurse to work Monday through Friday, providing basic on-site health services for employees. The company found Linda through a passive search online. The company regularly used the Internet to find people it might be interested in hiring, regardless of whether the candidate expressed interest in the company or not. It used an online service that made it possible to search resume databases and profiles on Websites, such as LinkedIn. The company used this system to build a list of potential candidates to have available for key positions, even when there were no job openings. This time, the system helped it find a match for an open position. Linda now had first-hand experience with exploring visible and hidden job markets for job opportunities.

Discussion Questions

1. Can you identify direct and indirect sources of job information available to Linda?
2. What other resources could Linda have used to further explore the hidden job market?
3. What do think are some advantages to an employee referral program for a company?

9.1 THE VALUE OF JOB EXPLORATION AND INFORMATION

It may seem to you that the job market is very visible. On a daily basis, you can scan the Internet classified ads and trade magazines. Community bulletin boards and postings in the campus career services office, in the department of unemployment security, and on companies' internal job-posting boards are but a few of the common places you may see notices of job openings.

Job hotlines now allow you to dial up jobs via the telephone 24 hours a day, and career days and job fairs are held regularly at schools and in the local community. Although these should be your first sources of job information, they are only the beginning of a comprehensive job search. In fact, only 10 to 20 percent of the job market is visible through these sources. This means that 80 to 90 percent of available jobs are not obvious to you through traditional sources. Job leads that are uncovered from untraditional sources are considered part of the hidden job market and the very hidden job market. Some common sources of job information in these markets are published resources, referral services, a direct approach, and networking.

Developing techniques to learn about openings and get interviews is important to a successful job search, but it requires work on your part. Being aware of circumstances that can help you find out about jobs and acting on opportunities as they become available will help you maximize the number of job opportunities available to you.

The following discussion of sourcing jobs in the visible job market, the hidden job market, and the very hidden job market illustrates a wide variety of techniques for accessing career opportunities as you prepare for your job search. Of all the methods used to access jobs and learn about career opportunities in your field, networking is the most effective. Most job vacancies are filled well before a job description is posted. It is estimated that 80 percent of jobs are found through personal networking rather than want ads. A company's current employees are among the best sources of referrals. Many employers report that 40 to 50 percent of jobs are filled more favorably by referred candidates than by those brought in through other methods.

In addition to the traditional networks you build with your institution's alumni and teachers, colleagues, friends, and community contacts, there are more formal network organizations. Examples of organized networking groups are women's networks and professional organizations, as well as diversity networks and professional organizations. More recently, transitioning military networks and professional organizations have emerged.

Virtual networks are prevalent on many major online career Websites and on college and university alumni Websites. These often provide chat rooms and message boards to allow for online discussion of contacts and career information.

Once you understand the role networking can play in your career decision making and when you are appropriately prepared for the experience, you will discover the high value of networking for your career planning and job search. Here are examples of some focused questions you might ask during a network exchange:

1. What are the key trends in this industry?
2. What are your major job responsibilities?
3. What has your career path been?
4. What do you enjoy most and least about your current position?
5. What have you learned?
6. Would you have done anything differently?
7. What are the major qualifications for a successful career in this field?
8. What advice can you give me on entering this field?
9. Are you aware of any current career opportunities with your company or with another company that I am qualified for?
10. Is there anyone else it might be useful for me to speak with?

9.2 THE VISIBLE JOB MARKET

The visible job market consists of those sources that are the most obvious and easily accessible. The Internet, the newspaper, career fairs, and your career services office are sources you normally associate with finding job information. The following sections offer some ways to access the visible job market.

PUBLISHED RESOURCES

When employers want to solicit the widest range of responses to available positions, they publish these job openings in the printed resources most widely read by job seekers. Following are some of these resources.

The Internet   Internet employment services are a popular means for firms to discover new talent. Most of the services provide classified job listings and advice on how to land a job.

Newspaper Classified Ads   You should use the classified ads not only to look for specific jobs but also to note which companies seem to be running ads

most often. The classified ads can bring to your attention the name of a company you are otherwise unfamiliar with. If you are seeking employment abroad, the classified section of newspapers from the country you wish to work in is the best indicator of current job openings and firms that are hiring. Whether in a domestic or international publication, classified ads are also an excellent source of information about qualifications for specific jobs. Reading the classifieds in the newspaper and online on a regular basis is essential to keeping current with the job market.

Job-Listing Bulletins and Newsletters Hundreds of independent publications list jobs weekly, monthly, or quarterly. Many colleges and universities publish online job postings for their alumni. Like the classifieds, these bulletins and newsletters are good indicators of employers who are currently hiring. Some companies will maintain an ad over a long period of time to generate a pool of qualified candidates to choose from when an actual position becomes available. Many job-listing bulletins are sold at newsstands and sometimes distributed in public places. These can be additional sources of job information to online postings.

Career Services Office Listings Whether on bulletin boards or in job books, current job opportunities are usually posted and maintained by career services offices. Although you should not limit yourself to this source, you should start to find job information through your school's career services office. Once you are aware of how much information you can obtain there on a regular basis, you will know what you need to do to supplement that information.

Internship Directories Books that list the names and addresses of firms with formal internship programs can be found in most bookstores and online. Usually these resources will list the contacts for hiring and the types of internships that exist. These listings can help you gain an overview of the types of jobs available at specific companies.

REFERRAL SERVICES

Many employers prefer to use an outside source to screen and refer candidates to their companies. For entry-level recruits, career services offices are the most commonly used source of candidate referrals. The following are referral services offered by career services offices.

Career Services Office Resume Referral Service Most schools offer employers the opportunity to ask for candidates to be prescreened by the career services office. In this case, the career services office prescreens candidates on the basis of qualifications defined by the employer and refers only qualified candidates directly to the employer.

Employee Referral Programs Many companies have employee referral programs. These are programs that reward current employees for referring qualified candidates to the company. This is helpful to the company because it can reduce the cost of recruiting and improve the quality of candidates. For the most part, an employee is not likely to recommend an unqualified candidate to a current employer because the quality of the referral can be a reflection on the employee. When the employer rewards a current employee for helping with the referral, the employee may feel more connected to the company. It is one of many motivational reward programs an employer can offer. If you are looking for a job, someone from a company in which you are interested may approach you about a job lead.

DIRECT APPROACH

Many companies provide students with opportunities to meet with them directly to discuss potential job openings. Perhaps the only time in your career when employers will come to you to speak about career opportunities is while you are in school. Following are common school recruiting programs in which employers participate.

Campus Interviews   Some schools invite companies to conduct job interviews for graduates at the school. This type of on-campus recruiting program is one of the most direct ways to secure an interview through your career services office.

Open Houses and Industry Nights   Many companies precede their day of interviews at the school with an open house for students who will be interviewed. The purpose of the open house is to provide information about the company's training programs, corporate structure, history, expansion plans, and career opportunities. Since this may be the first meeting you have with

the industry representative(s) from a particular company, you must make a positive first impression. Dress professionally when attending all open houses. Make an extra effort to ask questions during the question-and-answer period, and after the program introduce yourself to the industry representative(s). All these things will help make you more visible to the employer.

Job Fairs and Career Days   Many schools hold some type of career day to bring employers and students together. Although career days are mostly aimed at providing career information to students, the contacts you make with industry representatives during these programs are another source of job interviews for you. Many schools hold regional job fairs in conjunction with other schools in the area; these fairs bring a number of schools and their students together with major employers, and both employers and students benefit from a greater pool of jobs and job applicants. Most communities also host local job fairs for the general public in such facilities as the local civic or convention center. The Internet has even created its own job fairs for job seekers.

NETWORKING

Networking is the process of communicating your career goals to others who may be able to provide you with professional contacts you may need to help you reach your goals. The following are the more obvious professionals available to students for networking.

Teachers, Counselors, and Personal References   Teachers, counselors, and personal references can provide you with insight about jobs and offer advice about the jobs best suited for you. They can also refer you to career publications that will help you find out more about jobs in your field and tests that help you understand what jobs best fit your interests and personality.

Current Employer   If it is appropriate to do so, you can speak with your current employer about other job leads within or outside the company.

Cooperative Education and Internship Employer   Your cooperative education or internship employer can advise you on jobs available in his or her industry and company. He or she may also tell you the best way to find out about these jobs.

Progress Check Questions

1. Can you give an example of two published resources for sources of job information for your career field, either printed or online?

2. What are some ways you can use professional associations as a source of job information?

ACTIVITY 9.1

Accessing the Visible Job Market

Accessing the visible job market takes some knowledge of the resources available to you and some planning on how you will use these resources to uncover as many job leads as you can.

Review the types of resources available to you in the visible job market. Within each type, check one resource you think you will use. Then describe why you think the resources you checked will work best for you.

TYPES OF RESOURCES

Published Resources

❑ The Internet

❑ Newspaper classified ads

❑ Job-listing bulletins and newsletters

❑ Career services office listings

❑ Internship directories

❑ Bulletin board postings

Referral Services

❑ Career services office resume referral service

❑ Job hotlines

❑ Career services office practical training binder

Direct Approach

❑ Campus interviews

❑ Open houses and industry nights

❑ Job fairs and career days

Networking

❑ Teachers, counselors, and personal references

❑ Current employer

❑ Cooperative education and internship employer

Describe the reasons for your choices:
_____
_____
_____
_____

 ## 9.3 THE HIDDEN JOB MARKET

The hidden job market consists of sources of jobs that may be less obvious to you and may therefore require more of your initiative to find. For example, sourcing job information through professional associations or your local community may involve some planning on your part because you might not automatically think of these sources. The following are some ways to access the hidden job market.

PUBLISHED RESOURCES

There are many published resources that either post jobs or provide lists of potential employers that you might not ordinarily think about when you begin your job search. Knowing where to locate these resources can help you explore the hidden job market. The following publications listed are usually found in libraries, on the Internet, and may be available in your school's career services office.

Magazines and Trade Journals   Some magazines and trade journals have a section dedicated to classified ads. This can be a particularly helpful source of information if you are looking for a job abroad. If you don't have a contact who can send you this information regularly, you can probably access international publications at your local public or university library.

Professional and Trade Association Job Finders   Many professional and trade associations provide job information to their members. Many will also act as a referral source for members who are looking to fill vacant positions by passing on resumes from candidates. Whether you are a member looking to hire or be hired, you should inquire as to whether this service is available in your association or professional organization.

Business Directories   Business directories are good sources of information about companies' business standing. Before deciding to seek job information from a company, you will want to know that it is stable and has a solid future. Business directories are also a great way to research smaller successful firms that you may not otherwise know about.

Company Literature and Annual Reports   If you choose to go directly to a company for job information, you can learn a lot about the type of jobs that exist in the firm just by reading the company's literature and annual report. For example, an annual report with information about a company's products, customers, and future growth is a good indicator of existing jobs and new jobs that may emerge.

Telephone Directory   The yellow pages in your telephone directory are a great way to obtain a focused list of companies in your area by type of business.

Computerized Mailing Lists   Through professional associations, the chamber of commerce, or catalogs that specialize in job search products and resources, you may be able to purchase mailing lists of companies by industry.

Lists of New Firms with 100 Employees or Less   Small companies are probably the most overlooked source of job information because many of them are unknown and many job seekers assume the best information comes from larger corporations. Your chamber of commerce can supply you with lists of smaller companies that are operating in your area. In fact, as mentioned earlier, more jobs will be available with small companies than with large organizations over the next 6 to 10 years.

REFERRAL SERVICES

You may not be aware of the following referral services. They can, however, be an excellent source of available jobs and an indicator of which employers are hiring and what career fields are growing.

Employment Agencies Agencies are especially helpful to you once you have a few years of work experience. Some agencies are able to assist with entry-level positions, but most deal with advanced positions requiring at least two to three years' experience. It won't hurt to select one or two reputable employment agencies to submit resumes to during an entry-level job search. If you do have a lot of experience, use them more heavily. Just do not fall into the trap of depending solely on the agency to find you a job. And remember, be sure to ask if the employer will pay the placement fee if you are hired.

Government Employment Offices In many other countries, jobs are not advertised in the same way as in the United States. Job information may be centralized with government employment offices. International students wishing to pursue a career in their home country can do so through these offices.

Professional Associations Some of the professional associations in your career field are listed in the *Career Directions Handbook.* They can be extremely valuable sources of information to you throughout your career. For more contacts like these, refer to the *Encyclopedia of Associations*[1] in the reference area at your local library or on the Internet. Some professional associations publish jobs online; some actually provide employment services and some do not. The only way you will know is to write and ask. For example, if you are a member of the Future Business Leaders of America or the Distributive Education Clubs of America, write and ask for advice and any career literature that is available.

DIRECT APPROACH

A direct approach to uncovering jobs in the hidden job market involves your taking the initiative to contact companies on your own about possible job openings when the company has not invited you to inquire through company job postings, classified ads, and so on. The following are some ways to use the direct approach.

Walk-In Going into a company's human resource department for job information does not require an appointment. You may ask what jobs are currently available and obtain an application and company literature. Remember, the purpose is to obtain information; the walk-in approach is not a preferred way to obtain an interview.

Telemarketing Campaigns Get on the telephone and do some preliminary work for your job search. Call companies directly to see if they are actively seeking applicants in any particular area. Find out the name, title, and address of the person who may be responsible for hiring. You can create a job for yourself over the telephone if you are smart. When you call, know what you are going to say and be prepared to announce your qualifications and what you have to offer the company, rather than just asking if there are any jobs available. Many times employers will call a candidate in for an informational

---

[1] Dialog. (2009). Encyclopedia of Associations. Retrieved September 1, 2009, from http://library.dialog.com/bluesheets/html/bl0114.html.

interview if it sounds like the candidate might fit into the company somewhere. When you speak to someone on the telephone, you have an opportunity to create an impression that you cannot produce on a resume or a job application.

Volunteer, Temporary, or Part-Time Work   Volunteer, temporary, and part-time jobs are excellent sources of job information. They give you an opportunity to gain firsthand knowledge about certain jobs without requiring you to make a permanent commitment to the job. You have the opportunity to observe others in different positions and broaden your knowledge about careers in the company or industry you are in. Often these situations can provide you with job leads or even become full-time jobs.

Mass Mailings   At first, you may think mass mailings are a waste of time, but with this method you have a good chance of unearthing the job you want at a company you really never thought of working for. Visit your career services office, go to the library, use the yellow pages—do a variety of things—to find lists of potential employers. Then identify at least 20 that you may really be interested in; from there it's up to you. Mailing out 200 resumes and cover letters is not a bad idea if your field is especially competitive. When using the mass-mailing campaign, you may want to adjust your cover letter to suit particular types of employers.

Want Ads for Yourself   It is possible that you are in a field where job leads are not as abundant as in another, or perhaps you are involved in marketing or advertising and want to stand out to a prospective employer. Today, some job candidates are sourcing job leads by placing ads about their qualifications in the "Job Wanted" sections of the classifieds printed or online.

Former Employers   If you left a previous job in good standing, it can be helpful for you to contact your former employer for job information. You may be interested in returning to work at that company, or you may simply ask a former boss if he or she can refer you to a colleague for job information.

NETWORKING

We all have some contacts that we often overlook as possible sources of job leads. Although some people do not readily seek out these contacts to discuss job search and possible career opportunities, you can pursue networking opportunities for jobs with the following people.

Club and Organization Members   Speaking with members of clubs and organizations can help you learn about trends occurring in your industry and how these trends are affecting jobs. You can also learn about the companies that sponsor the clubs or organizations and explore job information.

Mentors   If you are fortunate enough to have a mentor, this person can share much information with you about his or her own career. In addition, your mentor can introduce you to other industry professionals who can be a useful source to you.

Relatives   Family members can provide job information to you because of the experiences they have had with their own jobs and because of what they can tell you about the companies they have worked for. They also may be able to refer you to other family members who can help you.

Friends and Neighbors   Friends can share information with you about their jobs or about what they have learned through their own job searches. By exchanging information about your experiences, you can both learn about the job market and talk about which jobs are most appealing and why. Even this informal process can help you sort out where your interests lie and what direction your job search may take.

Classmates Your classmates can be helpful to network with because they are probably experiencing the same anxiety, excitement, frustration, and sense of challenge that you are. They can share job information they have obtained through their experiences.

Community Contacts Contacts in your community can provide information about which companies might be moving into your area and what types of jobs they may bring. Community contacts are also helpful with explaining the types of jobs that may exist with nonprofit organizations. Some community contacts are the local chamber of commerce, your church, and local politicians.

Sporting Events Although a sporting event is not the first thing that comes to mind as a source of job information, it can be one. Accepting an invitation from or extending one to a businessperson you would like to network with can result in a fun time that is also productive.

Country Clubs and Health Clubs Joining a country club creates tremendous networking opportunities. Golf memberships are among the most popular with businesspeople. Health club memberships are also increasing in popularity with professionals because many companies now offer memberships as an employee benefit.

Fellow Job Seekers Keeping informed about how others are doing with their job search can provide you with information about companies that are hiring, the person responsible for hiring, and qualifications sought for different jobs. Perhaps someone you know may turn down a job offer, opening up the possibility for you to apply for that job yourself.

Fellow Employees You may learn that a fellow employee is leaving your company or being promoted, creating a job lead for you to act upon. Or you can simply learn about different job responsibilities from your coworkers.

Chamber of Commerce Your chamber of commerce can be an excellent source of job information if you take the initiative to find out about all the services and information it provides. In addition to having listings of company names and addresses, your chamber of commerce probably sponsors events for the local business community. These may include monthly after-hours receptions where professionals meet to discuss issues affecting their businesses and network with each other on an informal basis. Some chambers sponsor a state leadership institute to heighten businesspeople's awareness of issues facing their community. Any organized events that bring businesspeople together for a common reason are great networking opportunities.

ACTIVITY 9.2

Accessing the Hidden Job Market

Accessing the hidden job market takes some knowledge of the resources available to you and some planning on how you will use these resources to uncover as many job leads as you can.

Review the types of resources available to you in the hidden job market. Within each type, check one resource you think you will use. Then describe why you think the resource you checked will work best for you.

TYPES OF RESOURCES

Published Resources

❑ Magazines and trade journals

❑ Professional and trade associations' job finders

❑ Business directories

❑ Company literature and annual reports

Referral Services

❑ Employment agencies

❑ Government employment offices

❑ Professional associations

Direct Approach

❑ Walk-in

❑ Telemarketing campaigns

❑ Volunteer, temporary, or part-time work

Networking

❑ Club and organization members

❑ Mentors

❑ Relatives

❑ Friends and neighbors

❑ Classmates

❑ Community contacts

Describe the reasons for your choices:

_____

_____

_____

_____

Real Life Stories

Ann's Sources of Job Information

Ann was enrolled in a theater program and seeking an internship where she could gain some acting experience. She had tutored elementary school children part time for three years while she was in college. She became familiar with the characters in children's story books and thought about children's character entertainment as a career path to launch a future career in children's theater. Ann registered with the career services department at her school and was assigned to an internship at the library where she participated in character performances for children's plays at library and community events. She joined the acting club at school and, after two years of small parts in some plays, became the lead character in a campus performance of a well-known play. She received many letters of congratulations from members of the community. One came from the local performing arts center, encouraging Ann to audition for a part in an upcoming production. When she did not get the part, Ann applied to a position posted online as a teaching assistant in the theater department at a nearby community college. When she brought in a local television anchor to speak to her class, she found out about an opportunity to participate in a commercial for a local fundraising event. She passed on that opportunity to focus on her teaching job. Although she enjoyed teaching, she still wanted to be involved with children's theater someday and decided to keep exploring opportunities.

Ann knew that in her profession, many jobs were not advertised. She understood the importance of using a variety of sources to obtain information about opportunities for her to gain more experience.

Progress Check Questions

1. Can you describe some sources of job information that Ann used?
2. Can you identify some career fields that do not always advertise job opportunities?

CHAPTER SUMMARY

Any good job search begins with a thorough understanding of which jobs exist in your field and what resources are available for sourcing jobs that might interest you. Even with all the published online and printed materials pertaining to jobs and the many well-advertised career fairs, a majority of the job market is still not accessible through these traditional means. In addition to published resources, you can use a direct approach and networking to access the hidden job market. Your ability to access the hidden job market is critical because you want to be sure to explore as many options as possible to obtain career information and create job leads. There are literally hundreds of online career resources that provide job information. By deciding which resources you need for the career field you are interested in and how you can access them, you can begin to develop a targeted plan to keep current on job information in your field. Being aware of how to explore the hidden job market is particularly helpful during a recession or other situations that cause the job market to weaken. When the job market is weak, there is sometimes not a need to publicize jobs as extensively as in a good market because open positions are easier to fill due to the greater number of people available for employment. By acting on the many existing opportunities to enter the hidden job market, you put yourself in better control of finding of a job you want and creating more options to choose from.

REFLECTION EXERCISE

SOURCES OF JOB INFORMATION AND CAREER DECISION MAKING

What am I trying to decide?

_____

_____

What do I need to know?

_____

_____

Why do I need to know it?

_____

_____

How will it help me make a more informed decision?

_____

_____

Why do I need to know it now?

_____

_____

How can I obtain what I need to know?

_____

_____

People _____

Experience _____

Research _____

Who are my best resources for the information I need?

_____

_____

Why do I think they are the right resources?

_____

_____

Resumes and Job Applications

After completing this chapter, you will:

1. **Determine** when to use different resume styles and practice creating each one

2. **Differentiate** between electronic resume formats and create an electronic resume

3. **Know** how to create an effective paper resume

4. **Complete** a sample job application

Before attempting to apply for any job, you should be able to prepare a professional resume and a concise job application. Both are very often the first impression a potential employer has of you. Preparing a resume that is targeted to a specific company or position you are interested in can help your resume stand out and portray you as a serious candidate to a potential employer.

To target your resume to your specific employers, first determine which resume style best demonstrates your unique background. Match your skills and experiences with a resume style that emphasizes your strengths. Chronological and functional resumes are two examples of frequently used resume styles. Reviewing sample resumes will help you practice writing your own resume and select a style that works best for you.

There are many ways to transmit your resume to prospective employers. Whether you decide to provide a hard copy or an electronic copy of your resume, you will benefit from being familiar with the many types of computer files in which you can prepare and transmit your resume.

Like your resume, a job application should provide a professional and accurate picture of you. Knowing what parts of a job application are important and how your answers can impact your job search will help you make a positive impression on your application.

CASE STUDY

Jack took one last look at his resume before going to the career fair scheduled the next day. Jack first learned how to write a resume in his freshman year Professional Development class. At the time, he had developed a chronological resume. He had limited work experience to tout on his resume. His various jobs as a waiter, camp counselor, and part-time worker at the volunteer center developed nicely into a chronological resume that neatly showed his work history. Over time, Jack developed new transferable and technical skills from his internship, volunteer work and specialized courses. He was pleased to now be able to write a functional resume highlighting his more advanced and varied skills. He was sure to reference his language skills. He spoke and wrote both Spanish and Italian very well. He listed special accomplishments, including being selected to represent his school at a special ceremony recognizing outstanding service to AmeriCorp. Jack also provided a short, bulleted list of technical skills he had gained from work and through his coursework.

It was time to graduate, and Jack wanted to create a wide range of job options in case an offer from one of his top five companies didn't come through. All five companies would be at the career fair. He printed multiple copies of his paper resume to bring with him. He had taken the time to create targeted resumes for the five companies he was most interested in. Jack was able to do this by using key words from each company's Website and job posting that best fit his qualifications. He had also uploaded his e-resume into several online tracking systems.

At the career fair, Jack first went to the companies that he had applied to online. Only one of the company representatives was aware of his online application. He introduced himself to the others and gave them a hard copy of his resume. Two said they were interested in interviewing Jack now that they had met him and seen his resume. Several companies didn't take a paper copy of Jack's resume but asked him to post his resume on their company's resume bank. These companies had a policy to not accept paper resumes. Two companies preferred receiving an e-mail with a resume attachment, and one small business only wanted a paper copy. The company was too small to use an electronic system.

By the time Jack connected with all the companies he was interested in, he was pleased that he was prepared to follow up so quickly with each of these different requests. He received a call a few days later asking for a reference that could be contacted. When Jack said that his references were listed on his resume, he learned that two of them couldn't be reached at the contact information he had provided. When he asked if his e-resume had been received, he was told that it had not arrived and that occasionally e-mails with attachments were filtered out as junk mail. Jack received three interviews and two job offers, including an offer from one his five targeted companies.

Discussion Questions

1. What things did Jack do to make his resume stand out?
2. Do you think Jack's impressive background could stand out as clearly as he did in person at the career fair? Why or why not?
3. Do you know how the companies you are interested in will prefer you to submit your resume?

 ## 10.1 RESUME STYLES

A resume is both a factual presentation of yourself and an opportunity for self-promotion. Employers will use your resume to see whether you have the educational background, previous work experience, and professional objectives needed to be successful in the job for which you are applying. Since employers like to be able to scan resumes quickly to determine applicants' eligibility for a job, your resume should be brief, to the point, and formatted for easy reading. Although the length and style will depend on how much work experience you have, your resume should be a concise, error-free, attractive outline of your relevant job experiences, skills, accomplishments, and academic credentials. While your resume should be personalized to reflect your qualifications and professional interests, it should fit on one page, or be no more than two pages. The two basic styles of resumes used most frequently in a job search are the chronological resume and the functional resume.

The *chronological resume* lists your work experience and educational history in chronological order, that is, by date. This type of resume is excellent if you are entering the job market for the first time or are changing jobs within a given career field, because it highlights the education and work experience you have in your field. Sometimes your education is more important than your work experience when you are seeking a new job, especially if your education emphasizes for the employer the career direction you wish to take and your work experience is unrelated or minimal.

The *functional resume* organizes your experience according to specific skills or functions. This format is appropriate if you are changing careers or reentering the workforce after a period of absence, because it emphasizes your skills and abilities and downplays any gaps in employment or any unrelated work experience. This resume is especially effective if you have a lengthy work history. Most employers value previous work experience, both in and outside of the field. Experience reflects your work ethic and commitment to improving professional skills.

ORGANIZATION OF YOUR RESUME STYLE

Chronological and functional resumes usually organize information into the following categories.

Identification   Print your first name, middle initial, and last name at the top of the page.

Address   A correct address is critical information. A potential employer may want to send you a job offer or communicate with you for some other reason. Receiving that information will be extremely important to you. If you are not currently living at your permanent address, list both your temporary and permanent addresses.

Telephone Numbers   Like your address, your telephone number is critically important. Always include your area code. Do not assume the caller will know it. If you have no telephone or have an unlisted number that you prefer not to give out, leave the telephone number of a very reliable person who is home much of the time and can take messages for you without damaging your credibility. During your job search, check with that person regularly for messages. If you use an answering machine, be sure your greeting is professional and positive. If you have a fax machine, include your fax number.

E-mail Address   Many employers may prefer to follow up by e-mail. You should list your e-mail address in this section, but be sure not to list only your school e-mail address since it will probably expire at graduation. If you choose to use your school e-mail account during your job search as a student, feel free to do so, but be sure to back it up with a personal e-mail address that will stay with you after you graduate.

Professional Objective   Some employers suggest that a professional objective is not required on a resume because it may limit your chances of being considered for a wide range of jobs. On the other hand, there are those who feel your professional objective is an important part of your resume and should be included whether you are just starting out or making a next step in your career. Properly done, a professional objective indicates direction to an employer. You've gone to the trouble of deciding what you want to do; now you want to show the employer that you know what you want. A professional objective can be stated most clearly in one sentence, or no more than two sentences. Your objective should reflect your short- and long-term career goals and a realistic attitude. It should be broad enough to give you some flexibility but specific enough not to make it appear that you are floundering with your career direction.

The following are examples of good professional objectives:

- An entry-level job as an information coordinator leading to a career doing market research in the travel industry
- An entry-level job as a store manager trainee leading to a career in retail operations

The following are examples of poor professional objectives:

- An entry-level job as a store manager trainee leading to a retail buying career. (This is inappropriate because it is not a correct career path. If a buying track is what you want, you must start off on a buying track, as opposed to a management track.)
- An entry-level position in a growing company with an opportunity for advancement. (This is too general; it does not indicate that you have thought about any real direction.)

Education   Don't leave anything out. You want to account the best you can for how you have spent your time. If you attended a school but did not complete a diploma, certificate, or degree, then list it as a place you attended. List your high school only if you participated in a vocational program that is relevant to your career field.

Courses (Optional)   Courses are especially helpful to list if you are an entry-level applicant without a lot of work experience and if you have taken highly specialized courses that will help you on the job.

Special Skills (Optional)   You should list any special skills you have that are relevant to the job you are seeking. Business writing and computer skills are two examples. You don't want to list personal characteristics in this area. Save talking about your personality for the cover letter.

Work Experience   Don't make assumptions for employers and leave out certain experiences because you think they won't be valuable. Chances are, if you think this way, an employer won't value them either. It is important not to leave big gaps of time on your resume. You should list most of the experiences you have had and be prepared to convince an employer that you have learned from each one of them. Whether these experiences have been part-time or full-time jobs, it is vital for you to examine what you might have gained from each experience. Many times an employer sees someone who has worked as a waiter or waitress for three summers and subsequently asks about the job.

The employer then waits for the applicant to talk about his or her experiences as a server—working with the public; working under pressure; working nights, weekends, and holidays—only to find the applicant apologizing for lack of work experience related to his or her chosen career. Making the connection between many types of experiences to the job you are applying for can help you convince an employer that you have important transferable skills. Certainly, if you worked to support your college education, that should be noted on your resume. For example, stating "Earned 80 percent of college tuition through part-time employment" spells initiative, determination, and responsibility.

Work experience gained through internships, externships, or cooperative education programs may also be included in the Work Experience section of your resume. Since the purpose of participating in one of these programs is to gain employment skills, be sure to include all the responsibilities you had as part of your job, just as you do when listing a part-time, full-time, or summer job. Too often, students overlook how valuable these experiences are to a prospective employer. Many students list these experiences in the Education section. It is much more effective to include your internship, externship, or cooperative education experience under Work Experience.

International Experience (Optional)   Usually, international experience is described in the section of the resume where the experience belongs (e.g., Education or Work Experience) as opposed to being listed in a separate section. It is acceptable, however, to add a section called International Experience, with a summary of your job(s), if you know that an employer is looking specifically for someone with such experience.

Extracurricular Activities and Hobbies (Optional)   Your extracurricular activities and hobbies demonstrate leadership potential, interpersonal skills, initiative, creativity, and ability to plan and organize. They also show that when there's nothing to do, you choose to make valuable use of your time rather than seeing it as an opportunity to do nothing. This may be an important characteristic to the manager who wants employees to take initiative and do well with minimum supervision.

References (Optional)   You should always be prepared to list references. Have the courtesy to call or write to the person you'd like to be a reference for you. It is not essential to actually list references on your resume, but you should at least add the line "References available upon request." When you do this, type up your list of references on a separate sheet of paper headed "References for _____ (your name)." This list does not have to be mailed out with your resume, but you should take it with you on a job interview.

Special Distinctions (Optional)   Special distinctions may include honors and awards you have received, competitions you have won, work that you have had published, press releases about any media appearances you have made, or a foreign language you speak. If any of these accomplishments are part of your background, you may add a Special Distinctions section to your resume. This would normally be placed after the Work Experience section.

Community Service and Volunteer Work (Optional)   If you have participated in any type of community service or volunteer work, include a description of such work on your resume. Many employers now look at this involvement as important because of the initiative and commitment it demonstrates. Many companies also are conscious of their social responsibility in the community and want employees who will represent them through community service and volunteer work. Remember to write the description of your experience using action words to describe the employment skills you used to perform the work you did. Your description of community service or volunteer work may be placed after the Work Experience section.

The following pages present formats and samples for both chronological and functional resumes.

FIGURE 10.1

Format for a Chronological Resume

YOUR NAME

Permanent Address: **Temporary Address:**

Street address   Street address

City, State, Zip   City, State, Zip

Phone number (with area code)   Phone number (with area code)

Fax number (with area code)   Fax number (with area code)

E-mail address   E-mail address

Professional Objective:

State the type of position you are applying for and your long-term goal. You may include indications of wanting growth and challenge in your objective.

Education:

List professional training and/or college(s) you graduated from first. If you attended a college but did not complete the program you were in, you may list the college and dates attended without indicating a degree. List your high school only if you were in a special program of some kind (honors, tech-prep, etc.). Underline names of schools.

Courses: (*Optional*)

List no more than six; list only those that have something to do with the position for which you are applying.

Special Skills: (*Optional*)

Skills you have developed may be *technical* (word processing, desktop publishing, shorthand), *interpersonal* (teamwork, teaching, public speaking), or *thinking skills* (creativity, problem solving, decision making).

Work Experience:

Include part-time, full-time, and summer work, as well as internships, externships, and cooperative education experience, with brief descriptions and dates of employment. List the most recent job first and work back. Underline names of employers. If your employment history includes many short-term jobs, use the following rules:

1. List those relevant to the position for which you are applying.
2. List those you held for the longest periods of time.

Community Service/Volunteer Work: (*Optional*)

International Experience: (*Optional*)

Special Distinctions: (*Optional*)

Extracurricular Activities/Hobbies: (*Optional*)

List any organizations individually along with your responsibilities. Then list hobbies and special interests that might be pertinent to the position for which you are applying. Also list others that seem less relevant, since they will indicate your diversity in a variety of areas.

References: (*Optional*)

State "References available upon request." On a separate sheet of paper, list at least three. Be sure to get permission in advance. List teachers, friends, or former employers (but not relatives). Include names, titles, addresses, and telephone numbers with area codes.

Portfolio: (*Optional*)

If you have a career portfolio, state "Portfolio available upon request." Provide the link here if you have an e-portfolio.

FIGURE 10.2

Sample Chronological Resume

JENNIFER M. GORDON

Permanent Address:
64 Potter Street
Sodus, NY 14551
Phone: (315) 585-6609
Fax: (315) 585-4434
E-mail: jgordon@univ.edu

Temporary Address:
5 Washington Avenue
Providence, RI 02903
Phone: (401) 598-0101
Fax: (401) 598-1010
E-mail: jgordon@univ.edu

Professional Objective:

To obtain a sous-chef position in a large-volume restaurant leading to an executive chef's position for an upscale, themed restaurant.

Education:

Johnson & Wales University, Providence, RI 02903
B.S. Culinary Arts, 2012

Wayne Morgan High School, Sodus, NY 14551
Tech-prep program, Diploma 2008

Special Skills:

Garde-manger	Menu design	Purchasing and receiving
Wood grilling	Ice carving	Food cost control

Work Experience:

2009–present Goldenquill Restaurant, East Providence, RI 02906
Line Cook.
Assist sous chef at sauté and fry station and with grilling and broiling in 100-seat seafood restaurant.

Summer 2009 Acres Country Club, Cape Cod, MA 03421
Prep Cook.
Rotated between garde-manger, sauce, and grilling stations. Supervised four dishwashers and two kitchen workers. Received and purchased food products.

March 2009–June 2009 Salina Foodservice Corporation, Dallas, TX 43431
Cooperative Education Experience
Line Cook.
Assisted head cook with preparing meals for corporate dining room at downtown Dallas bank. Prepared daily "heart healthy" menus. Did cooking demonstrations for spouses' program during bank's annual meeting.

Sept. 2008–March 2009 Johnson & Wales University, Providence, RI 02903
Pasta Place Restaurant.
Prepared pasta menus for students' lunches and dinners at university student dining facility.

Community Service/Volunteer Work:

Sept. 2006–March 2007 Meals on Wheels, Providence, RI 02903
Cook.
Cooked dinners for clients needing special assistance with meal preparation.

Special Distinctions:

- Employee of the Month, May 2009, Salina Foodservice Corporation
- Distinguished Visiting Chef Scholarship recipient
- 3rd place, National High School Recipe Contest

Extracurricular Activities/Hobbies:

Secretary, Chippers Club
Vice President, VICA (Vocational Industrial Clubs of America)

References available upon request.

Portfolio available upon request.

FIGURE 10.3

Format for a Functional Resume

YOUR NAME

Permanent Address:
Street address
City, State, Zip
Phone number (with area code)
Fax number (with area code)
E-mail address

Temporary Address:
Street address
City, State, Zip
Phone number (with area code)
Fax number (with area code)
E-mail address

Professional Objective:
State the type of position you are applying for and your long-term goal. You may include indications of wanting growth and challenge in your objective.

Professional Experience and Skills:
List (and discuss, if necessary) all of the professional skills you can bring to an employer as a result of the different experiences you have had. These may include personal and interpersonal skills that are helpful to your career but should also stress your technical skills. Think about all of the skills you have acquired, and focus on those you think are transferable to other jobs.

Employment History:
List the jobs you have had, including your present position, in order by date, starting with your most recent job. You may omit any jobs you held for just a few months or any that are completely unrelated to the job you are seeking. It is not necessary to provide a detailed description of the jobs you held, but do list your job titles and place of employment along with the dates employed. Underline names of employers. (Remember, the information should be presented in such a way that the reader can focus first on your professional experience and skills.)

Community Service/Volunteer Work: (*Optional*)

Family Care/Household Management Experience: (*Optional*)

International Experience: (*Optional*)

Special Distinctions: (*Optional*)

Education:
List professional training and/or college(s) first and then high school attended, with date of graduation along with degree and major. Underline names of schools. List most recent program first and work backward, in order.

Courses: (*Optional*)
If listing courses helps clarify some of your specific skills, then list them following the same rule as noted in the chronological resume. Most skills can be listed in the section on professional experience and skills.

References: (*Optional*)
Follow the rule noted on the chronological resume.

Portfolio: (*Optional*)
Follow the rule noted on the chronological resume.

FIGURE 10.4

Sample Functional Resume

ROSE MARTINSON
43 Racine Avenue
Skokie, Illinois 60077
(847) 546-7898
Fax: (847) 546-7022
E-mail: rose97@xyzmail.com

Professional Objective:

To obtain a position within a major corporation, which will benefit from my administrative, communication, and interpersonal skills.

Relevant Experience And Skills:

Production

- Generated all personal and business correspondence via Microsoft Word.
- Processed over 25,000 full- and part-time job opportunities annually.
- Arranged hotel and travel accommodations for executive staff.
- Complete knowledge of Microsoft Office.

Planning/Promotion

- Coordinated daily schedules of management staff.
- Supervised four clerical assistants.
- Initiated and implemented new filing system and interoffice communication procedural manual.
- Assisted in formulation of marketing strategies.
- Aided in generation of promotional materials, serving as liaison for professional photographers, printers, and media personnel.
- Coordinated planning and execution of one-day conference on stress management.

Employment History:

2009–present	Northwestern University, Evanston, IL
	Administrative Assistant to Graduate Career Services
2008–2009	The Field Foundation, Chicago, IL
	Administrative Assistant to Director of Administrative Services
2007–2008	Howard T. Mack. Inc., Skokie, IL
	Administrative Assistant to Associate Human Resources Director

Education:

2008	Bryant & Stratton, Buffalo, NY
	B.S. Administrative Management

References available upon request.

Portfolio available upon request.

1. Do you think that a functional or chronological resume is better for you at this time? Why?

2. If you are not looking for a full-time job, what are some other ways that you might use an updated resume at this time?

MATCHING RESUME STYLE TO SKILLS AND EXPERIENCE

Each type of experience develops particular set of skills. Use the following guide to help you match the best resume style to the types of experience and skills you have.

NOTES | Choosing Resume Formats

Experience	Recommended Resume Format

Educational Experience
Skill Sets:
  Basic skills
  Thinking skills
  Personal qualities
  Academic achievement
  Professionalism
  Technical skills
  Financial responsibility
  References
	Chronological

Work Experience
Skill Sets:
  Basic skills
  Thinking skills
  Personal qualities
  Technical skills
  Professionalism leadership and management skills
  Financial responsibility
  Career planning
  Job search skills
  Human resource skills
  Career management
  Financial management
  Clerical and research skills
	Chronological or functional

Community Service/Volunteer Work
Skill Sets:
  Leadership and management
  Personal qualities
  Teaching
  Human resource skills
  Clerical and research skills
	Functional

International Experience
Skill Sets:
  Global perspective
  Personal qualities
	Functional

Military Experience
Skill Sets:
  Leadership and management skills
  Technical skills
  Teaching skills
	Chronological or functional

Human resource skills
Clerical and research skills
Personal qualities

Family Care and Household Management   Functional
Skill Sets:
   Thinking skills
   Personal qualities
   Financial responsibility
   Teaching
   Financial management
   Leadership and management

Most of us gain our experience at school or work, in the community, or at home. Some also gain experience through the military or international travel. Before deciding which type of resume you will use and the skills you should stress on it, assess which experiences should be emphasized the most on your resume.

ACTIVITY 10.1

Assessing Your Experience

Which of the following most clearly represents the experiences on which you are basing your resume? Place a 1 in the area(s) from which you have gained the most experience, a 2 in the area(s) from which you have gained some experience, and a 3 in the area(s) from which you have gained little or no experience.

Education and Academic Achievement

❑ Community service and volunteer work

❑ Work experience

❑ International experience

❑ Family care and household management

❑ Military

Review your assessment. The areas you have numbered 1 or 2 are the experiences on which you will build your resume. After reviewing the preceding table and checklist, which resume format will you use? Why?

ACTIVITY 10.2

Resume Preparation Checklist

Before printing the final copy of your resume, review this resume preparation checklist to be sure your resume is ready to present to a prospective employer. Place a check next to the steps you have already completed.

❑ My most current address, phone numbers (land and cell), and e-mail address are listed.

❑ My professional objective is clearly stated.

❑ My resume is no more than two pages in length.

❑ I've chosen the proper format for my resume.

❑ My resume contains appropriate key words.

❑ I have emphasized all my strengths.

❑ All my major accomplishments are listed.

❑ I have used numbers, percentages, and other details to describe how my accomplishments will add value to a company.

❑ My resume can be easily scanned to pick up key words.

❑ I've chosen white, off-white, blue, or gray resume paper of good stock.

❑ Someone else has proofread my resume.

> ❑ My resume contains at least one or two special skills or special distinctions that help me stand out among other applicants.
>
> If one or more of the preceding steps has not been taken, do not print and distribute your resume. Complete all missing steps, and you will feel confident about your final product.

Progress Check Questions

1. Are there times when your resume might be longer than two pages? Discuss when this might be appropriate.

2. Do you have anything on your resume that might require an explanation during your interview, such as gaps in employment dates or a job from which you were fired that could come up in conversation? If yes, mark it as something you need to include in your interview preparation in Chapter 12.

 10.2 ELECTRONIC RESUMES (E-RESUMES)

Your resume should be readily available so that you are prepared to promote your credentials in your interviews or in response to online job postings which can lead to interviews. Preparing your resume in both electronic and paper formats will help keep you flexible enough to share it in whichever way is appropriate for individual employers.

E-RESUMES

E-resumes are commonly used as an attachment to an e-mail or to upload into a resume data bank. Results of an employer survey posted on Quintessential Careers indicate that 80 percent of employers like to receive resumes by e-mail.[1]

Resume templates and data banks are often used on specific company Websites to collect applications for employment online. These companies will usually use their own Website to post vacant positions and then require candidates to apply online so that applicant data and profiles can be sourced electronically. Online applications hosted directly on company Websites usually include an e-form, or template, which is formatted to accept candidate information electronically. Major online job search Websites such as http://www .monster.com/ and http://www.careerbuilder.com/ use a similar process.

Most resume templates available online are ready to process resumes prepared in an electronic file format called ASCII or plain text.

ASCII and Plain Text   Electronic resumes are usually formatted in ASCII (plain text) and pasted into the body of an e-mail message or entered directly into an online form. You can prepare your ASCII version of your resume with or without line breaks as part of the formatting. When preparing an e-resume to be pasted into the body of an e-mail message, you need to use line breaks. ASCII resumes prepared without line breaks are compatible for uploading to resume banks online. There are many Websites that provide detailed instructions on how to prepare ASCII file e-resumes. A little further in the chapter, you are provided some simple steps on how to create an ASCII file e-resume from MS Word documents.

MS Word File   Microsoft (MS) Word is Microsoft's version of a word processing software program and is one of the most widely requested resume formats. This is because a resume prepared in MS Word can be printed for hard-copy submission and, in most cases, it can be sent electronically. MS Word allows you to create and format your resume in Microsoft Office.

---

[1] QuintCareers.com. (2009). Quintessential Careers. Retrieved September 15, 2009 from www.quintessentialcareers .com.

You should be aware that not every recipient of your resume may have word processing software that is compatible with MS Word. If this is the case, your word document might not be able to be read. When sending your resume electronically, you should know how to convert your MS Word document to ASCII (plain text) or a PDF (portable document file) to ensure your copy will be easily transmitted electronically. Most resumes start in MS Word format. Using MS Word processing software enables you to have control and flexibility in developing your resume. It provides a more easily read and more professional version than some electronic versions.

PDF Files PDF stands for portable document format. A PDF file preserves the words, format, images, and layout of your e-resume when you transmit it electronically. To create a PDF file version of your resume you will need access to Adobe Reader software in your computer.

Web Resumes and HTML Files HTML file formats enable your resume to exist as a Web page.

NOTES | Resume File Formats

ASCII (with line breaks)	Can be pasted into the body of an e-mail message.
ASCII (without line breaks)	Can be pasted into resume templates in resume banks.
Microsoft Word or PDF	Can be sent as an attachment to an e-mail message.
Web-based or HTML	Visual, video, and sound capability. Can be uploaded to certain resume banks and social networking sites or housed on the Internet as its own URL.

KEY WORDS FOR E-RESUMES

Electronic resumes are most effective when key words are used throughout the text. Key words are usually nouns that describe skills and experience sought by a potential employer. If the key words in your resume match the skills and experiences of the job, it is selected and ranked by a computer. Those selected and ranked are read by a person who will decide whether or not you qualify for an interview based on your resume.

There are a number of ways to determine key words to use in your e-resume. You can include nouns found in job postings that match the position you are looking for. You can also review the list of transferable skills found in Chapter 2 and identify those that apply to you for inclusion on your resume. There are many Websites that list key words for you to review, including some Websites that list key words targeted to specific industries.

When developing an e-resume, it is important to incorporate the key words that appropriately represent your skills and experiences to maximize the number of matches that can be made to jobs you qualify for.

ACTIVITY 10.3

Create Your E-resume

Online resume tutorials on Websites like http://www.careerperfect.com/, http://www.monster.com/, and http://www.quintcareers.com/ are examples of online resources that contain information about the most current technology options for developing your e-resume. Working with your instructor, decide on what file format is right for you and select an online tool to help you practice developing an e-resume of your choice.

FIGURE 10.5

Sample ASCII (Plain Text, with Line Breaks) E-resume

```
Carla Mendez
Phone:(555) 555-5555
E-Mail: carlamendez@aol.com

Professional Objective: Director of National Recruiting

*** Professional Profile

College relations manager with proven results in traditional and
electronic recruiting, training, marketing and sales.

Experience with applying employment law for hiring international
students and developing general recruitment policies and procedures.

Proven leader/strong communication and interpersonal skills.

Proficient with Microsoft Office and HRIS systems.

***Work Experience

Flagship Hotel Company - Orlando, Florida
College Relations Manager (2009-present)
Direct and manage college recruiting for 24 hotels.
Recruit, hire and train staff.
Supervise 4 recruitment coordinators.
Conduct on-boarding orientation for new hires.
Work with hotel managers to plan quarterly recruitment needs.
Provide input into recruitment marketing materials, including company
website.

*Recruited 26 new college graduates of which 18 have been promoted.

*Wrote a new orientation program specifically for college graduates.

*Introduced new orientation program to regional managers.

*Received talent management award at annual corporate meeting.

Linkpro Temporary Staffing - Key West, Florida
Assistant Manager  (2007-2009)
Managed operations and supervised staff at the central office.
Conducted training of staff at 7 satellite locations. Managed payroll,
site leases and financial reports.

*Managed contract negotiations.

*Developed prospective client list and planned and tracked sales calls.

*Developed advertising and marketing plan that doubled the client base.

Clohan Security Company - Miami, Florida
Assistant Manager  (2005-2007)
Assisted with managing the human resource functions. Screened
applicants, conducted initial interviews, and made hiring
recommendations.

Beneficient Hospital - Miami, Florida
Human Resource Intern  (2004-2005)
Screened applicant tracking system to identify potential candidates for
department managers. Greeted visitors, answered phones and organized
meeting requests.

*** Education

FLORIDA INTERNATIONAL UNIVERSITY - Miami, Florida
Bachelor of Science in Business Management  (2005)

PROFESSIONAL DEVELOPMENT

* Internet Hiring

* Applicant Tracking Systems

* Leadership Miami graduate

* HR Certificate

*** Affiliations

Society for Human Resource Management

*** References provided on request
```

Since the resume in Figure 10.5 was prepared with line breaks, it can be pasted into the body of an e-mail message.

FIGURE 10.6

SAMPLE ASCII (Plain Text, Without Line Breaks) E-resume

```
Carla Mendez
Phone:(555) 555-5555
E-Mail: carlamendez@aol.com

Professional Objective: Director of National Recruiting

*** Professional Profile

College relations manager with proven results in traditional and
electronic recruiting, training, marketing and sales.

Experience with applying employment law for hiring international
students and developing general recruitment policies and procedures.

Proven leader/strong communication and interpersonal skills.

Proficient with Microsoft Office and HRIS systems.

***Work Experience

Flagship Hotel Company - Orlando, Florida
College Relations Manager (2009-present)
Direct and manage college recruiting for 24 hotels.
Recruit, hire and train staff.
Supervise 4 recruitment coordinators.
Conduct on-boarding orientation for new hires.
Work with hotel managers to plan quarterly recruitment needs.
Provide input into recruitment marketing materials, including company
Website.
*Recruited 26 new college graduates of which 18 have been promoted.
*Wrote a new orientation program specifically for college graduates.
*Introduced new orientation program to regional managers.
*Received talent management award at annual corporate meeting.

Linkpro Temporary Staffing - Key West, Florida
Assistant Manager  (2007-2009)
Managed operations and supervised staff at the central office.
Conducted training of staff at 7 satellite locations. Managed payroll,
site leases and financial reports.
*Managed contract negotiations.
*Developed prospective client list and planned and tracked sales calls.
*Developed advertising and marketing plan that doubled the client base.

Clohan Security Company - Miami, Florida
Assistant Manager  (2005-2007)
Assisted with managing the human resource functions. Screened
applicants, conducted initial interviews, and made hiring
recommendations.

Beneficient Hospital - Miami, Florida
Human Resource Intern  (2004-2005)
Screened applicant tracking system to identify potential candidates for
department managers. Greeted visitors, answered phones and organized
meeting requests.

*** Education

FLORIDA INTERNATIONAL UNIVERSITY - Miami, Florida
Bachelor of Science in Business Management  (2005)

PROFESSIONAL DEVELOPMENT

* Internet Hiring
* Applicant Tracking Systems
* Leadership Miami graduate
* HR Certificate

*** Affiliations
Society for Human Resource Management

*** References provided on request
```

Since the resume in Figure 10.6 was prepared without line breaks, it can be cut and pasted into resume templates and e-forms in online resume banks.

FIGURE 10.7

Sample Resume pasted within an E-mail Message

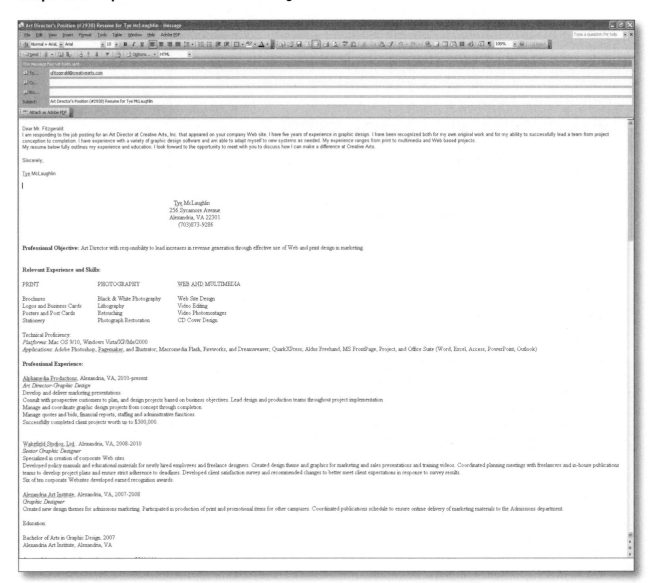

Real Life Stories

Eric and Lisa

Eric had just lost his job with a high-tech start company he had been with for two years. He was actively seeking a new job, using his expertise in the data storage industry. Eric circulated his resume with members of his industry trade group, an important part of his career network, and also posted his resume online. He also decided to file for unemployment. When he did, he did not realize that his resume automatically was sent to an online job resource developed by the Department of Labor. Eric received a job offer for a software engineer's position that was posted on the job bank. He accepted the offer and started the job within three weeks of posting his resume online. Eric's experience is an example of how applicant tracking systems can work well to electronically match job seekers' skills and experiences with specific job requirements.

Lisa

Lisa successfully used her online resume and job search follow-up advice she had received to obtain the internship she wanted with a public relations agency. The agency specifically requested applicants to submit plain text resumes online. After posting her plain text resume, Lisa received a call for an interview. After her interview, she was told that she would be contacted directly by the hiring manager for a second interview. Lisa asked for the name and e-mail address of the hiring manager. When she did not hear anything for a few days, Lisa e-mailed the hiring manager explaining she was following up from her first interview. She attached an MS Word document copy of her resume to the e-mail. She was asked back for a second interview. During the interview, Lisa noticed that the hiring manager had a printed copy of the MS Word version of her resume as opposed to the plain text version that prompted her first interview. Lisa was offered the internship position and later reflected on how important it was to be prepared to forward her resume in multiple formats to accommodate different situations in her job search.

Source: Accessed September 4, 2009, from http://money.cnn.com/magazines/moneymag/moneymag_

archive/2004/04/01/365028/index.htm and www.examiner.com/x-828-Entry-Level-Careers-Examiner~y2009m9d4-

Success-stories-from-my-first-year-as-an-Examiner.

10.3 PAPER RESUMES

While you will generally find an employer preference for e-resumes in your job search, hard-copy paper resumes are appropriate for targeted situations. You can mail or fax your paper version or present it to individuals at interviews, career fairs, networking events, and career coaching sessions.

Paper resumes can be prepared on your computer using Microsoft Word (.doc), Word-Perfect (.wpd), Rich Text Format (.rtf), or Portable Document Format (.pdf) formats.

NOTES   Paper Resume

When to Use a Paper Resume

- Mail
- Fax
- Person to person

NOTES   File Formats for Paper Resumes

Microsoft Word	(.doc)
WordPerfect	(.wpd)
Rich Text Format	(.rtf)
Portable Document	Format (.pdf)

FIGURE 10.8

Sample Chronological Print Resume—Recent Graduate

Source: © Career-Resumes, 2009. www.career-resumes.com.

JENNIFER L. NEWGRAD

5555 E. Hedgebrook Dr. ~ Sea Cove, TX 77000 ~ (555) 555-5555 ~ jnewgrad@aol.com

Career Focus

A position in Sales or Account Management

Strengths

- Friendly, enthusiastic and persuasive in sales situations — successful in promoting items with highest profit potential
- Excellent communication skills and a professional demeanor gained through extensive interaction with the public, leadership roles in college activities, and domestic and international travel.
- Unique combination of creativity and analytical skills with a high math aptitude and detail orientation.
- Computer proficient in MS Office 2000, PhotoShop, and Internet research on Mac and PC platforms.
- Recognized for reliability and "getting the job done" through persistence and a strong work ethic.

Education

<u>Texas A&M University</u> – College Station, TX
Bachelor of Business Administration, Marketing (November 2011)
Held numerous leadership positions in Alpha Kappa Psi, National Professional Business Fraternity
Educated children about community business as a Junior Achievement volunteer

Relevant Coursework:

Marketing ~ Advertising ~ Marketing Research ~ Marketing Management ~ European Marketing Strategy
Sales Management ~ Product Management ~ Operations Management ~ Scientific and Technical Writing
The Management Process ~ Strategic Management ~ Legal and Social Environment of Business ~ Business
Finance ~ Accounting ~ Business Math I & II ~ Design Foundations ~ Economics

Studied International Marketing in Eastern Europe through the university's Study Abroad program

Experience

<u>Morgan's Seafood Houses, Inc.</u> – Kemah and Houston, TX   9/09 to Present
Hostess / Shift Leader / Food Sales & Service
Earned living expenses during college through part-time employment in a variety of customer service positions for three Morgan's-owned restaurants. Accepted full-time employment after graduation and currently serve as Hostess for the flagship location and restaurant headquarters.

Implement menu changes and promotions, set customer service standards, and assist in training for other hostesses. Handle customer complaints with professionalism and a positive attitude in fast paced, stressful situations.

- Selected to work with corporate chef and management to design marketing and customer service strategies and improvements.
- Promoted to Shift Leader for excellence in service, sales, and leadership — successful in upselling drink items and persuading customers to order high dollar menu items and add-ons.

<u>Dynamic Marketing</u> – Houston, TX   Summer 2009
Recruiting Assistant
Assisted Human Resources in recruiting sales representatives to market cutlery products. Provided additional clerical and administrative support as needed, including taking telephone orders from customers and calculating individual sales volumes for each sales representative.

Available to travel and/or relocate

FIGURE 10.9

FIGURE 10.9

Sample Chronological Print Resume

Judy Epstein

Permanent Address:
89 Stallworth Drive
Boston, MA 89498
Phone: (508) 675-9387
E-mail: jepstein@cox.com

Professional Objective:
Jr. Staff Accountant's position with a national insurance or financial services firm with the opportunity to service multiple units.

Education:
Collins College, Boston, MA
B.S. Accounting, 2012

Relevant Coursework:

Accounting Information Systems	Cost Accounting
Computerized Financial Accounting	Managerial Accounting
Introduction to Financial Statements	Intermediate Accounting I & II

Work Experience:

2009–present: Goldcircle Bank, Quincy, MA
Part-time teller

Summer 2009 Brinker's Insurance Company, Boston, MA
Summer Internship Performed bookkeeping functions and monitored monthly budget reports. Assisted with processing insurance claims. Maintained updates to client profiles in ACCESS database. Worked with clients to ensure all necessary paperwork was available to process claims. Updated Employee Handbook. Performed general office work as needed.

September 2008– Collins College Purchasing Department
May 2009 *Student Assistant/College Work-Study Program*
Completed purchase orders. Coordinated classroom equipment inventories with facilities department to ensure classrooms were properly equipped.

Summer 2008 Camino's Italian Restaurant
Hostess

Community Service/Volunteer Work:

September 2007– Boys and Girls Clubs of America, Quincy, MA
May 2008

Extracurricular Activities:
Vice President of the Accounting Club
Member of DECA (Distributive Education Clubs of America)
Coach for girls' volleyball team
Fitness trainer

References available upon request

Sample Print Functional Resume

Hilmy Tecora

Permanent Address:

962 Summerdale Drive,
Pittsburg, PA 15122
Phone: (412) 483-9730
E-mail: htecora@gmail.com

Professional Objective:

To obtain a Web Developer position to support growth and development, and increased productivity of IT functions.

Relevant Experience and Skills:

Web Development	Knowledge of Section 508 and W3C Standards
Web Page Design	Architecture and Accessibility Techniques
Analytical Problem Solver	Presentation and Training Skills

Technical Skills:

Programming/Scripting Languages: HTML, XHTML, JavaScript
Database Applications: SQL, SQL/PL, Oracle, Access
Software Applications/Programs: Dreamweaver, Flash, Fireworks, Adobe Photoshop
Operating System/Platforms: Unix and Windows 2007

Professional Experience:

Cyrus Systems, Pittsburg, PA (2009–present)
Web Developer: Manage the maintenance, development, and enhancement of applications that interface with an Oracle database. Create, update, and maintain Web pages. Perform JavaScript and PDF conversions. Train staff in Flash and Fireworks applications.
Jr. Systems Programmer: Developed and coded Web-based applications and user interfaces. Technical team member responsible for developing Web, database, data search and retrieval applications.
Code Systems Securities, Denver, CO (2008–2009)
Technical Support Assistant: Generally assisted IT department with a variety of requests and interfaces with user groups. Supported the Help Desk. Monitored maintenance reports and tracked trouble shooting results on a monthly basis.

Education:

Cardon Community College, Denver, CO
B.S.Information Systems Programming (2008)
Student of the Year Award, 2007 and 2008

FIGURE 10-11

Sample Print Functional Resume

Lorinda Messina, MT (ASCP)

Permanent Address:
231 Maple Ave.
Long Island, NY 11111
Phone: (555) 555-5555
E-mail: lmessina@yahoo.com

Professional Objective
- Medical Technologist's position at a leading medical center

Special Distinctions
- Experienced medical technologist with ASCP certification, three years of experience as an NYU Medical Center lab technologist and bachelor's degree in medical technology.
- Excellent clinical laboratory skills, with commended performance conducting/analyzing laboratory assays and resolving complex clinical and instrument problems.
- Accurate, reliable, diligent and focused on the timely, quality completion of all lab procedures. Work well under pressure and time constraints within high-volume environments.

Work Experience
Medical Technologist
5/2010–Present, NYU Medical Center, New York, NY
Collect and prepare specimens and perform laboratory procedures used in the diagnosis, treatment, and prevention of disease. Verify, record, and report lab results on all performed tests. Ensure compliance with government requirements, hospital policies, and laboratory procedures, including maintaining the cleanliness of lab equipment, instruments, and work area.

Key Contributions
- Executed and analyzed tests in areas including chemistry, hematology, urinalysis, serology, histology, and bacteriology to aid physicians in diagnosing and treating disease.
- Consistently commended for the timely, high-quality completion of both routine and special laboratory assays of patient specimens (including blood and other body fluids, skin scrapings, and surgical specimens).
- Ensured test-result validity before recording/reporting results, earning a reputation for meticulous attention to detail.
- Demonstrated the ability to communicate test results effectively with physicians, pathologists, and nursing staff as a member of an interdisciplinary team focused on providing exemplary quality of care.
- Evaluated quality control within laboratory using standard laboratory test and measurement controls, and maintained compliance with CLIA, OSHA, safety, and risk-management guidelines.

Clinical Training
2/2009–5/2010, St. Vincent's Hospital Medical Center, New York, NY
Completed 15-month clinical training program at St. Vincent's Microbiology Department.

Key Contributions
- Operated and calibrated an assortment of laboratory/testing equipment and performed various chemical, microscopic, and bacteriologic tests.
- Performed stat and routine testing on a variety of specimens quickly and accurately.
- Maintained lab equipment and troubleshot/resolved instrument problems.
- Quickly mastered Meditech system.

Education
9/2006–5/2010: College of Long Island, Staten Island, NY
- BS degree in Medical Technology with honors (GPA: 3.6)

Certifications
- American Society for Clinical Pathology (ASCP) — Medical Technologist (MT), 2010, Chicago, IL
- Basic Life Support (BLS), 2010, New York, NY
- CPR and First Aid Certification, 2010, New York, NY

Skills

Skill Name	Skill Level
Clinical assays	Intermediate
Clinical microbiology	Intermediate
Lab equipment calibration	Intermediate
CLIA and OSHA compliance	Intermediate
Test result validity verification	Intermediate
Lab testing and reporting	Intermediate
Quality control	Intermediate

Additional Information
Available for all shifts and extended work hours. Relocating to Chicago, IL.

10.4 JOB APPLICATIONS

Employers commonly require completed job applications as part of the job search process. They are used by human resources departments for candidates who apply for a job in person at a company. Job applications are often used during interviews conducted at your school. When you are asked to complete a job application prior to an interview, you should submit your resume along with it, to be sure that your qualifications are presented in the best light. One purpose of the job application is to obtain factual information about you (e.g., Social Security number, emergency information, family relationships) that can be used for payroll or health insurance purposes if you are hired. Although the other purpose of the job application is to obtain information about your employment history, your professional qualifications are usually expressed better in your resume.

On a job application, you are simply presenting information an employer needs to see to determine whether you should be considered for a particular job. The job application is a screening device. It does not get you the job. Sometimes you will be asked to complete a job application after you've been hired so that the actual information about you needed by the human resources department can be recorded and used to process the necessary paperwork to start you as a new employee. You will want to ensure that your job application is the best one an employer sees.

The following are the main parts of a typical job application.

Identification

Name

Social Security number

Personal Data

Alien registration number of immigration status

Address

Telephone number

E-mail address

Emergency information

Health

General health

Workers' compensation

Attendance

Educational History

Education and formal training

Future schooling

Job Interest

Position desired

Salary desired

Availability

Transportation

Experience

Work experience

Military experience

Volunteer activities

Certification, registration, and licenses

Professional associations

Clubs and organizations

Hobbies, interests, and leisure-time activities
Other skills

Miscellaneous
Future plans
References
Crime convictions

POINTS TO REMEMBER WHEN COMPLETING A JOB APPLICATION

Name   Be sure to *print* your name where asked on the application and *sign* neatly on the signature line. You should carefully read and verify all statements on the application before signing it. Never list a nickname. Always use your complete legal name.

Social Security Number   Be sure to print your Social Security number so that it is readable and *correct!* Many companies use their employees' Social Security numbers in filing and computer systems. An error in your Social Security number could cause problems with your payments, benefits, taxes, retirement, and unemployment account. If you do not have a Social Security number, you should apply now at the nearest Social Security office.

Address   Before you list your address, read the instructions. Then be prepared to put all your data in the correct spaces. If the application does not ask for a certain order, list the information in the following order: street address, rural route or box number, city, state, and zip code. Consider your answer when asked how long you have lived at a certain address. This information will give employers an impression of your stability.

Telephone Number   A source of frustration for an employer is wanting to reach a good candidate and not being able to do so because the candidate has either forgotten to leave a telephone number or has left an incorrect one. List a phone number that is likely to be answered during the day. If no one will be answering your phone, or if you do not have a phone, list the number of someone who can accept messages for you. Choose someone who will be polite, take your message accurately, and get the message to you very quickly. If you are using an answering machine or your cell phone to accept your messages, be sure to create a positive impression on the caller by recording a professional-sounding message.

E-mail Address   Clearly spell out your e-mail address using proper letter cases (i.e., capital versus lowercase) and punctuation (e.g., dashes, periods, underscores).

Date and Place of Birth   You may be asked to give the date of your birth on some applications. It is important that you give the right information. This date is used to compute your insurance and retirement plans after you are hired. You can be fired for falsifying information on a job application. Remember that the law will be on your side if you are *denied* a job because of your age.

Proof of Age   You may be asked to prove your age for some employers. Most employers accept a driver's license as proof of age. If you do not have a driver's license, get a copy of your birth certificate or any other legal document that shows your age.

Citizenship   You may be asked to indicate whether you can provide proof of citizenship if you are hired.

General Health   It will benefit you the most if you can list your health as excellent. If you have a health problem that will not affect your ability to do the job you want, do not note any negative information on your application. Leave the health sections blank if necessary, and be prepared to discuss your health during an interview. If you have a health problem, ask your doctor if it will in any way impair your ability to perform your job. If your doctor thinks the problem would be limiting, ask for advice on how to handle this on a job application.

Education and Formal Training   You should be able to account for all the time you spent in school or in training. This information could be important in explaining gaps in your employment history. It will also clearly indicate to employers whether or not you meet the primary requirements for the job that is available.

Salary Desired   If you have not recently researched the job market, be careful how you answer this question. You do not want to undersell yourself or ask for such a high salary that you rule yourself out of the competition. You can research the job market by following these suggestions:

Read want ads that list salaries for similar positions.

Call your local employment office or job career services office and ask the salary range for the type of job you are seeking.

Talk with people who do the kind of work you want.

You may list a specific salary, give a high–low range, or leave the space blank. Another alternative is to respond with the word *open*. This is a positive word. It will not commit you to a future either too low or too high. When considering a salary offer, don't forget to consider the benefits as well as the base salary. Added benefits can make one salary more valuable than a slightly higher one without benefits. Mentally adjust your desired salary according to the benefits; then state the salary you want.

Work Experience   You should be well prepared to list your work history. List the data for your most recent job first. List your next most recent job in the next space provided, and so on. If you have no work experience, leave the spaces blank and be prepared to offset this during an interview.

Professional Organizations   Employers may be interested in the professional organizations to which you belong. Such membership is especially important if the organization and job are directly related.

Hobbies, Interests, and Leisure-Time Activities   What you do with your free time tells an employer much about your interests and drive. An employer may have a special interest in you if your hobby relates closely to your job.

References   Consider the following people to be your references:

Former employers, supervisors, and coworkers

Former teachers, instructors, and professors

Your minister, priest, or rabbi

Acquaintances who have job titles indicating responsibility

Long-time acquaintances

Many job seekers think that employers do *not* contact references. This is a myth. Employers *often* contact references—especially when the job includes significant responsibility.

After preparing all the information that might be asked of you on a job application, be sure to have your prepared details with you on every job search. Every employer differs in whether or not a job application is required in addition to a resume. You should always be prepared to complete an accurate and detailed job description when asked by an employer. The following are some guidelines for properly completing a job application.

Use a Pen   Do not use a pencil; use only a black or blue pen. Your pen should let you print neatly without blobs, smudges, or smears. You may want to use a fine-point pen. This kind of pen makes it easier to print small when you must write in small blanks or boxes. It is wise to carry a spare pen with the same ink color and line width as your first pen.

Bring Your Resume   If you prefer, you may carry an extra resume with you to use as a reminder of important information as well. In fact, it is wise to be prepared to present a resume should you obtain an immediate interview.

Follow Instructions   Be sure to read all the instructions before writing anything on an application. Many applications begin with general instructions, such as "Print in ink," or "To be handprinted in ink," or "Typewritten." Separate instructions may tell you not to put any data in certain spaces.

Following instructions is important. Employers want to hire people who can follow instructions on the job. Employers will not have a high regard for your dependability and skill if you cannot follow instructions on an application.

The Dash   Some application questions *will not apply to you.* Make a short dash (—) after each of these questions. The dash is simple; it tells the employer you have read the question but it does not apply to you.

Blank Spaces   It is sometimes better to leave a blank space on your application. An application will not necessarily get you a job, but it can keep you from being considered for a job. If an honest answer to an application question is negative or can easily be misunderstood, leave this item blank. Do not even make a dash in this space. You can explain the blank during the interview if necessary. In this way, the blank will not automatically be used to screen you from a job for which you might otherwise qualify.

ACTIVITY 10.4

Sample Job Application

Study the following application for employment to get an idea of what a typical job application looks like. Fill in each section accurately. Make sure you understand the questions you are required to answer, and be sure you feel comfortable with each response.

Once you have completed the job application, give it to someone to review. Discuss which sections you had the most difficulty with and why. Get input from others on how to handle any sections about which you are uncertain.

XYZ CORPORATION

Application for Employment

INCOMPLETE APPLICATIONS WILL NOT BE CONSIDERED

NAME (Last First Middle)	Date
Permanent Address Street City State Zip	Area Code Phone Number Cell Number
Temporary Address Street City State Zip	E-Mail Address
Birth Date Male ❑ Female ❑	Social Security Number

Are you applying for Full-Time ❑   Part-Time ❑   Seasonal ❑   Other? ❑

EDUCATIONAL HISTORY

School	Name and Location	Major	Grades High Good Aver.	Circle Highest Grade Completed	Type of Degree or Certificate Recvd.	Date of Leaving
High				9 10 11 12		
Trade				1 2 3 4		
College				1 2 3 4		
Postgrad				1 2 3 4		
Other training or skills (factory or office machines operated, special courses)						
List computer skills (such as competency with software packages)						

WE ARE AN EQUAL OPPORTUNITY EMPLOYER

EMPLOYMENT HISTORY

READ CAREFULLY: Starting with your present or most recent job, working backward; account for all time, including periods of unemployment (include five-year employment history).

Name, Address, Phone		Dates		Position, Duties, Supervisor	Base Wage/Salary	Reason for Leaving
		Month	Year			
	From				Starting	
	To				Final	
	From				Starting	
	To				Final	
	From				Starting	
	To				Final	
	From				Starting	
	To				Final	

Person to notify in case of emergency	Name	Address	City	State	Zip	Area Code Phone

JOB INTEREST

Have you ever been employed by XYZ Corporation?   Yes   No
Have you ever applied to XYZ Corporation?   Yes   No
In what types of work are you interested?   Starting wage expected? $ per
How were you referred?   If by newspaper or agency, give name

Can you work:

Saturday ❏ Yes   Sunday ❏ Yes   Weekdays ❏ Yes   Evenings ❏ Yes   Holidays ❏ Yes   Daytime ❏ Yes
       ❏ No   ❏ No   ❏ No   ❏ No   ❏ No   ❏ No
or Night Hours? ❏ Yes
                ❏ No

PERSONAL DATA

Citizen of USA?   Yes ❏   No ❏
If hired, can you furnish proof that you are eligible to work in the U.S.?
Have you ever collected workers' compensation?   Yes ❏   No ❏   State of health: Fair ❏   Good ❏   Excellent ❏
Have you ever been convicted of any crime other than a minor traffic violation?   Yes ❏   No ❏
If yes, when, where, and disposition?
Do you have any relatives or acquaintances employed by XYZ Corporation?   Yes ❏   No ❏   Location:
If yes, give names:

A professionally prepared resume is essential to any job search. Next to the interview, it is the tool most widely used by employers to evaluate the qualifications of job candidates.

Choosing a resume style that best portrays your qualifications is an essential first step. You can create a resume that stands out from others by taking the time to target your resume to a specific job or company. When used appropriately, power words and key words can help you tailor your resume to match key words in job postings or on the Website for the company you are interested in.

Practice writing your resume several times before you print or post your final copy. Have it reviewed by an instructor or another person who knows you and can provide input.

Once you have selected your resume style, it is best to prepare your resume in different electronic file formats. You will find that employers have preferences for the ways they would like your resume transmitted to them. If you have a paper resume and an e-resume that can be transmitted by e-mail and one that can be used with online resume banks, you will be prepared to share your resume as individual employers request.

While employer requirements for job applications vary, you should always be prepared to complete an accurate and thorough history of yourself to a prospective employer. Many employers will require you to complete their job application online. As with your resume, if you are transmitting your job application electronically, be prepared to use key words that will help your application be recognized among others as a best fit for the position you are applying to. Taking the time to think about how to prepare your resume and job applications can help you obtain job interviews for positions that best match your qualifications.

RESUMES AND JOB APPLICATIONS AND CAREER DECISION MAKING

Based on what you learned about resumes in this chapter, think about what decisions you need to make about developing your resume.

What am I trying to decide?

_____

_____

What do I need to know?

_____

_____

Why do I need to know it?

_____

_____

How will it help me make a more informed decision?

_____

_____

Why do I need to know it now?

_____

_____

How can I obtain what I need to know?

_____

_____

People _____

Experience _____

Research _____

Who are my best resources for the information I need?

_____

_____

Why do I think they are the right resources?

_____

_____

Letters

After completing this chapter you will:

1 **Identify** guidelines for writing job search letters

2 **Recognize** and effectively write the kinds of letters you may use during your job search

During your job search, letter writing is an important form of communicating with an employer. By corresponding directly with an employer over time, you demonstrate a sustained interest in the job and reveal something about your personality and professional goals. The prime reason for writing a letter as you initiate your job search is to secure a job interview. If your background and work experience are comparable to those of other candidates, it is your cover letter that will distinguish you from everyone else. The cover letter reveals the reason you want to work for the company and gives you an opportunity to talk about your positive traits and what you can bring to the employer. The clarity, conciseness, and professionalism of your letter can make a positive first impression on an employer who has not yet met you. In addition to the cover letter, there are several other letters that you will likely write before, during, and after your job search, including letters of application for specific positions, internships, or co-ops; letters of inquiry; networking letters; letters for a change of career; letters to request recommendations; thank-you letters; and letters to accept, reject, or resign from a position. It is imperative that you also be able to write proper electronic letters. You should be able to recognize the differences between each of these types and write each one effectively.

CASE STUDY

Maura learned about the importance of a well-written cover letter to her job search in her career development and business communications classes. Maura always knew that cover letters could be a good introduction to a resume when applying for a job. But she never considered other types of letters in her job search and why they are important. For example, taking the time to write a letter of refusal to an employer regarding a job offer that you decide not to accept, or writing a networking letter to use in your career network to help you obtain an interview with a company you would love to work for. Maura discovered that, when prepared well, job search letters can help you make a positive impression with employers. Now that she was preparing for her job search, Maura wanted to focus on preparing letters that would capture employers' interest in her unique qualifications.

In her career development class, Maura received a good grade for the sample cover letter she wrote as part of a homework assignment. At the career fairs she attended, she made a point of collecting the business cards of individual company representatives. Maura focused on writing cover letters to accompany her resume that she would send to the 10 companies that interested her most.

For those 10 companies, Maura targeted her cover letters by including the company name, the title of the position she was interested in, and some specific reasons why she wanted to work for that particular company. She researched the job descriptions posted on the companies' Websites to identify key words that she could use in her letters that matched some of the skills and other qualifications she felt matched the specific job requirements. She researched the names and correct titles of the contact people she was writing to and their e-mail addresses. She also obtained their street address. Maura had a head start on correct contact information with the business cards she had collected at the career fairs. When the contact information was difficult to obtain, she either called the company directly or went online and found that by going to the LinkedIn Website, she was able to obtain some of the contact information she was looking for. She planned on sending her letters online, but was also preparing a hard copy to mail to each employer as a back up. Her instructor told her that sometimes e-mails with attachments get filtered or cannot be opened by the recipient. Her mailed copies would ensure that she made the connections she wanted in the event that her electronic letter was not received.

Maura prepared another short list of companies she might be interested in and monitored job postings online on a regular basis. Her plan was to use the general cover letter she had prepared in her career development class to respond to additional opportunities as they became available. Maura tried to use the editing tools available to her online to avoid spelling, punctuation, and grammar errors on her document and also had her business communications instructor review her documents for accuracy and correctness.

Maura was confident that she had prepared cover letters that could make her qualifications stand out from others applying for the same jobs. She received a job interview, and eventually, a job offer from one of the 10 companies she was most interested in. The hiring manager commented that he was impressed that Maura had taken the time to properly address him, specifically, in the letter and tailor her cover letter to include specific references to the position and the company. Her extra effort demonstrated her genuine interest in working with the company and highlighted her qualifications for the specific position she was interested in.

Discussion Questions

1. What steps did Maura take to ensure her cover letters to her preferred employers were targeted to attract their attention?
2. Was Maura's strategy to use her general cover letter for the rest of her job search a good decision?
3. Do you think that Maura was right to include highlights of her skills and qualifications in her cover letter, in addition to including them on her resume?

11.1 GUIDELINES FOR WRITING JOB SEARCH LETTERS

Writing letters as part of the job search can be one of your most valuable efforts. It can also be one of the most difficult. The following are the basic guidelines:

- Be brief and to the point.
- Use a standard business letter format.
- Make sure you address the letter to the proper individual and use his or her proper title.
- Make absolutely no errors in grammar, punctuation, spelling, or typing. An error could automatically rule you out of consideration.

BE BRIEF AND TO THE POINT

Think about what you want to say before you compose your letter. Be sure to think about presenting information about yourself that will really spark interest in you as a serious job candidate. Don't repeat the detailed experience listed in your resume; summarize it. In your resume, what you write is important; in your cover letter, how you write the highlights from your resume is important.

It takes practice to create a well-written letter. Don't get frustrated if writing doesn't come easily to you and you have trouble with your cover letter at first. Seek out some help from your teacher, parents, or professional contacts, and you will be sure to end up with a document you are proud of.

USE STANDARD BUSINESS LETTER FORMAT

Your cover letter should be a professional business letter. There are sample formats for you to follow in this chapter. If you are not accustomed to business writing, these formats provide basic guidelines for you to follow. There are many reference books available in the library on effective business letter writing that give helpful hints on how to compose a letter that has a proper business format and elicits interest in the reader. By reviewing the sample formats in this chapter and completing the activities, you will be able to structure your cover letter properly.

ADDRESS THE LETTER TO THE PROPER INDIVIDUAL

It is important to personalize your letter by addressing it directly to the appropriate individual and using their proper title. You may find this person's name and title listed in a classified ad, a job vacancy bulletin, or a business directory. If the name of the contact person is not listed, or if you have heard about the job from another source, call the company and ask for the name and title of the person to write to. You may also want to ask for the person's proper address, because he or she may not be located at the main address listed for the company; many times a company has offices or buildings spread out in various locations. At all costs, avoid writing cover letters that begin with "Dear Sir or Madam" or "To Whom It May Concern." This type of general salutation may cause the reader to feel you have not taken much time to research the company or that you are not seriously considering that particular company in your job search. We all like to be acknowledged by name, and we all like our names to be spelled correctly; your prospective employer is no different.

MAKE ABSOLUTELY NO ERRORS

Your cover letter must be perfect. Most employers view the quality of your cover letter as a reflection of your professionalism, attention to detail, and written communication skills; therefore, even one error can cause an employer to pass on your application. Do not depend on only your own eyes to proofread your letter. You may be too close to your own work to see your mistakes. Have one or two other people read your letter and make necessary corrections. If you use a word processor to prepare your letter, do not depend totally on the spell-checker. A wrong word that is spelled properly but used out of context in your letter will be accepted by the spell-checker and will leave you with a mistake.

11.2 TYPES OF LETTERS

There are several types of letters you may likely write before, during, and after your job search. It is important that you have an understanding of each one and can recognize the differences between them in terms of format and content and when you should use each one.

NOTES | Letters You Should Know

You should know how to recognize and effectively write the following letters:

- Cover letters
    - Letter of application for a specific position
    - Letter of inquiry
    - Networking letter
- Career changer letter
- Letter to request a recommendation
- Thank-you letter following an interview
- Letter accepting a position
- Letter refusing a position
- Thank-you letter for a company visit
- Application letter for internship or co-operative education program
- Letter of resignation
- Electronic letters
    - E-mail with attached cover letter and resume
    - E-mail cover letter with attached resume

COVER LETTER

A cover letter is a letter that accompanies your resume. It is the main letter used in a job search. The purpose of the cover letter is to promote your qualifications to an employer so that you will obtain an interview. Employers can receive hundreds of resumes for a single job opening, depending on the type of job it is and on how many people are unemployed or looking to change their current jobs. When the resumes received show similar backgrounds among many candidates, employers look for some way to narrow down the field of applicants to be interviewed. A well-prepared cover letter can make you stand out favorably among other applicants and lead to your being selected for an interview.

Look at the sample format for cover letters in Figure 11.1. By using this as a guide for preparing your own cover letters, you will be sure to convey all the important information your prospective employer needs to know.

There are three types of cover letters. They are the letter of application for a specific position, the letter of inquiry, and the networking letter. The first is used when sending your resume in response to a specific position you know is available through the classified ads, through a job posting system at work, on the Internet, or by word of mouth. The second type is used when you are inquiring about the availability of employment at a firm. The third is used when you are contacting someone in your career network to apply for a particular position, ask for a job lead, or ask for an introduction to another contact. In each case, the cover letter is your tool for promoting your qualifications for employment, but you must approach writing these letters in slightly different ways.

FIGURE 11.1

Format for Cover Letters

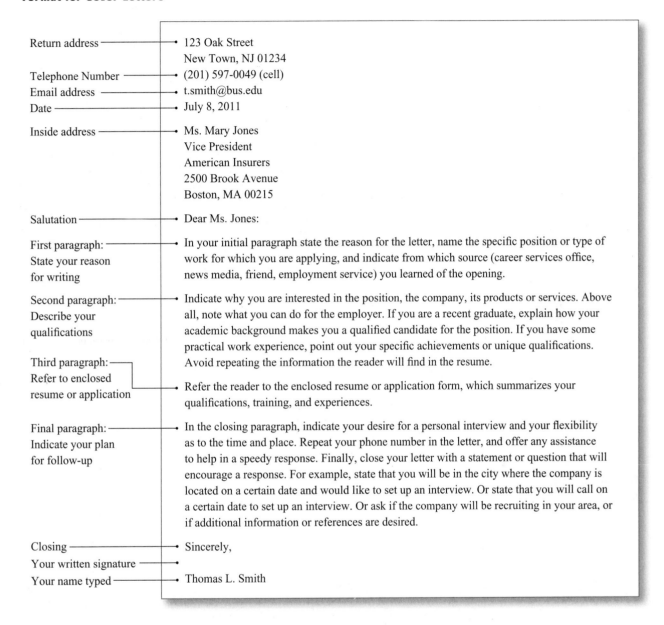

Return address — 123 Oak Street
New Town, NJ 01234

Telephone Number — (201) 597-0049 (cell)
Email address — t.smith@bus.edu
Date — July 8, 2011

Inside address — Ms. Mary Jones
Vice President
American Insurers
2500 Brook Avenue
Boston, MA 00215

Salutation — Dear Ms. Jones:

First paragraph:
State your reason
for writing — In your initial paragraph state the reason for the letter, name the specific position or type of work for which you are applying, and indicate from which source (career services office, news media, friend, employment service) you learned of the opening.

Second paragraph:
Describe your
qualifications — Indicate why you are interested in the position, the company, its products or services. Above all, note what you can do for the employer. If you are a recent graduate, explain how your academic background makes you a qualified candidate for the position. If you have some practical work experience, point out your specific achievements or unique qualifications. Avoid repeating the information the reader will find in the resume.

Third paragraph:
Refer to enclosed
resume or application — Refer the reader to the enclosed resume or application form, which summarizes your qualifications, training, and experiences.

Final paragraph:
Indicate your plan
for follow-up — In the closing paragraph, indicate your desire for a personal interview and your flexibility as to the time and place. Repeat your phone number in the letter, and offer any assistance to help in a speedy response. Finally, close your letter with a statement or question that will encourage a response. For example, state that you will be in the city where the company is located on a certain date and would like to set up an interview. Or state that you will call on a certain date to set up an interview. Or ask if the company will be recruiting in your area, or if additional information or references are desired.

Closing — Sincerely,
Your written signature —
Your name typed — Thomas L. Smith

Letter of Application for a Specific Position   This letter states your specific qualifications for the job for which you are applying. Always begin by addressing the letter to a specific person, using his or her full title. Be sure to enclose a typed copy of your resume, and say in the letter that you did so. State the position for which you are applying, and mention where you found out about the job (career services office, newspaper, etc.). Relate how your education has made you qualified for this position. State what you can offer rather than what you hope to gain. Unless requested to do so in the ad, do not mention a salary requirement in your letter; by being too high, or even too low, you can eliminate your chance for an interview. If the ad requires that you state a salary requirement, use the guidelines given in Chapter 10 for filling in that space in a job application. Request an interview at the employer's convenience, and follow up in approximately one week with a telephone call. Figure 11.2 is an example of a letter of application for a specific position.

Letter of Inquiry   Use this letter if a mass-mailing campaign is part of your job search. It is similar to a cold call in sales. You are writing to inquire whether or not

FIGURE 11.2

Format for Letter of Application for a Specific Position

Your home address
Telephone number
E-mail address

Inside address
(Always use individual's name)

Date

Dear _____:

I am writing in response to your ad in the *Boston Globe* on Sunday, August 6, 2011, for an administrative assistant for your executive offices.

Your company interests me because of your worldwide reputation and excellent history of stability. I have read about your plans to expand your business into the Southeast, and those plans for growth convince me that XYZ Corporation is a progressive company.

Enclosed is my resume. I am proficient with Microsoft 2007.

I have created intricate PowerPoint presentations, and Excel Worksheets. I also have created Access databases and have worked with Blackbaud fundraising software while on an internship involving a fundraising project. I completed a second internship with your firm last year.

I look forward to an interview and will call you shortly to arrange a convenient time.

Sincerely,

(written signature)

Your name typed

Enclosure

FIGURE 11.3

Format for Letter of Inquiry

Your address
E-mail address
Telephone number

Inside address
(Always use individual's name)

Date

Dear _____ :

I am writing to inquire about a career opportunity in marketing with your company.

At a recent career day held on my campus, I learned that XYZ Bank is expanding its branches throughout the Northeast. I have read about your profits over the past five years and see that XYZ Bank is a growth-oriented organization with a solid history.

My resume is enclosed for your information and highlights my work experience in the marketing field. My phone number and e-mail address are also listed. I look forward to an interview with you to further discuss how I think I can contribute to XYZ Bank.

Sincerely,

(written signature)

Your name typed

Enclosure

the company needs someone with your background. To your knowledge, there is not a specific position available. Address your letter to a specific person, and use his or her full title. You may need to call the company to find out the correct person's name and title. Enclose a copy of your resume, and say that you did so in the letter. State your interest in the company, referring to it by name. Briefly state how your background may benefit the company, mentioning your education and any skills gained through outside activities or part-time jobs. Ask for the opportunity to discuss your qualifications in person, at the employer's convenience. Figure 11.3 is an example of a Letter of Inquiry.

Networking Letter   Someone in your career network may have suggested you write to another member in your network or someone else they can refer you to. Your purpose might be to obtain information or to ask for a job lead. Figure 11.4 shows an outline of a networking letter, and Figure 11.5 shows a sample letter.

Your address
Telephone number
E-mail address

Date

Inside address
(Always use individual's name)

Dear_____:

I am writing at the recommendation of (name of person who referred you) who suggested I contact you regarding my job search. I have three years of part-time job experience in various technology related positions. My goal is to be a Software Engineer for Merckel, Inc. Since we are graduates of the same college and you have been with Merckel for two years, I thought you might tell me if you think I qualify for a position at the company. I understand there are many graduates from our college employed by Merckel.

I will graduate in March with my bachelors' degree in software engineering and feel there are a number of positions at your company that fit my qualifications. I have enclosed my resume for your information. My phone number and e-mail address are included.
I look forward to an interview to further discuss the contributions I think I can make to Merckel. If there is an individual within the company that you think I should contact directly regarding my job search, please be sure to let me know.

Thank you in advance for your help.

Sincerely,

(written signature)

Your name typed

FIGURE 11.4

Format for Networking Letter

FIGURE 11.5

Networking Letter Sample

84 Commanders Way
Annapolis, MD 21401
(410) 782-9184
d.bartnett@jwu.edu

November 7, 2011

Ms. Erica Downing, Esquire
Crane and Crane, Attorneys at Law
486 Regal Parkway
Baltimore, MD 21206

Dear Ms. Downing:

Tom Lester suggested I write you regarding the possibility of a position for a Paralegal at the new law office you will open in January. I am interested in working with Crane and Crane because of the fine reputation the firm has as the leading law firm in Maryland for bankruptcy and foreclosure work.

I am confident that my Paralegal degree and work experience gained through two internships have provided me specific skills needed by your firm.

Skills/qualifications	Example
• legal research	• researching legal journals to draft motion
• legal writing	• writing case notes
• computer skills	• XLNT writing
• meeting deadlines	• filing papers on deadline with courts

I have assisted attorneys with preparing for hearings and have the ability to prioritize work to accommodate case load requirements. I have experience with maintaining client databases. I created a new e-files system for the paralegals at one of my internship sites. The opening of your second office presents an opportunity for me to use my experience to establish a well organized, client-friendly office that reflects Crane and Crane's standards for quality.

Being part of your new office opening team would be an exciting and challenging experience for me. My resume, with contact information, is enclosed. Knowing you are frequently out of the office at hearings and with clients, I have copied Ms. Terri Burke, your office manager, should she be scheduling interview times with candidates for you. I will call next week if I do not hear from you or Ms. Burke sooner.

Thank you for your time.

Sincerely,

(written signature)

Dina Bartnett

cc: Ms. Terri Burke

Enclosure

Progress Check Questions

1. How many different situations can you think of where you might use a networking letter?
2. Have you updated your contact information in your career network files recently?

CAREER CHANGER LETTER

This type of letter is usually written by adult students who have returned to school and are now changing careers as a result of the additional skills and qualifications acquired by advanced education and previous work experience. These letters should focus on transferable skills. The use of bulleted points within the letter accentuates the transferable skills and emphasizes how they match specific skill requirements for the job.

FIGURE 11.6

Format for Career Changer Letter

Your address
Telephone number
E-mail address

Date

Inside address
(Always use individual's name)

Dear_____:

I am writing in response to the Corporate Event Planner position posted on your Website. Cranmore Industries has always been an employer of choice for me. I have followed your growing list of corporate clients and your introduction of your first international location in Italy, the site of the 2015 world sports competition. I know that it will take much advanced planning, staffing and training to prepare for servicing an event of this magnitude.

I am about to graduate with my degree in sports entertainment event management. I have worked as an administrative assistant in the corporate world for sixteen years and decided to return to school to obtain a degree to pursue my passion for a career as an events coordinator for a large, multinational company.

Enclosed is my resume. I am available for an interview upon request and look forward to the opportunity to discuss this opportunity with you directly. I feel confident that we will discover that Cranmore Industries and I are the right fit.

Sincerely,

(Written signature)

Elizabeth M. Cole

Enclosure

FIGURE 11.7

Career Changer Letter Sample

62 Indian Bend Court
Phoenix, AZ 85008
(602) 849-9624
l.diaz@asu.edu

March 24, 2011

Mr. Felipe Estrada
Vice President of Operations
Delta Pharmacy Corporation
1498 Comstock Parkway
Miami, FL 33101

Dear Mr. Estrada:

I am writing to apply for the Regional Store Manager position advertised on Monster.com on May 2nd. I have been following Delta Pharmacy's expansion plan to the Phoenix area, and am impressed with the company's strategic plan to be ranked among the top five pharmacy companies in the U.S. I have reviewed the job description that you have posted and am providing examples of my skills that match some of the job requirements.

Skills/qualifications	Examples
• speak and read Spanish fluently	• translated pharmaceutical representative's training manuals from English to Spanish
• pharmaceutical product knowledge	• semi-annual pharmaceutical sales convention
• time management	• Mind Tools software and personal digital assistant (PDA)
• cost control and revenue generation	• monitor generic drug prices vs. name brands • three year consecutive lead sales award

After spending fifteen years in pharmaceutical sales for Blake and Blake, I returned to school to pursue my degree in business management. After completing my degree in June, I am interested in applying my management skills and my sales experience to move from sales to a lead operations role. I am confident that I can build a strong team and manage the financial success of Delta's west coast group of stores.

I look forward to the opportunity to discuss this with you in person. I can be reached at the above phone number or e-mail address. My resume is enclosed.

Sincerely,

(Your written signature)

Lior Diaz

Enclosure

ACTIVITY 11.1

Preparing Your Cover Letter

Preparing your own cover letter is easy if you take the time to organize your thoughts and plan what you want to say in each part of the letter.

Select an employer to write to concerning your interest in employment. Decide what you want to say to your prospective employer. Then fill in each section below to create your own cover letter.

Return address _____

_____

_____

Telephone number _____

E-mail address _____

Date _____

_____

_____

Inside address _____

_____

_____

Salutation _____

First paragraph:
State your reason _____
for writing
_____

_____

Second paragraph:
Describe your _____
qualifications
_____

_____

Third paragraph:
Refer to enclosed _____
resume or application
_____

_____

Final paragraph:
Indicate your _____
plan for follow-up
_____

_____

Closing _____

Your written signature _____

Your name typed _____

LETTER TO REQUEST A RECOMMENDATION

This letter is written to people who will be able to recommend you for a position. Make a personal call in addition to writing the letter. Choose people you are sure will recommend you favorably. Identify yourself by name and make mention of how you know the person. If your name has changed since the time you first knew this person, mention the name by which he or she knew you. Ask permission to use this person's name as a reference in your job search. Make the contact friendly, but convince the person that this is important to you.

Send a copy of your resume to each person you would like to serve as a reference, and send updates as you make them. This will enable the person to be more comfortable and/or specific when talking about you to an employer. In addition to having someone write a letter of recommendation for you to present to a specific employer, you may also want to ask each person for an open letter of recommendation that can be used right away if you need it.

FIGURE 11.8

Format for Letter to Request a Recommendation

Your address

Date

Inside address

(Always use individual's name.)

Dear _____ :

I am currently conducting a job search and would like permission to give your name as a reference to some prospective employers.

I value the experience I gained when working for you last summer. Since you were my direct supervisor, you have firsthand knowledge of my skills, dependability, and ability to work well with others. Would you be willing to share your thoughts about my work performance with another employer by telephone or by writing a letter of reference for me to present on my interviews?

I can be reached at (telephone number, including area code). You can also contact me by e-mail at (e-mail address).

Thank you in advance for your cooperation.

Sincerely,

(written signature)

Your name typed

THANK-YOU LETTER FOLLOWING AN INTERVIEW

This letter is written after the interview to acknowledge the interviewer's time and cooperation. This is a good way to ensure that your interviewer will remember you. Be sure to send the letter right after the interview, and thank the interviewer for his or her time. Restate the position for which you applied, and give the date and/or place of the interview. In your letter mention one positive thing that happened during your interview. Express your interest in the opportunities offered in an enthusiastic way. Be sure to include your telephone number and return address. Without this information, an employer may not be able to contact you and you could lose out on a job offer.

To help in writing the thank-you letter, make sure you keep current and accurate records of every interview: the date, time, location, interviewer, and any special information concerning the company or the job itself.

FIGURE 11.9

Format for Thank-You Letter Following an Interview

Your home address
Telephone number
E-mail address

Inside address
(Always use individual's name.)

Date

Dear _____ :

I appreciated the opportunity to talk with you on (date) about the Account Representative position at your company. The information you shared with me about (company name) was excellent, and I am excited about the possibility of applying my education and experience to the position we discussed. I am confident that my sales experience with ABC Food Marketing Inc. will allow me to be among the more qualified candidates for the position.

If I can provide you with any additional information, please let me know. I look forward to hearing from you soon.

Sincerely,

(written signature)

Your name typed

Real Life Stories

Craig's Career Networking Letters
Craig was about to graduate with a degree in Homeland Security and Public Safety.

His goal was to obtain an entry-level position with the Department of Homeland Security. He knew that it might be difficult to stand out among the thousands of candidates applying each year. After Craig followed the instructions to apply online on the Department's Website, he wanted to draw attention to his application. He took advantage of his career network and wrote a letter to a friend currently working at the Department, who had graduated from his school the year before. Craig asked his friend for the recruiting manager's contact information and then wrote her a targeted letter of application.

Craig also wrote a letter to his friend and e-mailed his resume and asked her to share it directly with the recruiting manager. His friend said that she would be sure to communicate that Craig was one of the top graduates from the school's program that year and that Craig had already completed his application online.

Craig did receive a call for an interview and later received a job offer, which he accepted. He recognized the value of his personalized career networking letters and made a commitment to use targeted letters as a way to maintain and develop connections in his career network.

LETTER ACCEPTING A POSITION

This letter is written after you have agreed to accept an offer for a specific position. Whether a job offer comes to you orally or in writing, answer the offer immediately. Be direct about accepting, and restate the specific position you have accepted. Be sure to express your appreciation for the opportunity your employer has given you, and express your eagerness to begin your new job.

Resist the temptation to sound either overly grateful or reticent about your abilities to fulfill the job requirement. A straightforward, pleasant, confident response is all that is needed.

FIGURE 11.10

Format for Letter Accepting a Position

Your home address
Telephone number
E-mail address

Inside address
(Always use individual's name.)

Date

Dear _____ :

I am very pleased to accept your offer (state offer) as outlined in your letter of (date).
(Include all details of offer—location, starting salary, starting date.)
(Mention enclosures—application, resume, employee forms, or other information—and any related commentary.)

I look forward to meeting the challenges of the job, and I shall make every attempt to fulfill your expectations.

Sincerely,

(written signature)

Your name typed

Enclosures

LETTER REFUSING A POSITION

This letter is written after you have definitely decided not to accept the particular position offered. You should always write this letter to an employer, because by doing so, you make a favorable impression. Someday you may again be applying for a job at that company, and it is good to be remembered as a professional person. Answer the offer immediately. Don't be embarrassed to tell the employer that you have decided not to accept the job offer. Be direct with the answer, but soften your tone to show appreciation for the offer. Be concise and make the letter simple. Express your thanks, remembering that you may want to reapply for a future position with the same company.

FIGURE 11.11

Format for Letter Refusing a Position

Your home address
Telephone number
E-mail address

Inside address
(Always use individual's name.)

Date

Dear _____ :

Thank you for your letter of (date) offering me the position of (state position).

After considerable thought, I have decided not to accept your offer of employment as outlined in your letter. This has been a very difficult decision for me. However, I feel I have made the correct one for this point in my career.

Thank you for your time, effort, and consideration. Your confidence in me is sincerely appreciated.

Sincerely,

(written signature)

Your name typed

THANK-YOU LETTER FOR A COMPANY VISIT

Address these letters to the specific person or people who hosted you. State your appreciation for their valuable time. Comment on what impressed you the most and on what you learned from the visit.

FIGURE 11.12

Format for Thank-You Letter for a Company Visit

Your address
Telephone number
E-mail address

Inside address
(Always use individual's name.)

Date

Dear _____ :

Thank you for the tour you provided for our event planning class on Wednesday.

It was interesting to learn more about the many types of corporate events held at your company. I was impressed by the teamwork among your staff.

While I was there, Ms. Crane mentioned that there was a part-time job open for a sales assistant in your events planning office. I am interested in the job and have enclosed a copy of my resume for your consideration.

Sincerely,

(written signature)

Your name typed

Enclosure

APPLICATION LETTER FOR INTERNSHIP OR CO-OPERATIVE EDUCATION PROGRAM

Address the letter to the hiring authority and/or person involved in the selection process. Enclose a typed copy of your resume, and include references whether they are typed separately or included in your resume. State why you would like to be considered for the program. State the kind of professional experience you hope to gain and how you will use this experience to reach your career goal. Finally, state what qualifications you can bring to the employer.

FIGURE 11.13

Format for Application Letter for Internship or Co-operative Education Program

Your address
Telephone number
E-mail address

Inside address
(Always, use individual's name.)

Date

Dear _____ :

I am writing this letter to apply to the (name of school's internship program or cooperative education program).

This program offers me an opportunity to strengthen my current work history by giving me more focused experience in my career field. I feel this would give me an advantage over other students when I seek full-time employment.

Enclosed is my resume. I have 1 year of part-time work experience in accounting and strong Microsoft Office skills. I am available for an interview at your request. I look forward to the opportunity to meet with you.

Sincerely,

(written signature)

Your name typed

Enclosure

ACTIVITY 11.2

Practice Writing Cover Letters

The following is a list of the types of cover letters discussed in this chapter. Place a check next to the type of letter you would like to practice writing; then fill in each section of the letter format provided.

❑ Letter of application for a specific position

❑ Letter of inquiry

❑ Networking letter

❑ Request for a recommendation

❑ Career changer letter

❑ Thank-you letter following an interview

❑ Letter accepting a position

❑ Letter refusing a position

❑ Thank-you letter for a company visit

❑ Application letter for internship or co-operative education program

❑ Letter of resignation

Return address ⎯⎯⎯⎯⎯

Telephone number ⎯⎯⎯
E-mail address ⎯⎯⎯⎯⎯
Date ⎯⎯⎯⎯⎯⎯⎯⎯

Inside address ⎯⎯⎯⎯

Salutation ⎯⎯⎯⎯⎯⎯

First paragraph:
State your reason
for writing.

Second paragraph:
Describe your
qualifications.

Third paragraph:
Refer to enclosed
resume or application.

Final paragraph:
Indicate your
plan for follow-up.

Closing ⎯⎯⎯⎯⎯⎯
Your written signature ⎯
Your name typed ⎯⎯⎯

Have someone critique your letter for content and check for grammar, punctuation, and spelling.

LETTER OF RESIGNATION

This letter can be written to officially notify your employer of your decision to leave the company. Regardless of the reason why you are leaving, you should write a resignation in a positive tone. For example, if you are leaving to begin a new job or to relocate to another city, and you are leaving the company on good terms, you can indicate the reason for your leaving in the letter. If you have not had the best experience at the company, avoid mentioning any details, especially referring negatively to the company or your boss or coworkers. Once your letter is received, it is a permanent record of one of the last forms of your communication with the company. In the future, a negative letter could hurt your chances of ever returning to the company or obtaining a good reference.

FIGURE 11.14

Letter of Resignation Sample

Richard D. Eaton
24 Terrace Street
Boston, MA 02982
(508)592-9567
reaton@abc.com

Ms. Carol Faulkner
Director of Management Information Systems
TechCorp
1818 Tech Parkway
Boston, MA 02982

June 2, 2011

Dear Ms. Faulkner:

This letter is to confirm my decision to leave TechCorp on June 30, 2010. I have accepted a management position at Software Inc. I feel this career opportunity provides me new growth potential. My experience with TechCorp has been an asset to my career. I have learned technical skills and developed new, improved leadership skills through my work with members of the operations team.

Thank you for the career opportunity TechCorp has provided me. Best wishes!

Sincerely,

(written signature)

Richard D. Eaton

ELECTRONIC LETTERS

Just as you can source job information on the Internet and transmit your resume to companies on electronic employment services, so can you transmit your cover letter or letter of application via electronic mail. Like your resume, your cover letter can be scanned into applicant tracking systems, allowing key words in the letter to sort your qualifications into the pool of other available candidates. The selection of key words on the cover letter is critical to its usefulness.

A cover letter takes as much electronic storage as a resume and is usually stored with your resume. The letter needs some distinctive terminology for it to be retrieved. Like your electronic resume, your electronic cover letter will be retrieved by recruiters on the basis of key words. Keywords to include in your electronic cover letter may be taken from the help-wanted ad you are responding to or may be tied to someone who referred you for the job. For example, listing the name of the newspaper in which the ad

FIGURE 11.15

Sample E-mail with Attached Cover Letter and Resume

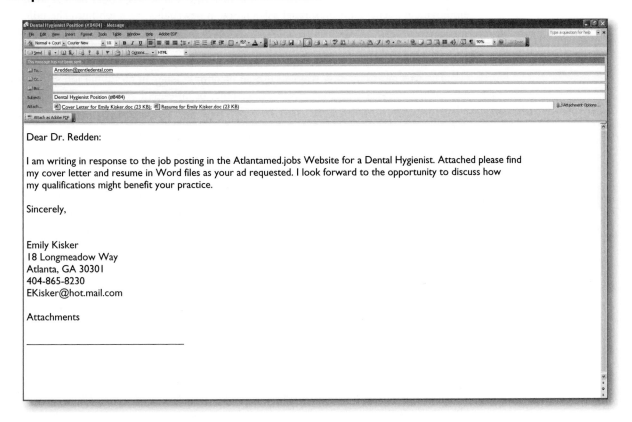

Dear Dr. Redden:

I am writing in response to the job posting in the Atlantamed.jobs Website for a Dental Hygienist. Attached please find my cover letter and resume in Word files as your ad requested. I look forward to the opportunity to discuss how my qualifications might benefit your practice.

Sincerely,

Emily Kisker
18 Longmeadow Way
Atlanta, GA 30301
404-865-8230
EKisker@hot.mail.com

Attachments

_____

FIGURE 11.16

Sample E-mail Cover Letter with Attached Resume

Dear Dr. Redden:

Chloe recommended I forward my resume to your office immediately for consideration for your dental hygienist position.
After reviewing your practice's Website and talking to your office manager over the phone, I find my skills fit well with your need for another dental hygienist in your growing operation. My AS degree in Dental Hygiene will be completed December of this year, and I look forward to putting my well-honed skills to work.
My resume is attached to this message per the instructions on your Website. I welcome the opportunity to talk to you about joining your team to help provide great care to your clients. I'll check on the status of your opening early next week.

Sincerely,

Emily Kisker
18 Longmeadow Way
Atlanta, GA 30301
404-865-8230
EKisker@hot.mail.com

Resume attached

- -

appeared, along with some of the same words used in the ad, would cause your cover letter to be directly retrieved for that job. This is because most recruiters use systems with which they can select a source for the resume. That source could be a school, an employment agency, a professional association, a newspaper, or a job fair. The point is to write your cover letter using as many key words as you can predict will be important. Then retrieval becomes easy, and your chance of being in the final cut of candidates is increased.

The two most common ways to use an electronic letter in an online job search are an e-mail with attached cover letter and resume, or an e-mail cover letter with resume attachment.

E-mail with Attached Cover Letter and Resume   This involves attaching a cover letter and resume, created as Word documents, to an e-mail message addressed to the employer. See Figure 11.15.

E-mail Cover Letter with Attached Resume   This involves writing an e-mail cover letter and including the text of your cover letter directly in the body of your e-mail message addressed to the employer and then attaching your resume, prepared in Word. See Figure 11.16.

When attaching a cover letter created in a word-processing document to an e-mail message to an employer, follow the guidelines provided in this chapter for text and format for traditional letters.

The guidelines for writing your message in the body of your e-mail are somewhat different. The following are tips for writing an effective e-mail letter.

Set up a Personal E-mail Account   Do not use your current employer's mail system for your job search. Most employers use e-mail scanning systems to monitor employees' e-mails. You may not want your employer to know you are seeking a new position, and you should not use your time on your current job to look for a new one. Doing this could put your current job at risk.

Send Your Message from a Serious E-mail Address   Use an e-mail address like JTJones876@. . . . If you want to include a little marketing, use an address like JTJones876-MBA@. . . or JTJones876-CSPro@. . . . Don't use your smarty-pants@. . . or bigboozer@. . . account for your job search. Messages from informal e-mail addresses may look like junk e-mail (or jokes) and be deleted or ignored.

Have an Effective Subject   Headline your message in the subject line to catch the reader's attention. For example, an effective follow-up to a job interview might be "Interested Candidate for Accounting Position" as opposed to "Interview Follow-up."

Send Your Message to the Appropriate Addressee   If there is a specified recipient in the job posting, want ad, or instructions on the Website, use that addressee. Otherwise, try to obtain a person's name and e-mail address to use, preferably the hiring manager or human resources recruiter.

Use Short Paragraphs   E-mail messages need plenty of white space to be easy to read. Break big paragraphs into smaller ones. Summarize and highlight important points with bulleted lists.

Keep the Message Short   Long messages are not as likely to be read, especially in e-mail form.

The letters you create during your job search are critical because they sell your resume and ultimately help differentiate you from other candidates with similar backgrounds. You should recognize that there are many opportunities, in addition to a letter of application, for letters to help you connect effectively with companies that are potential employers now, and in the future.

Whether you are searching for an internship, asking for a recommendation, or applying for a job, a well-composed letter can give you a competitive edge. You should remember, however, that your letter must always be a truthful representation of your qualifications and background. To create a letter that promotes your strengths, you must first have acquired competitive skills and qualifications from your educational and work experiences. Letters give you the opportunity to emphasize your work experience, highlight your interest in a particular company, and express your unique personality. In many ways, the letters you write are the most critical elements of a successful job search, because they can reveal more about you as a person than your resume can. Whether sent as hard copy or transmitted electronically, a well-put-together letter during your job search can draw the favorable attention you need to obtain a job interview.

LETTERS AND CAREER DECISION MAKING

Based on what you learned about job search letters in this chapter, answer the following questions.

What am I trying to decide?

_____

_____

What do I need to know?

_____

_____

Why do I need to know it?

_____

_____

How will it help me make a more informed decision?

_____

_____

Why do I need to know it now?

_____

_____

How can I obtain what I need to know?

_____

_____

People _____

Experience _____

Research _____

Who are my best resources for the information I need?

_____

_____

Why do I think they are the right resources?

_____

_____

Successful Interviews

After completing this chapter, you will:

1   **Identify** preliminary steps to take to secure an interview

2   **Practice** and prepare for different types of interviews

3   **Recognize** how to conduct yourself during an interview

4   **Evaluate** your performance after the interview and conduct appropriate follow-up

5   **Identify** both successful and unsuccessful interview examples

The job interview is the most widely used process for screening job candidates and hiring new employees. In many ways, it provides the most direct information about the candidate's background, personality, and style. The interview is an oral test. Understanding how to best prepare for and follow-up on interviews is critical to your success. New technology provides alternative ways to bring candidates and employers together for the interviewing process. Regardless of the medium used, the basic guidelines for a successful interview remain the same. Remember, the purpose of a successful job interview is to receive a job offer.

CASE STUDY

Naomi spent five years working as a guide with a tour company. She was doing extremely well. When the company offered her a promotion with a significant salary increase, she declined. She realized that she was tired of the demanding schedule that consisted of constant travel. Deciding to make a career change, Naomi enrolled in college to pursue a degree in art.

Naomi applied for a job online, using her Web resume, at the corporate office of a greeting card company. She posted selected photos she had taken of many of the international travel destinations she had traveled to. Naomi learned that she loved photography and used her photo collection to create a card collection. At first she presented the cards as gifts to relatives and friends. Eventually her collection was sold at several tourist and airport gift shops. She saw the entry-level job in the art department as an opportunity to further develop an interest, gain some experience in a new field, and earn money to pay for her tuition. She followed up her online application with a telephone call to the company to secure a job interview. Though she did not know the full scope of the company's plans, goals, financial stability, or customer base, she felt she knew enough from the job posting to go on her interview.

When she arrived, she was surprised to see the company had a much more formal environment than she expected. Two other candidates in the reception area were dressed more professionally than Naomi. She assumed that because the position was in the art department that she would be interviewing in a more casual environment.

Her interviewer began by telling Naomi how impressed she was with her photography samples posted on her Web resume. She remarked that they demonstrated her artistic talent and that her card collection revealed her creative side. When she asked Naomi why she was interested in the company, Naomi explained that she was most interested in a job to help pay for her tuition. Naomi explained her previous salary and said she hoped to earn the same in a new job.

Within a week, Naomi was contacted by the company and told she was not being asked back for a second interview. Naomi was disappointed and surprised. She thought the interviewer was really impressed with her.

Naomi called the interviewer and asked if she would be willing to provide feedback on her interview. She was told that her salary expectations were too high and that she was probably better suited for a more casual work environment. Members of the art department frequently participated in meetings in-house and off-site, and often interfaced with current and prospective clients running focus groups on proposed art copy and messaging. They needed to know how to dress professionally on these occasions, even though the art department itself was very casual.

The interviewer was impressed with her follow-up and invited her back for a second interview. When they met the second time, Naomi learned that the lower salary was not negotiable. She had to face the fact that she was switching career paths and sometimes that meant having to accept an adjusted salary to gain entry into a new field. She learned that the company had a tuition reimbursement program that could cover much of her tuition expense. Naomi agreed to stay with the company after completing her degree if the company provided educational assistance. Naomi was now on a new career path that she was more passionate about with a plan on how to accomplish her goal.

Discussion Questions

1. How could Naomi have been better prepared for her first interview?
2. Why do you think Naomi was finally offered a second interview?
3. What decisions did Naomi have to make as she changed her career path?

 ## 12.1 STEPS TO TAKE BEFORE THE INTERVIEW

Securing an interview takes planning, preparation, research, and communication. While obtaining a meeting with the employer of your choice may seem daunting, there are several steps you can take and resources you can use to make the process easier.

SECURING A JOB INTERVIEW

There are three main sources for securing a job interview: telephone calls, writing letters, and through the Internet. All three approaches will probably require you to apply your networking skills to personalize your approach and maximize the relationships you have built in your career network

Telephone Calls   The telephone may be the quickest and most effective way to show your interest in a position as soon as you learn it has become available. By being among the first to respond, you are more likely to secure an interview before the interview schedule is filled. When you call:

- State the reason for your call. Say that you are applying for a job.

  "I am responding to the position advertised in the Sun Journal for a Management Trainee."

- Ask if you have reached the right person or need to be connected to another person or department.

  "Have I reached the right contact person to discuss this position?"

- Briefly state a few of your qualifications, but do not ramble on about everything on your resume. Leave room for the company to want to learn more about you in person.

  "I have two years of work experience and a degree in accounting. I find your company interesting because I know two of your staff members who highly regard their experience with your company."

This is a perfect time to use your career networking message that you created in Chapter 7.

- State your availability for an interview.

  "I can make myself available for an interview at your earliest convenience."

- Confirm the interview time, date, and location or other follow-up. Telephone calls can be used to respond to a job posting you have read or make an inquiry about available positions that are unadvertised. It is also a good idea to call as a follow-up to a letter and resume you previously sent by postal mail or e-mail.

Letters Writing a letter tailored to a particular employer and position is the most effective way to obtain a job interview through written communication. Sometimes, you may find that mass mailings to a large group of employers may be helpful to uncovering unadvertised positions, but this is not as personal as tailoring your letter and can be less effective. Targeted letters are better than mass mailings, but it doesn't hurt to do both. You can review how to write job search letters in Chapter 11.

Internet Most large employers require you to first post your resume or job application online before they will arrange an interview with you. Don't be discouraged if this slows down the process of securing an interview. Complete whatever online application requirements there are and then follow up with a phone call. Be sure to start your call by stating that you have already completed the online requirement so you can get to a discussion about arranging an interview.

In addition to applying directly on company Websites, you may also use the Internet to send your resume directly online to an employer with a targeted message describing your readiness for the position. This can be very helpful.

When you apply online and then try to secure an interview, follow the same procedure as you would over the phone or in a letter. Send an e-mail to the company telling them you have applied and that you are interested in an interview. Some companies may see your extra effort as a sign of initiative and real interest in the company

Other Resources The career services office at your school may provide you with help in contacting prospective employers for an interview. This can be done through individual business contacts that they have or through career events sponsored by the office. Industry open houses, career fairs, and industry guest speakers are all ways that your career services office might help you with obtaining a job interview.

The alumni relations office at your campus may have an online resource and sponsor alumni events that connect you to alumni who can assist you with obtaining interviews.

Your faculty members may provide you with industry-specific leads to job interviews and may be helpful in making your initial introduction to the company. Employers do notice when you secure a job interview on your own because it demonstrates your interest, motivation, and initiative, all qualities that your prospective employers look for when comparing you with other job candidates.

RESEARCHING COMPANIES

An important step in your interview preparation is conducting company research. Understanding the culture, profitability, career paths, and reputation of a prospective employer helps you determine how to best prepare to answer and ask questions during your interview.

How to Research a Company   There are various options available to you to conduct company research. The most effective ways include person-to-person contact and published resources, including those on the Internet.

Person to Person   Current or former employees of the company are generally good resources for learning about the company. They can share first-hand experience with you and provide advice on what to look for when considering the company for employment.

Career services staff or faculty can also be helpful. They should have access to company information provided to them directly by employers, particularly about the type of candidate that best fits their company. Graduates from your school may share information about the company's reputation, competition, and experiences they have heard about if they have not personally worked at the company.

Published Resources   Company literature that is available printed or online can be very informative and provide you with the specific information you need about a company to help you decide if you want to interview with the company and to help you tailor your interview preparation to the company. These resources include trade publications, business magazines, and newspapers and periodicals.

Internet Resources   Company Websites and commercial job search Websites are great resources for conducting company research when preparing for a job interview.

You may be preparing to interview with a small company and require company research that is more tailored to smaller businesses.

NOTES	Career Opportunities with Small Businesses

"According to the U.S. Small Business Administration, small businesses represent more than 99.7 percent of all employees, employ more than half of all private sector employees, pay 44.5 percent of the total U.S. private payroll and generate 75 percent of new jobs annually."[1]

Web resources such as The Riley Guide and The Inc. 500 might be helpful with researching smaller companies, including nonprofits. Both can be found by using your favorite online search engine, and searching the phrase "Riley Guide," or "The Inc. 500."

You can also learn more about current activities with small companies by reading local newspapers and journals and by reviewing the local chamber of commerce Website.

Blogs and message boards can sometimes provide information about companies that might be helpful to your job interview. For example, Morgan Stanley has used vault.com to establish the Vault Morgan Stanley Board. It was established for prospective candidates to view Morgan Stanley's job profiles, how it hires, the company's onboarding program, and other valuable career information.[2]

Blogs sometimes provide information about company culture, policies, and approach to career pathing. Remember to always communicate in a professional manner when using online tools because companies can readily view comments from viewers. Your company research should include a wide variety of company information to include:

---

[1] CreativePro.com. (2009). "The Art of Business: Small (Business) Is Beautiful." Retrieved September 1, 2009, from www.creativepro.com/article/the-art-of-business-small-business-is-beautiful-.

[2] Business Wire. (2000). "MBA Message Board Hits No.1 on Vault.com's Electronic Watercooler." Retrieved September 1, 2009, from http://findarticles.com/p/articles/mi_m0EIN/is_2000_Jan_12/ai_58540071/.

Evaluating Company Standing   Look at the company's annual financial report and determine the following: Private or publicly owned? What information can I obtain from privately owned companies? Growth rate? Expansion? Analyze the competition. How much competition? Reputations?

Organizational Framework   Look at the company's organizational chart thoroughly and determine the following: Degree of individual responsibility? Centralized or decentralized? What is the chain of command? What is the system for promotions within the company?

Philosophy and Policies   Consider the philosophies of the company. Are they practiced as stated? Do you agree with what is practiced? Is the company production or people oriented? Is the management traditional or progressive? Are you allowed to read the company's policies? Do you agree with them?

Geography   Where is the company's market—international or domestic? What is the direction and rate of expansion? Do you know where you will be located? How often is relocation required for promotion? How much travel is involved?

Management Development   How much training is provided by the company? Is continuing education endorsed? Does the company have a human resources program? What support groups are available?

Salary and Benefits   How open is the company about salary? How does it compare with the industry average? How are raises determined? What is the maximum earning potential?

Read the company's benefits and consider the following: insurance package (reputation of insurance company), travel pay, sick leave, training pay, overtime, vacation, family leave, relocation fee, holidays, continuing education, profit sharing, and retirement. On the average, benefits will equal about 25 to 30 percent of the salary.

ACTIVITY 12.1

Company Research Profile

Select a company that you think you might want to work for. Decide which resources will be most helpful and research as much as you can about the company. Make notes on what you find. When you finish, review details about the company to determine if you want to pursue an interview. If you do, you will have completed a major part of your interview preparation.

Company name _____

Research Area	Your comments
Company Standing	
Reputation	_____
Growth rate	_____
Customer base	_____
Privately or publicly owned	_____
Size (annual profits, number of employees and locations)	_____
Competition	_____
Organizational Structure	
Centralized/decentralized	_____
Degree of individual authority	_____
Degree of individual decision making	_____
Policy development	_____
Organizational charts	_____
Job descriptions	_____
Philosophies and Policies	
How is success defined?	_____
Role of employee development	_____

Inclusivness _____

Traditional or progressive management style _____

Geography

Global, national, local presence _____

How much travel is involved? _____

How often is relocation required for promotion? _____

Is the training period at a central location? _____

Are there plans for expansion? _____

Career Development

Company training program _____

Support for continuing education _____

Process for performance review _____

Mentoring programs _____

Corporate Culture

Diversity programs _____

Community commitment _____

Fair treatment of employees _____

Work-life balance _____

Informal or formal environment _____

Salary and Benefits

Salary comparison with other companies _____

Process for salary reviews _____

Tuition reimbursement _____

Family leave _____

Relocation expenses _____

Health coverage _____

Retirement planning _____

Flexibility of benefits package _____

PREPARING FOR A JOB INTERVIEW

Successful interviews are the result of good preparation. Preparation gives you not only the information and the appearance you need but, more important, the confidence to succeed.

Think of preparing for an interview like preparing for a final exam. If you start studying well in advance, it helps. If you get enough of a head start on studying, you may not have to cram the night before. What this means is that you can get to sleep on time, and you can probably get up in time to have breakfast and freshen up properly so that you will arrive on time and feel good when you sit down for the exam. There will be an air of calmness and confidence that will help you think straight throughout the exam. You will leave knowing that regardless of the outcome, you gave it your best shot—you did the best you could. If you give the same preparation to an interview, you will gain the same satisfaction.

NOTES | Preparing for an Interview

The three keys to interviewing success:

1. Preparation ➜ Know yourself
2. Preparation ➜ Know your career goals
3. Preparation ➜ Know your employer

The various forms of preparation for your interview are situational knowledge, mental preparation, physical preparation, and written preparation.

Situational Knowledge   Be sure you can answer yes to the following questions:

* Do you know where the company is located?
* Do you know how long it will take you to get there?
* Do you know where you will park?
* Do you know what office to go to?
* Do you know the name and title of the person with whom you will be interviewing?
* Do you have the phone number of the company so that you can call if you are going to be late for any reason?
* Do you know if you will be interviewing with more than one person?

Mental Preparation   Mental preparation for a job interview involves several areas. It involves your knowledge of the company, the position for which you are applying, and the career path you wish to follow, as well as your mental attitude about work in general, your expectations about the job, and your confidence in your ability to do the job.

Knowledge about the company serves many purposes on a job interview. First, it confirms your real interest in working for the company. Second, it provides you with a frame of reference for the interview. For example, if you are extremely nervous about your interview, you may want to jot down some questions about the information you read. Maybe it is to clarify something you did not really understand, or maybe it is to find out something you want to know that could not be found in the literature. By having a frame of reference from which to ask questions on the interview, you will feel more relaxed. You will be able to pick up the ball when there is a lag in conversation during the interview or have something to respond to if the interviewer asks you if you have any questions. The interview should be a conversation between two people. You shouldn't let yourself be talked at because you are too shy to ask questions. Remember, this is an investment for both you and the company. You have as much right to evaluate the opportunities being discussed as the interviewer has to evaluate you.

Third, having knowledge of the company before the interview puts you in a convincing position that shows the employer you really want to work with that company. Equipped with the proper knowledge, you can bring the company name into your responses and conversations. You can clearly and specifically state the reasons you want to work for that company and the reasons you would be an asset to the company. This is most difficult to do without being able to incorporate specific information about the company. You already learned how to use the sales process on a job interview. Convincing is the key word. Genuinely convincing is most important.

Part of mental preparation for an interview is having a clear understanding about the job for which you are interviewing. Time after time, interviewers comment that applicants don't really understand the nature of the job for which they are applying. Typically, the employer may ask, "What do you see yourself doing every day as a (title of the job)?" The one area in which applicants fall short is lack of specific information available to really answer questions effectively. And yet, isn't it critical to know what you are getting into when you choose a career field? The information provided in the *Career Directions Handbook* should give you the information you need about the job for which you are interviewing. You used this information once in deciding on your career goal; use it again to make yourself more convincing on your job interview. Be able to speak comfortably about the job you are applying for as it relates to your career field and the professional objectives you have developed. Let the interviewer know that you have thought about the big picture and that the decisions you are making are a part of an overall plan. Employers like to see applicants who have career direction.

Finally, your mental attitude about work will be evaluated in your interview. You should be enthusiastic about the challenges your career presents to you, as opposed to the person who does not see the value of work beyond the paycheck. If you emanate motivation and enthusiasm about work, the employer will see that you might be able to make some valuable contributions to the company. Your work ethic is important.

The employer will evaluate your expectations about the job as well. Demonstrate realistic attitudes about the responsibilities and authority you hope for as well as the starting salary you expect to earn. Be confident in your ability to do the job.

Physical Preparation   Physical preparation for a job interview reinforces your mental preparation.

- Present a professional image—then enhance it! Bring your resume and references in a leather-bound folder. Properly arrange your portfolio if this is part of your presentation; have a pen with you, and bring extra copies of your resume. Also have with you a small index card with all the pertinent data to allow you to quickly and efficiently complete a job application if you are required to do so.
- Wear little jewelry, just enough to enhance your presentation of yourself but not so much that it becomes the focus of attention.
- Arrive 15 minutes early.
- Relax. If you are nervous and worried about what to do with your hands, put some paperclips in your pocket. Unobtrusively playing with them can help reduce nervousness and eliminate restless hand movements.
- Smile.
- Be energetic.

Written Preparation   Make sure you have the proper street directions to the company. It is not inappropriate to bring notes with you on an interview. Bring notes from your company research in case you need them. Prepare a brief list of questions to have with you. Write down any miscellaneous information that does not appear on your resume that you feel might be worth bringing up at the interview. Summarize the details of the job as you perceive them from the ad you read or the information you researched. This information should not prove to be a distraction during the interview, but rather, a help should you need it. Study it. Review it. Rehearse it mentally. Rehearse the information in a conversational style that is clear, confident, and convincing.

Self-Preparation Summary

- Is my goal clear to me? If not, it will not be clear to an employer.
- Have I decided if and where I am willing to relocate?
- Have I decided how much I need to earn to meet my living expenses?
- Have I researched the company?
- Have I tried to find the name and title of the person that I will be interviewing with?
- Can I now explain to an employer why I want to work for this company?
- Can I also explain to an employer why the company should hire me?
- Do I have the proper outfits to wear on my interviews?
- Will I be well groomed, alert, and on time for my interview?
- Is my resume ready?
- Have I developed a positive attitude so that the interview will be successful?

Finally, the best preparation for a successful job interview is knowing yourself and being able to tell an employer about how you think your career choice is a good fit for you.

In Chapter 2, you learned how the Myers-Briggs Type Indicator can help you learn more about who you are and what career paths are best suited for you. If you have completed the inventory, review your results again before your interview. It can help you prepare to discuss your career choice and fit during your interview. It is not too late to think about completing the inventory as part of your interview preparation, if you have not already done so. Be sure to work with a professional in your career services office or another professional career counselor who can help guide you through completing the inventory and interpreting the results with you.

12.2 THE INTERVIEW

When you meet the recruiter, shake his or her hand firmly, maintain eye contact, offer a pleasant but professional smile, and say, "Hello, I'm (your name). It's good to meet you, (Mr., Ms., or Mrs. recruiter's name)." Wait for the recruiter to indicate you should sit down, or wait for him or her to sit down before you do so.

During the interview maintain a positive attitude, good posture, an interested manner, a good appearance, a pleasant look on your face, eye contact with the recruiter, and confidence. Be yourself. This is what recruiters look for! The recruiter will be assessing your responses on the following topics:

- Why you want this kind of employment
- Ultimate goal
- Relocation
- Social, civic activities
- Future career goals
- Job or career
- Reason for wanting to work for the company
- Quality of professional training
- Past experiences
- How you heard about this company

TYPES OF INTERVIEWS

Interviews fall into several categories. There are interviews you participate in to gather information or practice your interviewing skills. When you interview with employers, you will find that there are many different approaches that they can take with the interviewing process, depending on what best meets their company's needs.
The following is a discussion about:

- Informational interviews
- Traditional interviews
- Group interviews
- Mock interviews
- Multiple interviews
- Telephone interviews
- Behavioral-based interviews

NOTES	Types of Interviews
Informational interviews	Multiple interviews
Traditional interviews	Telephone interviews
Group interviews	Behavioral-based interviews
Mock interviews	

INFORMATIONAL INTERVIEWS

An informational interview is designed to help you gather more information about an industry, a specific employer, or a type of job. There are two types of informational interviews. The first involves your interviewing an employer about which jobs are generally available for someone with your background and finding out more about the company itself. You may obtain more knowledge about the career paths in your field and the qualifications sought by a particular company.

The second type of informational interview involves your speaking to someone who is already working in your chosen career and has the job you think you want. During this interview you can clarify your career goal and gain a better understanding of the day-to-day responsibilities of a particular job.

Informational interviews are helpful because they provide you with an up-to-date perspective on your industry and on your desired job. By having a general feeling for what is happening in these areas, you will be better prepared for your traditional job interviews.

Procedures for Arranging and Conducting Informational Interviews

- Compile a list of employers for the occupations in your career field. Use business directories, the Encyclopedia of Associations, the yellow pages of cities across the United States, or other sources. Note employers' locations, phone numbers, types of businesses, product lines, and other relevant information. Include alumni from your school on your list. Check with your alumni or career services office for names of past graduates who would be willing to help you out.
- Review your list of employers, and mark those you consider the most attractive.
- If possible, compare employer locations with other members of your class. Coordinating trips to visit the same city with a classmate may reduce travel costs.
- On your list, mark those employers located where you are able to travel and visit.
- Draft a separate list of employers to contact for arranging interviews. Base your new list on the occupations you are considering the most seriously, the new employers that appear the most attractive to you, and your ability to travel.
- Before contacting employing organizations, consider the following issues: When can the interviews be conducted? Other commitments may conflict or need to be rescheduled. Interviews should be scheduled to allow more than adequate time to locate destinations, accommodate delays, conduct the interviews, and take advantage of invitations to extend your visit or tour employers' facilities.
- What people are available for interviews? This can be checked by telephoning the employer to explain your needs. Public relations or human resources offices are good sources for this information.
- How can you know if the person you ask for an interview is able to give you the kind of information you are seeking? Verify that the person you contact actually works in the occupation you are assessing. Clearly explain your needs and objectives before requesting an interview.
- Where should the interviews be conducted? Request that interviews be conducted in locations allowing privacy and freedom from distraction. The people you interview may agree to provide tours of their workplaces. Your interviews should be conducted close enough to actual work settings for you to be able to observe them at some point during your visits.
- Schedule your informational interviews. Whenever possible, make your arrangements directly with the people you plan to interview. Explain the nature of your search and your reasons for requesting an interview. You should find most people open to talking with you about their occupation.
- Leave your phone number or e-mail address so your interview subjects are able to contact you if rescheduling becomes necessary.

- If you have not had experience in interviewing for information, you may want to practice mock interviewing with a classmate, friend, or relative.

- Be familiar enough with the questions you want to ask so that you will not continually need to refer to a list during the interviews. This will help you achieve a more natural, relaxed, and spontaneous conversation with your interview subjects. This style of interview is likely to provide more honest, candid, and complete information than a straight question-and-answer interview format.

- Reconfirm interview times, dates, and locations on the day before each scheduled interview.

- At the conclusion of each visit, ask your subject for the names of other people who can provide information about the occupations in your targeted range of occupations. Obtaining permission to use your subjects' names can help in arranging future interviews.

- After each interview, take time to send a thank-you letter to your subject. Courtesy is a good habit, and you want to be remembered favorably by your subjects' organizations.

The following questions are for you to ask an employer on an informational interview. They give you an idea of the kind of information you can obtain from an employer about the career and job you think you are interested in. You can use this form to collect information when conducting an informational interview with an employer.

ACTIVITY 12.2

Conducting an Informational Interview— Questions to Ask

Name of the person to be interviewed: _____

Job title: _____

Write comments and additional interview questions in the spaces provided.

_____

What do you like about your career? Why?

_____

What are the activities and responsibilities connected with your job? Could you describe your job routine for a typical day or week?

_____

Do the activities and responsibilities of your career vary depending on the employer, or are they generally the same? In what ways could your job situation be different from those of others in your career?

_____

Do the responsibilities in your career remain constant, or do they increase over time?

_____

What skills are necessary to perform your job activities?

_____

What certifications and education does your career require?

_____

Do the training requirements for your career vary from employer to employer?

_____

How much variety is connected with your work routine?

_____

How would you describe your actual work setting or workplace?

_____

What opportunities are there in your job for sharing ideas, acquiring new skills, and learning from your coworkers or supervisors?

_____

How competitive is entry into your field? What is the outlook for openings in your field over the next few years?

_____

What is the usual progression of jobs and assignments for people in your occupation? What career paths can people follow?

_____

Is yours considered a staff (management) or a line (support) position? If a line position, what other people do you supervise?

_____

What qualities do employers look for in job applicants who want to enter your career?

_____

What are the goals of your organization? How would you describe its overall philosophy and objectives?

_____

This interview began with the question, "What do you like about your career?" What do you not like about your career? What job frustrations and negative points should I know about before deciding whether to enter this field?

_____

To what extent are the advantages and disadvantages of your particular job attributable to your particular place of employment?

_____

Do you know the names of employers other than your own who hire people in your career? Do you know of any sources I could consult to locate still more employers?

_____

Can you recommend the names of other people I can consult to find out more about your field? May I use your name to introduce myself?

_____

TRADITIONAL JOB INTERVIEWS

A traditional job interview is one in which you meet your interviewer, in person, to be interviewed for an actual job. This may occur at your school, on-site at the company, or on-site at a job fair. While the goal of an informational interview is to gather information and to practice your interviewing skills, the goal of a traditional job interview is to obtain an actual job offer.

GROUP INTERVIEWS

Group interviews are interviews that include a number of job candidates in the same interview setting at one time. Group interviews may be held for two reasons. Some companies that have many openings for the same type of position, may find it faster and more economical to interview a group of candidates at the same time. The other purpose of group interviews is for the employer to observe how individuals conduct themselves in group settings. For example, an employer can observe how well you interact with others. They may also want to observe how well you are able to compete with other candidates and what strategies you use to stand out among the group. Some things you can do to stand out include:

- Participate in discussions. Sitting quietly will not give any indication to others what you are thinking or how well you can articulate your opinions. This is an opportunity to demonstrate your communication skills.
- Do not dominate the conversation. Remember that part of demonstrating good communication skills is showing that you are a good listener as well. Don't interrupt others when they are speaking.

- Ask questions. Asking questions shows that you are engaged in the conversation. You can ask questions to clarify something you don't understand or to find out something you don't know.

- Disagree tactfully. Don't be afraid to disagree on issues you feel strongly about. This can work in your favor by showing that you are confident, but only if you are tactful in how you present your opinion.

Some group interviews include candidates being put in smaller teams and being led through problem-solving or decision-making exercises as a group. Here the employer may be looking to see who has the best ability to persuade others in the group or who emerges as the leader.

No matter how group interviews are conducted, they are usually an opportunity to show how well you handle pressure and still stand out, in a positive way, among the group. One last thought. Everyone can't be the leader and not all positions require those skills. If you are the type of person who will emerge as a good team contributor or individual performer, that can work as well. This will just help the employer to know which type of role you are best suited for.

MOCK INTERVIEWS

A mock interview is simply a practice interview. It can be conducted by an instructor, a friend, a classmate, or even an employer who is not the same as the one you are preparing to interview with for a job. Sometimes employers will help students practice mock interviews during classroom presentations or at career fairs.

Having your instructor demonstrate a mock interview with a member of your class can be very effective. If you have a portfolio, use a mock interview to practice your portfolio presentation.

You can videotape a mock interview and learn what works well in an interview by observing the person being videotaped. Whether in person or by video, a mock interview is excellent practice for preparing for your actual job interview.

ACTIVITY 12.3

Practice a Mock Interview

Ask someone to give you a mock interview: an instructor, a friend, a relative, or, of course, a member of your school's career services office.

- Review the 20 questions typically asked by interviewers.
- Rehearse the answers mentally.
- Look over your resume.

Give the person who will interview you a list of questions most frequently asked on an interview. Let that person conduct the interview and evaluate you by using the following Mock Interview Evaluation Form.

Go through as many mock interviews as you think necessary to master the interviewing process.

Mock Interview Evaluation

Outstanding   Very Good   Good
Needs Improvement   Unsatisfactory

Communication skills _____

Appearance _____

Enthusiasm _____

Initial impression/clothing _____

Poise/confidence _____

```
Preparation _____

Comments and evaluation _____

    Interviewed by: _____

    Date: _____
```

For further practice you can also use you favorite online search engine to search "virtual interview." Several career search Websites, such as Monster.com, provide virtual interviews, which are great for honing your skills.

MULTIPLE INTERVIEWS

When you interview with a company, you may be asked to participate in more than one interview if you become a strong candidate for a particular job. Your initial interview is the most critical because it is your first time to generate serious interest in you from the employer. When you succeed in making a favorable impression on an initial interview, an employer may ask you to visit the company for a second or third interview. The focus of each of these interviews will be a little different as you move from gaining an employer's initial interest in you to convincing the employer that your qualifications are better than those of any other candidates. Multiple interviews are usually common for candidates who are being seriously considered by a prospective employer to fill a position.

The Initial Interview   The following table is a summary of the five stages of an initial interview, detailing the topics the interviewer will cover in each and what the interviewer will be looking for from you.

NOTES	**Stages and Topics Covered during the Initial Interview**	
Stages	**Interviewer Topics**	**Interviewer Looks for**
First impressions	Introduction and greeting Small talk about traffic conditions, the weather, record of the basketball team, and the like	Firm handshake, eye contact Appearance and dress appropriate to the business, not college, setting Ease in social situations, good manners, poise
	Education	
Your record	Reasons for choice of school and major Grades, effort required to earn them Special areas of interest	Intellectual abilities Breadth and depth of knowledge Relevance of course work to career interests
	Courses enjoyed most and least, reasons Special achievements, toughest problems Value of education as career preparation Interaction with instructors	Special or general interests Value placed on achievement Willingness to work hard Relation between ability and achievement
	High school record, important test scores	Reaction to authority Ability to cope with problems Sensible use of resources (time, energy, money)

Work Experience

	Nature of jobs held	High energy level, vitality, enthusiasm
	Why undertaken	Leadership, interest in responsibility
	Level of responsibility reached	Willingness to follow directions
	Duties liked most and least	Ability to get along with others
	Supervisory experience	Seriousness of purpose
	Relations with others	Ability to motivate oneself to make things happen
		Positive, can-do attitude

Activities and Interests

	Role in extracurricular, athletic, community, and social service activities	Diversity of interests
	Personal interests—hobbies, cultural interests, sports	Awareness of world outside the classroom
		Social conscience, good citizenship
Your career goals	Type of work desired	Realistic knowledge of strengths and weaknesses
	Immediate objectives	Preparation for employment
	Long-term objectives	Knowledge of opportunities
	Interest in this company	Seriousness of purpose: career-oriented rather than job-oriented
	Other companies being considered	Knowledge of the company
	Desire for further education, training	Real interest in the company
	Geographic preferences and limitations	Work interests in line with talents
	Attitude toward relocation	Company's chance to get and keep you
	Health factors that might affect job performance	
The company	Company opportunities	Informed and relevant questions
	Where you might fit in	Indicators of interest in answers
	Current and future projects	Appropriate, but not undue, interest in salary or benefits
	Major divisions and departments	
	Training programs, educational and other benefits	
Conclusion	Further steps you should take (application form, transcript, references)	Candidate's attention to information as a sign of continued interest
	Further steps company will take, outline how application handled, to which departments it will be sent, time of notification of decision	
	Cordial farewell	

Second and Third Interviews Second and third interviews are sometimes conducted by a prospective employer to become more familiar with which candidates best fit the job.

Second interviews are conducted to allow the candidate and prospective employer the opportunity to discuss in greater detail the available job and whether or not the candidate's qualifications and career goals match the job opportunity. Second interviews help both the employer and the candidate determine if they are the right match for each other. These interviews are conducted in different ways. As the job candidate, you may be asked back to speak with your first interviewer again or to interview with others in the company. For example, if your first interviewer was with the human resources department, your second interview may be with the head of the department in which you would be working. Very often, the human resources department screens potential candidates for department heads to interview, and the department head makes the actual hiring decision.

On your second interview you may be interviewed both one-on-one and with a group of other candidates. This method is sometimes used to determine how well you interact with others. Bringing in a group of applicants is also a way for some companies to show the candidates the company and talk about its history or future. During the second interview, you should be prepared to ask a lot of the more detailed questions you didn't discuss the first time. It is more appropriate to discuss salary and benefits during a second interview than during the first interview.

Third interviews are not the norm, but many companies conduct them with the one or two top candidates for the job to make a final decision. By the third interview, many employers feel familiar enough with the candidate to extend a job offer. Benefits and salary are almost always discussed in detail during a third interview because by this time, the employer is dealing with only the most serious candidates.

TELEPHONE INTERVIEWS

Occasionally, you may be in a situation where your interview will be conducted by telephone. This sometimes happens when there is not enough time to wait to interview in person or when travel expenses are too costly to bring the interviewer and interviewee together in the same place. Although most job candidates are not hired after having a telephone interview only, this type of interview often precedes or follows an in-person interview for the reasons described earlier.

While making a positive first impression in person is sometimes challenging, it is even more challenging to make a positive first impression through a telephone interview because in this case, the employer does not have the benefit of observing your physical appearance or your body language, both of which play a major role in creating someone's impression of you.

To make your telephone interview successful, focus on these three things: voice quality, preparation, and attention to detail.

Voice Quality   When speaking on the telephone, be sure to project your voice, speak slowly, enunciate clearly, and sound enthusiastic.

Preparation   Try to be where you know you will be uninterrupted during your telephone interview. It would be helpful if you had access to a fax machine in the room or in a nearby room because you may be asked to fax another copy of your resume, a letter of reference, or some other document pertinent to your interview. You should have two copies of your resume with you, one handy for the fax machine and one for you to refer to as you describe your skills, experiences, and employment dates over the phone. You should also prepare some notes of key words or key points about yourself that you want to be sure to interject during the interview. Also prepare a list of questions you will want to ask the employer, and have it available to refer to.

Attention to Detail   Because you are not in the interviewer's office, you cannot be handed copies of information or business cards that give you the correct spelling, title, address, and telephone and fax numbers of your interviewer. You need this information to send him or her a thank-you letter. It is probably best to get all those details after the interview from a receptionist or secretary at the company, but be prepared to take the information from your interviewer if the situation arises. As a follow-up to your telephone interview, mail or fax a thank-you letter immediately and stress your willingness to meet in person.

BEHAVIORAL-BASED INTERVIEWS

The most recent recruiting trend by many major employers is the use of behavioral-based interviews. Consultants estimate that at least one-fourth of interviewers are using this approach, and the numbers are increasing. As Poised for the Future Company reports, research continues to prove that the result of behavioral-based versus traditional interviews is a lower cost per hire for the employer. For example, if the cost per hire is $7,500 ($2,000 for advertising, $2,500 for travel, $3,000 for training), the real cost per right hire is $53,571 if the traditional interview is the primary selection tool. If a behavioral interview approach is used (55 percent reliability), the real cost per right hire drops to $21,429.[3]

Behavioral-based interviews are based on the premise that past performance in a similar setting is the best predictor of future performance. Before a behavioral interview, hiring managers identify specific competencies or abilities needed to succeed in the available position. From these competencies, the interviewer develops a list of questions that are designed to elicit descriptions of skills candidates used in the past. After the interview, the interviewer can point to examples, provided by the candidate, of ways the candidate has previously demonstrated the competencies identified as most important to success in the available position. Based on this knowledge about the candidate, the interviewer's confidence that the person will do well on the job may be substantially increased. There may be one or more steps to a behavioral interview. Step one is usually the face-to-face interview. A second step could include a standardized test administered in person, online, or by telephone.

Face-to-Face Behavioral Interview Sample Questions

1. Describe a difficult problem you tried to solve. How did you identify the problem? How did you go about trying to solve it? *Employers are evaluating your problem-solving skills.*

2. Give me an example of a time when you went above and beyond the call of duty. *Employers are evaluating your motivation.*

3. Have you ever had to sell your idea to your coworker or group? How did you do it? Was the coworker or group sold on the idea? *Employers are evaluating your communication skills.*

4. Describe a time when you tried to persuade another person to do something that he or she was not very willing to do. *Employers are evaluating your leadership skills.*

5. Describe a time when you decided on your own that something needed to be done and you took on the task to get it done. *Employers are evaluating your initiative.*

A simple way to prepare for a behavioral-based interview is to use what is commonly referred to as the three-step STAR (Situation or Task, Action, Result) process. In the STAR process you will focus your responses to your interview questions by providing the following types of information:

Situation or task: Identify and explain a particular situation or task you have had previous experience with that best demonstrates how you might respond or perform in a similar situation.

Action: Identify and explain the specific action you took in response to the situation or task.

Result or outcome: Identify and explain the business result or outcome of your action.

The use of online job search tools streamlines the way employers connect with and initially screen job candidates in the employment process. When using online job search tools, remember that in most instances, the face-to-face interview will be a part of the follow-up if you become one of the top candidates eligible for the job. Employers use online job search tools to obtain a pool of initial candidates, but many still think there is still no substitute for good behavioral interviewing once the search has been narrowed down.

[3] I. S. Wolfe. (March 2003). "Lower Cost, Higher Accuracy," *Labor Storm Alert: Workforce Trends,* 2(3). Retrieved September 1, 2009, from www.super-solutions.com/pdfs/March_2003.pdf.

Follow-up Screening Test for Talent Profiles and Culture Fit

While many behavioral-based interviews involve only the first step, that of completing a face-to-face interview with a candidate, many involve a second phase, in the form of a standardized test to further qualify the candidate on the basis of talent profiles and culture fit with the organization. Many of these are telephone screening tests developed by outside organizations contracted by the employer. One example is a candidate screening tool available from the Gallup Organization, called the SRI, or Selection Research Instruments System. The SRI System is a series of interview questions that are behavioral based. In this case, Gallup may be contracted by an employer to develop profiles of successful candidates for key positions in the company. From that profile, Gallup designs a specific set of interview questions that will determine the candidate's culture fit for the company. A candidate's profile is determined by the answers provided to the screening questions.

The candidate's profile is then compared for a match with the predetermined profile of employees already successful in that job. Many times, a candidate may appear to be well qualified until she or he takes the SRI. For example, results may indicate that the candidate might become bored very quickly in a position that involves a lot of routine or that he or she might be underprepared to succeed in a highly competitive environment.

Results may also indicate that a candidate thrives best in a highly structured management culture, whereas the position available requires an independent worker because of the entrepreneurial nature of the company's work environment. Often candidates who seem to be the most qualified are not selected as a result of this type of screening. Because these types of screening interviews go beyond matching specific skills to evaluating natural talents and culture fit, they can be extremely beneficial. The results often ensure the candidate's job satisfaction, while at the same time improving the employer's retention rates for new hires.

Real Life Stories

Ken's Group Interview

Ken successfully completed his first interview with Magnus Resort and Entertainment Complex. He was applying for a job as a promotions coordinator for their group conventions division. The next steps in the process consisted of a candidate profile assessment and a group interview.

The group interview consisted of two parts, beginning with questions asked to the entire group that individuals could volunteer to answer. Each time Ken, and others, were about to respond, Tony spoke first. Toward the middle of the session, Ken decided to appropriately assert himself before Tony could jump in. Ken stood up, signaling he was about to speak, and proceeded to respond to some questions. It worked. Others began to participate more once Ken broke the pattern Tony set. Ken was recognized for the quality of his responses and his ability to manage a dominant group member.

In the second part of the interview, Ken was placed into a smaller group for a group exercise. One person role-played a client presentation, and others were asked to provide feedback. Ken listened to his presenter and then asked questions to ensure he understood some key points. He had some good ideas about how to improve the presentation, but thought it best to encourage other team members to provide their input before he spoke. The trainer for his group noticed Ken's ability to lead each member to participate in the discussion.

During the group interview, Ken demonstrated leadership, teamwork, and self-confidence. He stood out among the group without being domineering, earned the respect of the group, and proved to the trainer that he was well prepared for the promotions' leader position.

In his first interview, Ken showed an ability to answer interview questions well. In the second interview, he demonstrated interpersonal and communication skills in a real-life situation. His performance on his group interview and the results of his assessment, confirmed the first interviewer's impression that Ken was a good fit for the job and company.

INTERVIEW QUESTIONS

The types of questions an employer may ask during an interview may range from general questions to specific questions targeted to learn more about your ability to apply certain skills or respond effectively to a variety of workplace situations. The following discussion is focused on three types of interview questions: general, 21st Century and other skills, and behavioral-based. You will also learn about improper questions and questions about ethics that could be asked on an interview and review suggestions on how to handle them.

General Questions   The following are typically asked general questions aimed at getting to know about your background and career goals.

1. What kind of company or work environment are you looking for?
2. What kind of job or duties and responsibilities are you looking for?
3. Tell me a little bit about your professional training and/or your college experience.
4. Describe some of the part-time or summer jobs you've had in the past.
5. What is your academic and school record up till now?
6. Describe some of your extracurricular and student activities.
7. What do you consider to be some of your strong points?
8. What are some of your short- and long-term job goals?
9. Tell me about your past employers.
10. What do you know about this company?
11. What led you to choose your major field of study?
12. Why did you select your institution for your education?
13. What are the three most important accomplishments you have made thus far in your life?
14. What is the most difficult assignment you have tackled, and how did you resolve it?
15. Why should I hire you?
16. How would a friend, former employer, or instructor describe you?
17. Will you relocate and/or travel for your job?
18. Give an example of your ability to work with a team.
19. What are your salary expectations?
20. Are you willing to spend at least six months as a trainee?

There are not always right or wrong answers to interview questions. Practicing answers with someone else to be sure you have thought through your answers prior to an interview can be helpful. In a while you will have the opportunity to document your own answers to key questions. Before you do that, complete the following activity with one other person or a group so that you can discuss different opinions about how to answer some general questions.

ACTIVITY 12.4

Practice Responses to General Interview Questions

The following are some examples of answers to some of the general questions.

Review each option and select the reply you think would be most effective. Discuss your thoughts with others providing the reason for your choice. Your discussion might cause you to see things from a different perspective. In any case, this exercise will help you learn to develop thoughtful answers to some important questions.

1. What kind of company or work environment are you looking for?

   a. I do well working in a team environment. I can give you some examples of some of my best work that I did as part of a team.

   b. I enjoy working independently with little or no supervision.

   c. I think I would benefit from starting in a more structured environment until I am adjusted to my job and the company culture.

2. Tell me about your past employers.

   a. I'd rather not talk about my previous employer. I did not have a good experience with the company.

   b. I have learned something from my experiences with each employer that I think can help me in my next job.

   c. My internship employer taught me a lot about the industry and provided me great coaching on how to improve upon some of my weaknesses.

3. Why did you select your institution for your education?

   a. It was close to home.

   b. I received the financial aid I needed to afford my degree.

   c. The alumni are generally following great career paths because of the quality of their education and the school's reputation with employers.

4. Why should I hire you?

   a. I am confident my qualifications match the requirements of the job.

   b. XYZ company has emerged as my first choice because of your reputation and the opportunities for me to learn and gain more experience.

   c. I don't have a lot of experience, but I am willing to learn.

5. Will you relocate and/or travel for your job?

   a. I would relocate to a warmer climate.

   b. I would be prepared to relocate in two more years. I currently have personal commitments that require me to stay in this area until that time.

   c. I can travel as often as needed for the job, but I need my home base to be here.

6. What are your salary expectations?

   a. I am open. What does the position pay?

   b. I need to earn a minimum of $35,000 to eliminate debt I have incurred. I think this salary is in line with my education and work experience.

   c. I am most interested in your company and the position. Can we continue to talk about the position requirements and how I might be the best match for what your company needs?

7. Are you willing to spend at least six months as a trainee?

   a. It depends on what is involved.

   b. Yes.

   c. Yes, I would expect to be required to participate in some type of training program. Is training done at the location I will be assigned to work or will I need to travel to another location to complete the training?

8. What kind of job or duties are you looking for?

   a. I am willing to do anything to get my foot in the door.

   b. I am interested in the legal office coordinator's position posted on Monster.com because it will allow me to get started in a law firm where, eventually, I can apply my paralegal degree.

   c. What jobs do you think I qualify for?

Now that you have had some practice with answering general questions, you can prepare your own answers as preparation for your interviews. In the spaces provided, write down some key words or phrases that you will use to help deliver a strong response to each question or write complete answers, whichever is most helpful to you.

1. What kind of company or work environment are you looking for?
_____

2. What kind of job or duties and responsibilities are you looking for?
_____

3. Tell me a little bit about your professional training and/or your college experience.
_____

4. Describe some of the part-time and summer jobs you've had in the past.
_____

5. What is your academic and school record up till now?
_____

6. Describe some of your extracurricular and student activities.
_____

7. What do you consider some of your strong points?
_____

8. What are some of your short- and long-term job goals?
_____

9. Tell me about your past employers.
_____

10. What do you know about this company?
_____

11. What led you to choose your major field of study?
_____

12. Why did you select your institution for your education?
_____

13. What are your three most important accomplishments so far in your life?
_____

14. What is the most difficult assignment you have tackled, and how did you resolve it?
_____

15. Why should I hire you?
_____

16. How would a friend, former employer, or instructor describe you?
_____

17. Will you relocate and/or travel for your job?
_____

18. Give an example of your ability to work with a team.
_____

19. What are your salary expectations?
_____

20. Are you willing to spend at least six months as a trainee?
_____

Progress Check Questions

1. After practicing answers to general interview questions, do you feel better prepared and more confident in answering these questions on an interview?

2. Are there any answers that you modified from your original thinking after your discussions with others?

21ST Century Skills Interview Questions   In Chapter 2 you learned about the importance of developing key skills employers have identified as important to succeeding in today's workplace. Some interviewers may choose to ask questions targeted to those skills. The following are some examples of the types of questions that employers might ask to probe how prepared you are in these skill areas.

NOTES | Interview Questions for 21st Century Skills

SAMPLE QUESTIONS

Communication Skills

- When do you think it is best to communicate in writing?
- When do you handle communication face to face?
- Describe a time you used your communication skills to negotiate with an angry person.
- What do you do when you think someone is not listening to you?

Creative Thinking

- What's the best book you read last year? Tell me what you liked about it.
- What was the most creative thing you did in your last job?
- Describe an ideal work environment or "the perfect job."

Diversity

- What kinds of experiences have you had working with others with different backgrounds than your own?
- Tell me about a time you had to alter your work or personal style to meet a diversity need or challenge.
- How have you handled a situation when a colleague was not accepting of others' diversity?

Interpersonal Skills

- How would your coworkers describe your work style or work habits?
- What do you do when others resist your ideas or actions?
- Describe a difficult time you had dealing with an employee, customer, or coworker. Why was it difficult? How did you handle it? What was the outcome?

Teamwork

- Tell me about a time you pitched in to help finish a project even though it "wasn't your job." What was the result?
- Tell me what role you play within work groups and why.
- Have you ever been in a situation where you had to lead a group of peers? How did you handle it?
- Tell me about any problems you had and how you handled them.

Time Management

- Describe a time you identified a barrier to your (and others') productivity and what you did about it.
- What do you do when someone else is late and preventing you from accomplishing your tasks?
- When you have a lot of work to do, how do you get it all done. Give me an example.

Source: Society for Human Resource Management-will provide detail. Sample Interview Questions. Society for Human Resource Management. Alexandria, VA 2009.accessed 8/24/09. http://www.shrm.org/TemplatesTools/Samples/InterviewQuestions/Pages/default.aspx

Personal Ethics Questions   Many employers are interested in knowing how you might react to ethical decisions you may be faced with on the job. Your responses to these questions tell a lot about your own character and help an employer determine whether you are able to make decisions that are good for the company. Some of these questions do not always have clear-cut answers. You should be prepared to answer these types of questions.

ACTIVITY 12.6

Interview Questions about Personal Ethics

The following questions are examples of interview questions that can be asked to probe your ability to make ethical decisions at work.

1. If you saw a coworker doing something dishonest, what would you do?

2. What would you do if someone in management asked you to do something unethical?

3. In what business situations do you feel honesty is inappropriate?

Discuss your thoughts about how to answer these questions in a group. You will probably learn that there are different ways to approach the answers. What's important is recognizing that employers are interested in knowing as much as they can about potential candidates' ability to make good ethical decisions that will uphold the image and reputation of the company.

NOTES   Guide to Appropriate Preemployment Inquiries

Subject	Acceptable	Unacceptable
Experience	Applicant's work experience. Applicant's military experience in armed forces of United States, in a state militia (U.S.), or in a particular branch of U.S. armed forces.	Applicant's military experience (general). Type of military discharge.
Character	"Have you ever been convicted of any crime? If so, when, where, and what was the disposition of the case?"	"Have you ever been *arrested?*"
Relatives	Names of applicant's relatives already employed by this company. Name and address of parent or guardian if applicant is a minor.	Marital status or number of dependents. Name or address of relative, spouse, or children of adult applicant. "With whom do you reside?" "Do you live with your parents?"
Notice in case of emergency	Name and address of person to be notified in case of accident or emergency.	Name and address of relative to be notified in case of accident or emergency.
Organizations	Organizations, clubs, professional societies, or other associations of which applicant is a member, excluding any names the character of which indicates the race, religious creed, color, national origin, or ancestry of its members.	All organizations, clubs, societies, and lodges to which you belong.
References	"By whom were you referred for a position here?"	Requirement of submission of a religious reference.
Physical condition	"Do you have any physical condition which may limit your ability to perform the job applied for?" Statement by employer that offer may be made contingent on passing a physical examination.	"Do you have any physical disabilities?" Questions on general medical condition. Inquiries as to receipt of workers' compensation.
Miscellaneous	Notice to applicant that any misstatements or omissions of material facts in his or her application may be cause for dismissal.	Any inquiry that is not job related or necessary for determining an applicant's eligibility for employment.
Race or color	(None.)	Complexion, color of skin, or other questions directly or indirectly indicating race or color.

Subject	Acceptable	Unacceptable
Photograph	Statement that photograph may be required after employment.	Requirement that applicant affix a photograph to his or her application form.
		Request applicant, at his or her option, to submit photograph.
		Requirement of photograph after interview but before hiring.
Citizenship	Statement by employer that, if hired, applicant may be required to submit proof of citizenship.	Whether applicant or his parents or spouse are naturalized or native-born U.S. citizens.
		Date when applicant or parents or spouse acquired U.S. citizenship. Requirement that applicant produce his naturalization papers or first papers. Whether applicant's spouse or parents are citizens of the United States.
National origin or ancestry	Languages applicant reads, speaks, or writes fluently.	Applicant's nationality, lineage, ancestry, national origin, descent, or parentage.
		Date of arrival in United States or port of entry; how long a resident.
		Nationality of applicant's parents or spouse; maiden name of applicant's wife or mother.
		Language commonly used by applicant; "What is your mother tongue?"
		How applicant acquired ability to read, write, or speak a foreign language.
Education	Applicant's academic, vocational, or professional education; schools attended.	Date last attended high school.
Name	"Have you worked for this company under a different name?"	Former name of applicant whose name has been changed by court order or otherwise.
	"Have you ever been convicted of a crime under another name?"	
Address or duration of residence	Applicant's place of residence. How long applicant has been resident of this state or city.	

Subject	Acceptable	Unacceptable
Birthplace	(None.)	Birthplace of applicant.
		Birthplace of applicant's parents, spouse, or other relatives.
		Requirements that applicant submit a birth certificate, naturalization papers, or baptismal record.
Age	"Can you, after employment, submit a work permit if under 18?"	Questions which tend to identify applicants 40 to 64 years of age.
	"Are you over 18 years of age?"	
	"If hired, can you furnish proof of age?" or statement that hire is subject to verification that applicant's age meets legal requirements.	
Religion	(None.)	Applicant's religious denomination or affiliation, church, parish, pastor, or religious holidays observed.
		"Do you attend religious services or a house of worship?"
		Applicant may not be told that "this is a Catholic/Protestant/Jewish/atheist organization."
Work days and shifts	Statement by employer of regular days, hours, or shift to be worked.	

Improper Interview Questions   In an interview, an employer should avoid asking questions that are discriminatory. The focus of the interview questions should be on determining your ability to do the job.

If you think you have been asked an improper question, you have the option to respond or not respond. If you choose to answer the question, you should keep in mind that, without knowing it, you may be providing the wrong answer and this can disqualify you from further interviews.

Deciding not to answer the question is certainly acceptable. The key is how you phrase the answer. You do not want to appear to be uncooperative, confrontational, or defensive. Your best choice is to answer the question only as it applies to the job you are applying to.

NOTES | Handling Improper Interview Questions

If you think you have been asked an illegal question, you have the option to respond in one of three ways:

- Answer the question.
- Decline answering the question.
- Answer the question only as it might apply to the job.

Here are some examples:

1. Are you a U.S. citizen or what country are you from?

Answer: "I am authorized to work in the United States."

2. Who will take care of your children when you travel for your job?

Answer: "I am able to meet the travel and work schedule that this job requires."

3. How old are you?

Answer: "If I am hired, I am prepared to provide a copy of my birth certificate or other identification as needed to process my employment documents." Or, if applicable, "I am over the age of 18."

There are federal, state, and local laws that prohibit discrimination in employment to protect you from unfair or illegal hiring decisions by employers. There are many resources online that provide detailed information on how to avoid discrimination in the hiring process, while still providing an employer enough information about you to show you are qualified for the job. Most employers are well trained on how to conduct proper interviews. By being aware of and prepared to answer an improper question, you will be in better control of this situation if it happens to you.

WHAT TO FIND OUT DURING AN INTERVIEW

Don't forget to make the interview a two-way conversation: Ask questions, as well as answer them. Use the following list as a guide to the kinds of information you should find out.

- The exact job: its title and responsibilities, as well as the department in which you would work
- The fit of the department into the company structure: its purpose, its budget, and other departments with which it works
- Reporting structure: whether you would have one or more bosses
- Type of formal or informal training you would be given
- Whether you would be working on your own or as a member of a team
- Whether skills you learn on this job would prepare you for higher-level jobs
- How job performance is measured
- What your opportunities for advancement would be and where those who previously held your position are now
- What the salary for this position would be

Questions to Ask on an Interview

1. How did this position become available?
2. How is the person in this position evaluated?
3. What is the typical career path from this position?
4. Can you tell me if there is a formal training program or informal? Please explain.
5. What is the employee retention at the company?

6. What types of technology are used in this job? Throughout the company?

7. When would I have my first performance review?

8. Who will make the final hiring decision?

9. Are there other graduates from my institution employed here? In what jobs?

10. Are there expansion plans for the company? If yes, what new jobs would be created?

· ·

Progress Check Questions

1. Can you identify other questions you might ask during an interview?

2. What specific information do you need to know to properly follow up after an interview?

· ·

12.3 EVALUATE AND FOLLOW UP AFTER THE INTERVIEW

A successful interview does not end simply when you leave the interviewer's office. It is important to follow up with certain steps that will help you understand how the employer is evaluating you and how you are evaluating the company. Your evaluation by the employer continues after you leave the interview. Most interviewers have interview evaluation forms they complete on each job candidate. This helps the interviewer evaluate the candidate's qualifications for the job, compare each candidate's qualifications with those of all other job applicants, and remember important details about each individual interviewed.

The interviewer may also explain to you the company's other follow-up practices, which further screen candidates for how they fit the job.

NOTES | Means by Which Companies Rate Applicants

Evidence of ability	→	Grades, certifications, competency profiles
Desire to work	→	Part-time jobs, internships, cooperative education programs
Ambition	→	Future career plans
Ability to communicate	→	Interview
Acceptable personality	→	Interview
Character	→	Postinterview screening tests, background checks
Personal qualities	→	Postinterview screening tests
Financial competence	→	Credit rating
Reputation	→	References

NOTES | Words Employers Use to Rate Applicants

Appearance and manner	→	Well-groomed
		Professional presence
		Considerate
		Polite
Personality	→	Warm and friendly
		Attractive
		Attentive
		Responsive
		Enthusiastic

Intelligence	→	Mental organization
		Alertness
		Judgment
		Understanding
		Imagination
Attitude	→	Loyal
		Tactful
		Constructive
		Cooperative
		Reasonable
Self-expression	→	Clear and interesting
		Convincing
		Pleasant voice
Effectiveness	→	Reliable
		Trustworthy
		Industrious

⦿ NOTES | Employer's Interview Evaluation

A = Outstanding
B = Average
C = Below average

Appearance

	A	B	C
Grooming	___A	___B	___C
Posture	___A	___B	___C
Dress	___A	___B	___C
Manners	___A	___B	___C

Preparation for Interview

	A	B	C
Asked pertinent questions	___A	___B	___C
Resume	___A	___B	___C

Verbal Communication

	A	B	C
Conversational ability	___A	___B	___C
Expression	___A	___B	___C

Direction

	A	B	C
Well-defined goals	___A	___B	___C
Confidence level	___A	___B	___C
Realistic and practical	___A	___B	___C

Maturity

	A	B	C
Responsible	___A	___B	___C
Self-reliant	___A	___B	___C
Decisive	___A	___B	___C
Leader—school	___A	___B	___C
Leader—work	___A	___B	___C

Sincerity

	A	B	C
Genuine attitude	___A	___B	___C

Personality

	A	B	C
Enthusiastic	___A	___B	___C
Extroverted	___A	___B	___C
Motivated	___A	___B	___C
Aggressive	___A	___B	___C

Qualifications

Academic preparation	___A	___B	___C
Work experience	___A	___B	___C
Position match	___A	___B	___C

Overall Evaluation

Long-range potential	___A	___B	___C
Drive and ambition	___A	___B	___C
Ability and qualifications	___A	___B	___C

POSTINTERVIEW EMPLOYMENT SCREENING

Postinterview screening practices vary widely by type of industry, specific employer, and job type. Some of these screening tests and other practices are discussed in the following sections.

Tests for Personal Qualities   Employers rely on screening tools to assess various aspects of candidates' fitness for the job. An example of a company offering contracted services to major hiring firms is Batrus Hollweg. The Batrus Hollweg tools can assess indicators that drive employers' hiring decisions, including tests that assess a candidate's

- Honesty
- Ethical behavior
- Commitment to quality
- Communication ability
- Ability to relate to customers

Skills Tests   A wide variety of skills tests are available for most industries and job types. Some employers require a skills test as part of the employment screening process to determine how well prepared the candidate is to perform the specific tasks required for the job. You can research the types of skills tests that you might be asked to take on many job-search Websites. If you have taken any skills tests in school, be ready to share the results in the interviewing process. While most skills tests are written or available online, some employers ask candidates for an actual demonstration of skills that can be observed in person.

Credit Checks   Employers frequently check candidates' credit ratings as a routine part of an interview screening process. Employers may ask you if you know what they would find if they were able to obtain a copy of your credit report. The credit report, a personal financial report card, is often checked for a person who would be handling a company's finances and property. If a candidate is irresponsible in handling his or her own finances, employers will question whether company assets can be properly handled by that individual. Employers may ask your permission to check your credit rating as a normal part of the interview process. Having a good credit rating is an extremely important part of creating the right professional image in your job search.

Background Checks   Candidates who are well prepared and ready to discuss their personal history with an interviewer are those who do well. The reason employers conduct background checks is to probe for possible deceit, inconsistencies in responses on forms or applications, lies, or false representations of personal information. Background checks may include a review of any of the following:

- Employment history
- Military history

- Criminal history
- Education history
- Memberships in organizations
- Financial history
- Motor vehicle history
- Application process history

Among the most common misrepresentations made by job candidates are claiming unearned college degrees, disguising gaps in employment history, and falsifying salary claims. Although not every employer always conducts a background check on every applicant, you should build a history that will not include any behavior that could disqualify you from a job.

Drug Tests There is no specific prohibition of drug testing under federal law, although several states have imposed certain restrictions on the use of drug tests in the employment process. The drug test is the preemployment screening test that many college graduates are most concerned about. Following some simple advice can help you avoid being turned down for a job you really want because of drug use. The smartest plan you can have to pass a drug test is to simply stop any use of illegal drugs.

If, however, you have recently used drugs and are in the employment process, you should know that most substances will clear your body in under a week. If you do fail a drug test, you can ask to take it again. Some employers may not allow a second test, since it can be extremely expensive. If you really want a second test and the employer will not provide a second opportunity, you may offer to pay for the test yourself so that you can present the results to a prospective employer.

Reference Checks When you provide references to a prospective employer, you are providing the opportunity for that employer to either verify information you have provided, validate your match for a position, or inquire about your personal or professional reputation. Checking references is one of the most common practices used by hiring managers to avoid hiring mistakes.

Understanding in advance how postinterview screenings may qualify or disqualify you for a job is an important part of interview preparation.

FOLLOW-UP STRATEGIES

How you follow up after the interview is just as important as the preparation you did beforehand.

Follow-up begins as you end your interview with the employer. If it is unclear to you what will happen next, ask. The employer may indicate that he or she will get back to you in two or three weeks or by a certain date. If that is the case, you may want to ask whether you will be contacted by telephone or in writing. If by telephone, you will want to be sure to leave a number where you can be easily reached.

If the employer says that he or she would like you to get back to him or her after thinking about the interview to pursue things further, do it! The employer is not giving you the runaround but may be testing your initiative and your genuine interest in the company. The employer may even ask that you visit one of the company's locations before pursuing a second interview if you have not done so already. This is to be sure that you will understand the company style and the type of environment in which you may be working. If you are unsure of your interest in the company, this visit could be a deciding factor for you. In that case, it is a benefit to both you and the employer.

If an employer asks you to take initiative in any way, do it! If you are absolutely sure the job or the company is not right for you, don't waste the employer's time by taking the next step, but do send a thank-you letter acknowledging the time given to your first meeting. You do not want to burn any bridges as you move through your career. If an employer says nothing about follow-up, ask what you should do or expect next. If an employer does not get back to you in the time indicated, call. Be sure to wait for the designated amount of time to go by before calling.

When you go home after an interview, write down all the questions you can remember and what your responses were. This will help you remember what the employer told you and what you told the employer, in case any questions arise about what was communicated during the interview.

Always send a thank-you letter immediately after an interview. If you are interested in the job, the letter will jog the employer's mind about you as an applicant and will relate your interest in the job. Figure 12.1 Sample Thank you letter of Interest after a Job Interview provides an example of a follow-up letter after an interview. If you are not interested in the job, still send a thank-you letter for the time the employer took with you. A few years from now, that employer may be one you want to work for, and you would not want to have created a negative first impression of your professionalism.

ACTIVITY 12.7

Postinterview Company Evaluation

An important part of your follow-up after an interview is to evaluate how much the company's philosophy and needs match your own professional interests. By completing the Postinterview Company Evaluation, you can gain an understanding of the company that should be useful as you compare it with other firms you interview with. If you receive a job offer, this is one tool to help you decide whether or not to accept it.

Company name

_____

	Yes No	Comments
Company Standing		
Is the company public?	__ __	_____
Is the company private?	__ __	_____
Is the company an industry leader?	__ __	_____
Is the company growing?	__ __	_____
Does the company have a positive reputation?	__ __	_____
Organizational Framework		
Is the management mainly centralized?	__ __	_____
Is the management mainly decentralized?	__ __	_____
Is the company's advancement vertical?	__ __	_____
horizontal?	__ __	_____
frequent?	__ __	_____
Philosophies and Policies		
Do I agree with the company philosophy?	__ __	_____
Is the company production oriented?	__ __	_____
Is the company people oriented?	__ __	_____
Is the company's management traditional?	__ __	_____
Is the company's management progressive?	__ __	_____
Geography		
Is the job in a desired location?	__ __	_____
Is relocation required?	__ __	_____
Is travel required?	__ __	_____
Management Development		
Is there a formal training program?	__ __	_____
Is the majority of training hands-on?	__ __	_____

Is there a continuing education program?	__ __	_____
Is there a remedial training program?	__ __	_____
Is the evaluation system used as a management tool?	__ __	_____
Are there criteria to be met before salary increases are given?	__ __	_____
Are salary increases given on the basis of merit?	__ __	_____
Is there a maximum earning level?	__ __	_____
Does the company provide health insurance?	__ __	_____
dental insurance?	__ __	_____
sick leave?	__ __	_____

FIGURE 12.1

Sample Thank-You Letter of Interest after a Job Interview

Your address

Date

(Employer's name, title, address)

Dear (Ms. or Mr.) (Last name):

It was a pleasure meeting with you yesterday. My interview with you confirmed my interest in the international credit analyst's position at Finance Bank Inc. and confirmed my belief that I have the qualifications to do the job.

I am further interested in working at Finance Bank Inc. after observing the professional, results-oriented attitude in everyone I spoke with.

The international credit analyst's position would allow me to apply my strengths in computer programming, customer relations, and accounting procedures while at the same time expanding my knowledge of international banking. My ability to speak Spanish fluently should be particularly helpful in communicating with your new customers in Madrid.

I am very enthusiastic about joining the Finance Bank Inc. team and contributing to the development of your customer base in Europe. I have enclosed some more samples of financial models I have worked on and a copy of the customer service award I received from my co-op employer, NNC Bank in Boston.

If you have any further questions, please do not hesitate to contact me. I look forward to hearing from you soon.

Sincerely,

John L. Coburn

Enclosure

Progress Check Questions

1. If you know immediately after an interview that you do not want the job, should you notify the company or wait to see if you get the job offer? Discuss the reason for your answer.

2. Do you think you should apply again to a company if you are not offered a job the first time you apply? Discuss the reason for your answer.

12.4 THE INTERVIEW HALL OF FAME . . . AND SHAME

The Interview Hall of Fame and Shame depicts examples of some interviews that were successful and some that were not so successful. These stories demonstrate that certain things, when taken to an extreme, can hurt your chances of leaving an employer with a favorable impression. On the other hand, given the right balance between creativity and professionalism, you can develop some unique ways to stand out in a positive way when interviewing for a job.

For the best results, however, check first with your career services office to see if your strategies to impress an employer on your interview have a good chance of working.

HALL OF FAME CASE 1: JOHN—SOUS-CHEF

John was about to graduate from a two-year culinary arts program. He loved his profession, and it showed in the quality of his work. John had received good grades in school, had four years of part-time work experience in the food service industry, and had represented his school well by earning several gold and silver medals in national food competitions. At graduation, John was interviewing for his first full-time job with many companies visiting his campus. For one interview, John came to the career services, properly dressed and with resume in hand. He also carried with him a black box. The career services office director offered to store the box for John while he went on his interview. He declined the offer, stating he needed to bring it with him on his interview.

John was the last interviewee of the day. He went into the interviewing room, introduced himself, and before the interviewer could begin to ask questions, John opened the black box, producing the makings for a flaming dessert coffee. He said to the interviewer, "I know you've had a long day and that I am your last interview. I thought you'd like to sit back and relax a moment. While I prepare you some coffee, feel free to begin my interview." The interviewer smiled and immediately said, "You're hired."

HALL OF FAME CASE 2: SUSAN—ADVERTISING ASSISTANT

Susan was about to graduate from a two-year program in advertising and public relations. In addition to the job interviews she secured through her school's career services, Susan arranged her own interview with a top advertising firm in Manhattan. She realized the competition would be stiff because there were many applicants.

Susan decided to use her expertise in her field to create a unique approach for her interview. Two weeks before her scheduled interview, Susan sent a portfolio by mail to her prospective interviewer, asking that it be reviewed prior to her interview. Her portfolio contained samples of two promotional brochures she had designed for her advertising class. Also enclosed were a copy of an ad she had created for the company where she had completed her internship and other samples of her writing.

That same week, Susan remembered the name of a graduate of her school who worked for the company with which she would be interviewing. Susan telephoned that person, introduced herself, and informally acquired some information about the company. Finally, one week before her interview, Susan had a classmate videotape her class presentation on how to design an effective promotional brochure and mailed it to her prospective employer. By the time Susan arrived for her interview, she felt comfortable because she knew a little about the company and her interviewer knew something about her.

Susan's preparation allowed more time during the interview to discuss the details of the job. The originality Susan demonstrated in her job search, combined with her qualifications, led to a job offer, which she accepted. Employers appreciate creativity that is professional yet unique. This approach told the employer that Susan really wanted the job and that she had initiative and creative skills to bring to the company.

HALL OF FAME CASE 3: KIRSTEN—CORPORATE TRAVEL AGENT

After receiving her diploma in travel and tourism from a local travel school, Kirsten decided to continue at her job as a receptionist for a travel agency where she had worked while in school. After working there full-time for two months, Kirsten was fired because of a personality conflict she had with a coworker that led Kirsten to refuse to work on several projects with her. Before interviewing for her next job, Kirsten sought advice from her school's career services office on how to explain the fact that she had been fired from her job.

Part of Kirsten's corrective action was to complete a professional development workshop on teamwork and to obtain some temporary work, from which she received a positive evaluation on her ability to work with others. Equipped with demonstrated proof that she had addressed her problem, Kirsten began interviewing again for full-time employment.

When her next interviewer asked Kirsten why she had left her job, Kirsten said that she had been fired because she had had differences with a coworker that had led her to be uncooperative several times. Kirsten explained that there were no problems with her individual work performance and that she had taken steps in learning to be a good team worker.

Kirsten went on to discuss the positive side of the job she had and emphasized her accomplishments. She stated that she had sought advice from her school's career services office and now realized that despite her individual talents, her success depended on working well with others. Kirsten expressed sincere interest in the corporate travel agent's position and said she was ready to learn how to work better with others.

HALL OF SHAME CASE 1: DENNIS—SYSTEMS CONSULTANT

The career services director at XYZ Business School was successful in getting Technology Futures Corporation to recruit XYZ graduates for the first time. Five of the top students from the computer program were selected to interview with Technology Futures Corporation.

Dennis, one of the candidates, appeared to have the best qualifications. He was in his last year of the program, academically was one of the top five graduates in his major, had part-time job experience as a systems analyst, had successfully completed a computer internship, and was a lab assistant on campus. Dennis was articulate and projected a professional image. At the interview, Dennis was asked, "What type of environment do you like to work in?" The question was intended to determine how much supervision Dennis needed and if he could work well in a fast-paced environment. Dennis responded to the question as follows: "See this suit I have on? I never wear these. I program best in my jeans with a six-pack of beer." Thoroughly confused, the interviewer commented that Dennis seemed to have the appearance of one person and the personality of another. She decided he was not a match for their company because he did not appear ready to adapt to the corporate environment at Technology Futures Corporation.

When the career services director asked Dennis why he responded as he did, he answered, "I went to your professional development seminar, and you said to always be honest on an interview." Four years later, Dennis was hired to work at Technology Futures, after realizing that portraying a professional image is necessary in most corporate environments.

HALL OF SHAME CASE 2: LARRY—RETAIL BUYER

Larry was a retail management major from Brooklyn. He came to the career services office with a request to interview with Macy's department store for a buying position in their jewelry department. Larry first came to the career services office wearing two earrings on his left ear, expressing his desire to be a jewelry buyer because he liked jewelry. The career services director advised Larry to investigate the role of a buyer, explaining that it entailed excellent quantitative skills and business management expertise. She told Larry that if he tried to promote himself on the basis of his interest in jewelry, he would not be perceived as someone who really understood what the job entailed. Larry convinced the career services director that he understood and was scheduled for an interview.

On the day of the interview, Larry came to the interview dressed professionally and seemingly well prepared. Later, the interviewer came to the career services director to tell her that Larry would not be called back for a second interview because he had an unrealistic viewpoint of what a retail buyer does. In fact, before entering the interviewing office, Larry had slipped his earrings on and proceeded to tell the interviewer he liked jewelry and wanted to be a jewelry buyer. Larry did not get a job in the retail field that year. After trying two or three jobs, Larry established a career as a sales representative for a local manufacturing company. Having a clear understanding of what a job entails day to day is critical.

HALL OF SHAME CASE 3: CHERYL — ADMINISTRATIVE ASSISTANT

Cheryl saw a job posting on Monster.com for an administrative assistant at a bank. Since this was what she had trained to do at her school, Cheryl saw this job as a good opportunity to launch her career. A good student, Cheryl received A's and B's in almost all her classes. She did not have much part-time job experience. The only jobs she had had for the past two summers were as a waitress and a retail sales clerk.

When Cheryl began preparing for her interview, she reviewed the checklist given to her in her career development class. The checklist reminded her to wear her best dress or suit. Cheryl selected the new dress she had worn at her class formal the previous week. It was a straight, black dress with a low V back and sheer, long sleeves. She wore black hose and shoes and added a pearl necklace to complete her outfit.

When Cheryl went on her interview at the bank, she felt confident she would get the job. When she did not, she went to discuss with the career services director what might have gone wrong. The career services director called the person at the bank who had interviewed Cheryl and asked for her feedback on Cheryl's interview. The interviewer thought that Cheryl had interviewed well, but they were looking for a "different type" of person, one who would fit into the professional environment at their company. Cheryl had made the mistake of thinking that the dress appropriate for a social occasion was also best for her interview. The message given by a job candidate's appearance is powerful on an interview.

CHAPTER SUMMARY

The interviewing process is a key factor in most hiring decisions. Although you can't reliably predict the outcome of every interview, you stand the best chance of receiving a job offer if you have demonstrated initiative and preparation to a prospective employer.

Preparation before an interview is worth the time. Knowing how to secure an interview on your own through online and person-to-person resources will help you keep connected to and able to explore a variety of career opportunities. Researching companies prior to your interview can help you target the interview conversation and your questions specifically to the company. This is very important because employers want to know that you are considering employment with their firm based on company knowledge and your belief that you fit the company culture and have skills that can enhance their business. The type of interviews you have may vary from industry to industry and company to company. By being aware of some different types of interviews and practicing answers to important interview questions, you will be prepared for a successful interview. Looking your best and knowing what to ask during an interview will build your confidence as you go through the process. Finally, taking the initiative to follow up after the interview can also help you impress your prospective employer as someone who is a serious and competent candidate.

SUCCESSFUL INTERVIEWS AND CAREER DECISION MAKING

Based on what you learned about interviewing in this chapter, answer the following questions:

What am I trying to decide?

_____

_____

What do I need to know?

_____

_____

Why do I need to know it?

_____

_____

Will it help me make a more informed decision?

_____

_____

Why do I need to know it now?

_____

_____

How can I obtain what I need to know?

_____

_____

    People _____

    Experience _____

    Research_____

Who are my best resources for the information I need?

_____

_____

Why do I think they are the right resources?

_____

_____

Accepting or Rejecting a Job

13

After completing this chapter, you will:

1   **Identify** what you offer an employer

2   **Evaluate** what employers offer you

3   **Practice** salary negotiation

4   **Explain** how salary relates to cost of living and how to budget your first salary

5   **Evaluate** which job offers you will accept or reject

learning outcomes

Congratulations! You have received one or more job offers. You now need to decide which one you will accept. Accepting a job is a big step. It is a commitment. You must decide if the job represents the right match between you and your prospective employer. You must also consider whether or not the job brings you closer to your long-term career goal. As part of that process, you will need to review what you offer the employer, what the employer offers you, how much you will earn, and how that salary compares with the cost of living in the geographic location you will be in.

CASE STUDY

Mercedes had one more interview scheduled. It was with Danforth Financial Services where she had applied for a financial services position. Of all the companies she interviewed with, Danforth was her first choice. It was a medium-size company with several locations in the tristate area. Mercedes was attracted to the company based on the reputation of its training and mentoring programs. There were several career paths Mercedes could consider once she completed the training program. She knew several graduates from her school who enjoyed working at Danforth. Mercedes was interested in furthering her education and knew that Danforth would reimburse related expenses and allow her the time to pursue her goal. She also learned that she could continue her volunteer work for a few hours a week since Danforth supported the participation of its employees in community service initiatives.

On Tuesday, Mercedes received a job offer from a smaller company, Kyak Industries, to work in their finance department. Mercedes would spend six months rotating through different functions in the finance department. After six months, she would move on to be the Assistant Manager of Financial Services, a position she would likely be in for a number of years.

Kyak did not have a formal training program but would provide Mercedes reimbursement for continuing education. The starting salary at Kyak was higher than at Danforth. Mercedes considered taking the job at Kyak. She had until Friday to decide. Her second interview with Danforth was not until Monday. If her interview went well, she wondered if she would receive a job offer that day or would have to wait until after the interview.

Mercedes called and thanked Kyak Industries and told them she was thrilled with the job offer. She was honest with them and told them she was still interviewing and didn't feel she had all the information she needed to make a good decision. She thought it would be unprofessional to accept the position and then change her mind. She asked if she could respond the following Friday instead and they agreed.

When Mercedes interviewed with Danforth on Monday, they told her they would get back to her within a week with a final decision. Mercedes asked if they could tell her about the status of her application and told them that she needed to make some decisions by Friday of that week. Danforth made her a job offer on Thursday which she accepted. She felt good about being able to follow up with Kyak Industries on time. She felt even better about the way she handled the situation, knowing that she still had a positive image with Kyak Industries because she was honest and fair with them during her job search.

Discussion Questions

1. Do you think Mercedes made the right choice of company and job? Why or why not?
2. Do you think Mercedes should have tried to negotiate her starting salary with Danforth Financial Services?
3. Should Mercedes have accepted the position with Kyak to be on the safe side?

 ## 13.1 WHAT YOU OFFER THE EMPLOYER

You should be prepared to wait a while before receiving the job offer you want. The economy, geographic location, supply and demand, your experience, and how well you interview in your field will affect both how long it takes for you to receive a job offer and the number of job offers you receive. In some cases, you will find it better to accept a job that you do not consider ideal to get the experience you need and to demonstrate a realistic attitude about your readiness to fill certain positions. It takes some people longer than others to find the job they really want.

When you do receive a job offer, it is always good to review what you can bring to the job. This step is important because if you don't feel that what you have to offer matches what the employer is looking for, you probably will not be happy in your job. A review of what you offer the employer will help you decide which job offer is right for you. You should review the skills you have that can benefit the company. You will want to be sure that you have the opportunity to use at least some of your skills on the job. This will help you practice and improve your skills so that you become more valuable to your company and better prepared to accept new responsibilities throughout your career. You may also offer the company a positive and realistic attitude about the level of responsibility you will have in the job. Being realistic about what you expect in your job is important to your employer because it means you can be focused on and satisfied with your current job for a period of time. This means you will not be overly concerned with a promotion or salary increase before the appropriate time for these changes. Consider whether the job offered can be a stepping-stone to more responsibility in that job or in your next job. You should also offer your employer the reassurance that you can be committed to this job for at least a one- to two-year period.

Finally, in considering your job offer, you can express to an employer that this job offers you the chance to learn new skills and techniques and contribute to the company those you already have. Your willingness to learn from as well as contribute to the company is important to an employer because it means you are willing to grow to become a more valuable asset to the company. By thinking about what you offer the employer and the job, you can make a better decision about whether or not this opportunity is the right one for you.

 ## 13.2 WHAT THE EMPLOYER OFFERS YOU

Among the things to consider when deciding on a job offer is what the employer can offer you. To determine if this is the right career opportunity for you, consider how much you can learn and grow professionally (professional development), the current standing of the company (how is it doing?), and the compensation package.

PROFESSIONAL DEVELOPMENT

The very first thing you should think about is what you can learn in your new job. This is especially true when accepting your first job, because you will want this job to prepare you for future career opportunities. Many students underestimate the value of selecting a job based on the learning it can offer. You should consider the first job a stepping-stone in your career and focus primarily on how it will help you grow professionally. You can learn directly on the job or through training programs offered by the company. On the job, you will learn new skills and techniques, how to work better with others, and how to work better independently. By observing your coworkers and those in management or leadership positions, you can learn how the company operates and how certain situations are handled.

TRAINING PROGRAMS

Training programs vary from company to company. Before accepting a job, find out about any formal training the company may have. You should know the duration of the program, salary during the training phase, location of the training (on-site, home office, etc.), and what type of ongoing training will occur.

If training is done on the job, as opposed to in a formal program, this is fine in most cases. Just be sure to ask enough questions to get a feel for whether or not the training will be structured enough for your needs. If an employer offers you a lower salary to begin training on the job and says that it will increase to a certain amount after your training period, ask how long that will be. If you are accepting this as a condition of employment, you should be able to measure the time frame within which the change should occur. This will be important to you from a financial standpoint. You will then have an idea as to how long you will be working within a particular budget and be able to plan your personal and financial responsibilities based on that knowledge. On-the-job training and formal training programs can help you do a better job and will better prepare you for new opportunities that may interest you later on.

PROMOTIONAL OPPORTUNITY

Some companies have more predictable promotional routes than others. Some move employees through different grades or levels of jobs based on their seniority with the company. Others base promotions strictly on performance. The large ones may offer many employees the chance to move up, while smaller companies have less room at the top. Many have a formal, internal job-posting system to which employees may respond by applying for posted positions. Other companies fill positions by going directly to employees selected on the basis of good performance. Knowing the promotional procedures at a company before you accept a job will help you understand your chances for advancement within that company.

Before you accept a job, you should feel comfortable about the company's current status. This means knowing about such things as the financial stability of the company, plans for growth or expansion, reputation and standing with the competition, involvement with employees, and stability of the workforce. You can find this information in a company's corporate brochure and annual reports, in financial sections of many newspapers, or in business references such as those from Moody's Investors Service or Dun & Bradstreet (now known as D&B). Your local chamber of commerce may also be able to provide you with some of this information.

Financial Stability   You should know enough about the company to be reasonably sure it is financially healthy and will be in business in the future. When you've started your new job, you don't want to have to worry about whether your company will be around in a few years.

Growth or Expansion   A company that is growing or expanding may have a wider offering of long-term career opportunities than one that is stagnant. You want to know that the position you take will be made interesting and challenging because the company is active and growing. If the company is expanding, this may raise questions in your mind about possible future relocation or changes in responsibilities.

Reputation and Standing with the Competition   Knowing if the company has a reputation for good business practices is important because you want to be proud to be associated with your employer. Knowing how well the company stands with its competition may tell you something about its ability to stay in business despite competition from other companies. If the company continues to perform well in comparison with its competitors, you may feel more secure about the company's ability to stay in business and about your ability to keep your job.

Involvement with Employees and Stability of the Workforce   Some companies communicate with and involve employees in the company more than others do. Employees may be involved in providing ideas to improve the work environment or customer service, to cut costs, or to implement a new program. Working in a company that encourages employee participation can be interesting and professionally rewarding.

A company's low employee turnover may tell you that employees are generally happy with their jobs. A stable workforce usually indicates the company is a good one to work for.

NOTES	Key Immediate and Long-Range Factors to Consider	
Factor	**Immediate**	**Long-Range**
Job duties and tasks	Compensation	Career advancement
Development	Challenging work	Company growth
Mentoring	Training	Company values
Corporate culture	Supervision	Compensation
	Work environment	
	Commitment to diversity	

Source: U.S. Department of Labor, Bureau of Labor Statistics. Evaluating a Job Offer, 2009. Retrieved October 8, 2009 from http://www.bls.gov/oco/oco20046.htm.

Progress Check Questions

1. Of the three areas discussed that employers may offer you, which is most important to you and why?

2. What resources for information about companies that you reviewed in Chapter 9 can be helpful to you again, as you consider company standing in your decision to accept or reject a job?

ACTIVITY 13.1

What's Important to You in a Job?

1. Review the items in column 1 and, in the blanks, add any other factors you might use in deciding about a job.

2. In column 2, check off the items that would influence your decision about a job offer.

3. Use column 3 to prioritize the factors you've checked off; give each a letter.

   A I must have this (most important).
   B I really want this (important).
   C This would be nice to have (least important).

Column 1	Column 2	Column 3
Learn new skills	_____	_____
Interesting work	_____	_____
Responsibility	_____	_____
Job importance to the company	_____	_____
Authority level	_____	_____
Challenging work	_____	_____
Career progression	_____	_____
Work hours	_____	_____
Working conditions	_____	_____
Relationships with customers	_____	_____
Salary	_____	_____
Fringe benefits	_____	_____
Training program	_____	_____
Job location	_____	_____
Company size	_____	_____
Company reputation	_____	_____
Employee retention	_____	_____
Educational reimbursement	_____	_____

Source: U.S. Department of Labor, Bureau of Labor Statistics. Evaluating a Job Offer, 2009. Retrieved October 8, 2009 from http://www.bls.gov/oco/oco20046.htm.

BENEFITS

When considering a job offer, you need to evaluate how well the compensation package meets your needs. Understanding the many different types of compensation programs that exist will help you make a good career decision. You want to have a sense of financial security and know that your personal needs are being met. This sense of security will leave you free to concentrate on your job performance and professional development.

The first thing to be aware of is that compensation does not consist of salary alone, but is the combination of both the salary and the benefits offered to you. This is important because if you are tempted to accept a job that pays a high salary and has few benefits,

BENEFITS

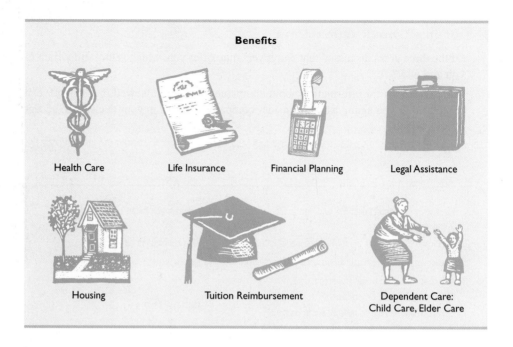

Benefits

Health Care   Life Insurance   Financial Planning   Legal Assistance

Housing   Tuition Reimbursement   Dependent Care:
Child Care, Elder Care

you may be required to pay a substantial amount of money for the benefits you need. You need to understand the value of the benefits offered to you, and then, by relating that to the salary, you can determine if this is the best compensation package for you. For example, the average cost paid by a company for a health insurance plan is approximately $7,307 per employee.[1] If you were offered a job that paid $35,000 per year at a company that did not pay for your health insurance, instead of $27,693 elsewhere, that extra $7,307 would not be an advantage to you. Not only would you have to pay your own health insurance with it, but you would also be taxed more on the higher salary. There are many other types of benefits. Some are financially beneficial and some provide you personal or professional assistance, while others simply offer a convenience or enjoyment of some kind.

Health Benefits Health benefits vary from company to company. Some firms pay this benefit in full; others provide partial payment, with the employee contributing the remaining portion; and some companies offer no health care coverage. Companies are paring costs by clamping down on health care benefits. As a result of annual premiums that are rising over 10 percent, many employers are now required to pay a larger share of these premiums. Today, an individual employee contribution to medical benefits can go as high as 40 percent. In addition, many employers require employees to undergo health assessments to qualify for health care coverage. Be sure to ask what is available and how extensive the coverage is so that you will know if you need to plan for any of this expense on your own.

Life Insurance Life insurance is usually available in most companies. The purpose of life insurance is to provide your dependents financial support in the event of your death.

Education and Training Education and training benefits may be available through a variety of programs. In addition, *tuition reimbursement* is frequently available. This is a great benefit for employees who wish to continue their formal education while working. The economic value of tuition reimbursement is tremendous, as the cost of education remains relatively high. *Seminars* or *conferences* are also popular forms of education and training in many companies. Offered for periods from as little as a few hours to a week or more, these are good vehicles for providing new skills to staff or keeping them updated in current issues and techniques in their field.

[1] New Jersey Business and Industry Association. (April 4, 2005). "2005 Health Benefits Survey: Exploding costs force many small businesses to drop coverage." Retrieved from www.nibia.org/.

Housing, Meals, and Transportation Housing, meals, and transportation are often referred to as living expenses. These costs are frequently covered in full for employees who must relocate temporarily or travel regularly for their jobs.

Travel Travel opportunities are often presented as benefits to employees. When travel is required for the job, companies usually reimburse employees for travel-related expenses. Sometimes trips are given away as bonuses or rewards for top performance.

Financial Counseling Financial counseling provides employees the opportunity to learn how to better manage their own personal finances. For example, advice may be given on budgeting, investing, or computing personal income tax returns. In some companies, employees have the option of buying stock in the company that earns a monetary return for the individual based on how well the company does financially.

Time Off Time off with pay is usually available through paid vacations. Most companies also allow a certain amount of sick leave, which is to be used in times of illness. Generally, sick days are not to be used to supplement vacation time, because they have the exclusive purpose of being available only if needed for sickness. Paid holidays are another form of time off with pay. Some companies provide only paid time off, which must accommodate both sick days and vacation days. Although you should not seem primarily interested in time off, before accepting a job it is good to ask enough questions to be sure you thoroughly understand the company's position on time off. This will allow you to plan your time well and not overextend yourself with more time off than is acceptable to the company.

Family Care Family care services are often available to support employees in caring for children or older family members. These may include such things as day care for children or summer camps.

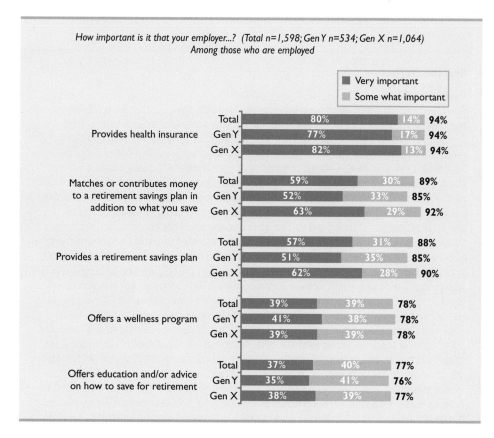

How important is it that your employer...? (Total n=1,598; Gen Y n=534; Gen X n=1,064)
Among those who are employed

■ Very important
■ Some what important

	Very important	Some what important	Total
Provides health insurance			
Total	80%	14%	94%
Gen Y	77%	17%	94%
Gen X	82%	13%	94%
Matches or contributes money to a retirement savings plan in addition to what you save			
Total	59%	30%	89%
Gen Y	52%	33%	85%
Gen X	63%	29%	92%
Provides a retirement savings plan			
Total	57%	31%	88%
Gen Y	51%	35%	85%
Gen X	62%	28%	90%
Offers a wellness program			
Total	39%	39%	78%
Gen Y	41%	38%	78%
Gen X	39%	39%	78%
Offers education and/or advice on how to save for retirement			
Total	37%	40%	77%
Gen Y	35%	41%	76%
Gen X	38%	39%	77%

FIGURE 13.1

Importance of Certain Workplace Benefits, by Generation

Other Benefits   Fitness and wellness programs may be available on the company's premises, or support may be provided for participating in off-site programs. Additional types of benefits may include a company car, club memberships, or discounts on products or services. These are usually referred to as "perks." Perks (short for the word *perquisites*) are benefits offered to provide a convenience, entertainment, or comfort of some kind. Although these are usually not as important to your final decision as the other benefits listed, when they do exist, such extras may entice you to take the job.

ACTIVITY 13.2

Benefits Checklist

Review the following list of benefits that may be offered to you by a prospective employer, and rank which benefits you think are most important. Begin by placing a 1 next to the benefit most important to you and end with a 10 next to the benefit that is least important to you.

❑ Salary ___
❑ Health benefits ___
❑ Life insurance ___
❑ Education and training ___

❑ Seminars or conferences ___
❑ Housing, meals, and
   transportation ___
❑ Travel ___

❑ Financial counseling ___
❑ Time off ___
❑ Family care ___

Discuss your choices with others in your class to see where you match or differ. You may find that choices will vary according to age, family situations, or current financial status.

Employers' traditional commitment to funding employee pension plans is changing in response to increasing costs for the company. Some companies are realizing benefit cost savings by deemphasizing or abolishing employee-funded pensions in favor of 401(k) savings plans, in which employees contribute to their retirement themselves and assume the investment risk.

Keep in mind that although this variety of benefits may be available to you, you must consider which ones you need at this point in your life to determine if the compensation package is for you.

Real Life Stories

Randy's Job Offers

Randy had two job offers. Both were in his career field with positions that were challenging and provided opportunities for career advancement over time. Altman Engineering, in his home town, offered a competitive starting salary. The job at Scranton Planning and Design required him to relocate. The job offered a lower starting salary, but had better group health insurance. During interviews, Randy observed that each company had very different working environments. At Altman, his work would primarily be conducted from the office and he would work under the direct supervision of a senior design engineer. Working in a closely supervised situation could provide some structure and a mentoring opportunity for Randy. If he took the job with Scranton Planning and Design, the company would pay his relocation expenses. While he was not sure he was ready to move, he was attracted to the working environment at Scranton. After an initial orientation period prescribed by the company, much of his work would be done in teams. Part of his time would be spent in the field working on project plans with clients. Randy was leaning toward accepting the job with Scranton, but was concerned about whether he could afford to move and work at a salary lower than what Altman offered. Randy made a list of the pros and cons of each job offer. He researched the cost of living differences associated with each location based on the salaries he was offered and calculated a first-year personal budget for each scenario. At Altman, he would need to contribute a significant portion of his salary to his employee contribution to the health care plan. At Scranton, the group health coverage was more comprehensive and paid by the company. Many of his friends suggested that health care coverage would be a more important factor in his job decisions as Randy grew older. In the process of computing his first-year budget, Randy realized that with the high cost of health care, even a small, unexpected medical emergency could be the one expense that he simply could not afford.

Randy accepted the job with Scranton. He was excited about the position, attracted to the work environment, and determined that the combined compensation and benefits were better. At first glance, the opportunity to stay and work in his home town seemed like the obvious choice, but when Randy took the time to weigh many factors into his decision, the job with Scranton Planning and Design was right for him.

13.3 NEGOTIATING SALARY

The salary offered you is certainly important; employees like to know they are paid what they are worth in the marketplace. Like benefits, the geographic location of the job can affect the total value of that salary, because in each area of the country living expenses vary. This means the same salary does not always have the same worth in different parts of the country. You may be willing to relocate and decide to take a job because it pays more than another, but the American Chamber of Commerce Researchers Association (now known as ACCRA) recommends: Don't jump at a high salary unless you know what it is really worth! Many firms are holding the line on base salaries and relying more on incentive compensation and bonuses, which can be varied from year to year.

SALARY DISCUSSION DOS AND DON'TS

DO: Research average salaries for your degree level, industry, and geographic area.

DON'T: Use national averages if you can get good information at a regional or local level.

DO: Use your research to set realistic salary expectations based on degree level, industry, and geographic area.

DON'T: Plan to ask for a salary that is unrealistic and appear uninformed about your career field. Expect salaries between small and large companies with similar positions and titles to be the same. The scope of responsibility may be very different even though job titles are similar.

DO: Know what you need to earn.

DON'T: Discuss your financial problems or situations with your interviewer.

DO: Try to find out if the company has standardized salary ranges by job title.

DON'T: Expect the salary offer to be beyond standard ranges set by the company.

DO: Set salary goals, but keep your career interests and goals first in mind. Stay committed to finding the job and company that best matches your career interests and abilities and consider the salary in this context.

DON'T: Use salary alone to determine the right career decision.

DO: Try to hold off on salary discussion until you receive a job offer.

DON'T: Consider any salary discussions final until you receive a specific offer.

DO: Answer the question.

DON'T: Say you are not prepared to discuss the question.

DO: Follow the interviewers lead and let him or her bring up the salary topic first.

DON'T: Bring up salary until your interviewer does.

DO: Act confident about the value you bring to the company.

DON'T: Apologize for lack of experience and communicate that you will accept any salary because of your minimal qualifications.

DO: Be reasonable when discussing salary and stay professional at all times.

DON'T: Show anger over disappointment that the salary does not meet you expectations.

DO: Ask when and what the formal salary review process is at the company.

DON'T: Don't ask the average percent of increases typically given because this can vary.

DO: Keep your career goal foremost in your overall discussion.

DON'T: Give up a better career opportunity for a small difference in salary, if you can afford it.

Bonuses Some companies have a bonus system in addition to the regular salary plan. If you earn a bonus, it is usually in addition to an annual salary increase. A bonus is usually a monetary reward paid to an individual for outstanding performance. Sign-on bonuses are often offered by some employers at hiring time when the candidate market is extremely competitive. In recent years, sign-on bonuses have become rare as a result of greater fluctuations in the economy and the labor market.

ACTIVITY 13.3

Practice Salary Negotiation

The following is a list of questions you might be asked about your salary expectations. Discuss the options for answers to salary-related questions your interviewer may ask and discuss which answers that you think are most appropriate. Discuss whether answering the question with a question might be appropriate.

1. What salary range are you looking for?
   - My research has shown that the mid-thirties is the average compensation for someone with my degree in this geographic location.
   - I am open.
   - I know that the mid-thirties is the average, but I feel my work experience qualifies me for a higher salary.
   - I am more interested in the position itself than the salary.
   - What is the current salary range offered by the company for someone with my qualifications?

2. How do benefits play into your salary considerations?
   - Certain benefits are more important to me than the salary.
   - Tuition reimbursement to support my educational investment is my biggest priority right now.
   - I am more interested in the position than the benefits.
   - I need to consider the whole compensation package, that is salary and benefits combined.
   - Are there opportunities to opt out of benefits that I don't need right now and keep those dollars as part of my salary?

3. Would you be willing to relocate for a position that pays more in another city at this time?
   - I would love to take advantage of that opportunity, but family and personal commitments will keep me in this area for another two years.
   - Yes, I am free and willing to relocate anywhere to have an opportunity to earn the salary I want.
   - It depends on how the larger salary compares to the different cost of living in that location.
   - I am more interested in the position than the salary.
   - If I take the job here, how long will it take and what is expected of me to reach that salary level?

4. Do you have an idea about how your salary might progress over your first few years on the job?
   - I expect to start at the entry level and then earn salary increases based on my job performance.
   - I would think that I would receive the average 4 percent increase each year that most companies are giving.
   - Not much, based on the starting salary you are offering.
   - I think my answer depends on whether or not your company has standardized salary ranges for different levels of jobs.
   - Can you tell me about career progression at your particular company and how that impacts compensation?

5. When you had your last salary review, do you know how your salary adjustment was determined?
   - I have only had temporary and part-time jobs so far as a student.
   - I have no idea, I was just happy to get a raise.
   - We don't have salary review meetings, we are just told what our raise is each year.
   - It was based on my performance review for the year. I received the company standard increase for the year and a 5% merit bonus for exceeding my goals.

13.4 COST OF LIVING AND BUDGETING

The following information will help you compare a salary offer for a job in one state with a salary offer from a job in a different state. The indeed.com Website (http://www.indeed.com/) provides you the ability to do your own salary comparisons by state as you evaluate your job offers.

Cost-of-living calculators can also help you determine if the salary of a potential job will be enough to maintain your desired standard of living or even enough to live on. A set salary in one part of the country that allows you to own a home and a car and put money in the bank may be just enough for you to rent an apartment in another part of the country. Since salaries can vary across the nation, it's important to know the average cost of living in an area before you accept a job. Use your favorite online search engine to search the phrase "salary calculator," and you will find several helpful results.

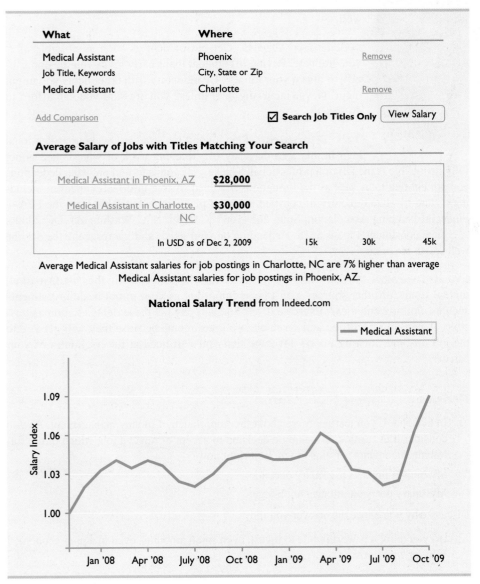

FIFURE 13.2

Salary Comparisons by State

BUDGETING YOUR FIRST SALARY

After you have viewed your salary offer with respect to the cost of living, you may want to actually calculate your potential budget based on that salary. After reviewing this potential budget, you will be able to see how your salary might be allocated to suit your individual financial needs.

Savings Plans Put yourself at the top of the list. Financial planners generally advise clients to put away 5 to 20 percent of every paycheck before they do anything else. Payroll deduction plans are a great way to do this. Because the money never touches your hands, the temptation to spend it is not there. Also, some employers offer special benefits to savers—such as IRAs, 401(k)s, or matching programs—by means of payroll deductions.

Reserve Funds Have your own slush fund. Having at least a month's salary in a liquid, money market–type account works well.

Avoiding Debt Get out of debt as soon as possible after you graduate. Paying off student loans early gives you the opportunity to invest your money. Be moderate with other debts you might incur. Never incur any debt unless you are sure you can afford to do so.

Tax Planning Plan a good tax strategy. Seeking professional help in this area may pay off. Keeping track of what is and is not fully deductible is the job of a professional. The key for you is to find out what deductions you are entitled to as well as the limitations involved. A free information packet, including a state-by-state directory of certified financial planners, is available from the FPA— Financial Planning Association, Suite 201, 1600 K Street, NW, Washington, DC 20006. A typical consultant's fee is $575. Depending on your needs and interests, the fee may be well worth the price.

Investments Invest early in your career. Investments in the stock market, mutual funds, or other sources won't be as important as your initial basic investments such as clothing and a car. Exercise discipline and pay off these debts as soon as possible. A working wardrobe and a vehicle are investments because they will get you to the job on time, looking good—leverage that you will need at the beginning of your career.

. . . .

Progress Check Questions

1. In Chapter 4, you learned more about the importance of money management. As you consider it in relation to making a decision to accept or reject a job, which of the following statements pertains to you best right now?

   My budget impacts my salary decision.

   My salary decision impacts my budget.

Discuss why you chose the answer you did.

2. Do you think it is worthwhile to invest, even small amounts, even in a poor economy? Why or why not?

. . . .

Fill in the appropriate amounts for each income or expense item as it relates to your own personal finances. At the end, you can compute your monthly net cash flow.

Monthly Income

Wages and salary   _____
Interest on savings, CDs, bonds   _____
Other   _____
   Total monthly income   _____

Monthly Expenses

Rent or mortgage   _____
Automobile loans   _____
Personal loans (student loans)   _____
Credit cards   _____
Income taxes   _____
Social Security   _____
Savings and investments   _____
Contributions   _____
Household maintenance   _____
Gas   _____
Electricity   _____
Telephone   _____
Water   _____
Transportation   _____
Food   _____
Clothing   _____
Medical   _____
Entertainment   _____
Other expenses   _____
     _____
     _____

Total monthly expenses   _____
Total monthly income   _____
Minus total monthly expenses   _____
Discretionary monthly income   _____

 13.5 ACCEPTING THE RIGHT JOB

Accepting the right job for the right reasons is critical to your career success and your personal happiness. If you select a job only for the benefits, you may not always be accepting the job that offers you the challenge or professional experience you need to move ahead in your career. To recognize a good job offer, you should first evaluate what you can learn. Continuing to learn with each job you take will keep your career moving in a positive direction.

Beyond professional growth, there are lifestyle considerations that have an impact on your decision. For example, your normal working hours and vacation time may be important to you if you want to keep a good balance between work and family and friends. If you have family responsibilities, child care or elder care services may be important to you. With the rising costs of health benefits, you may choose a job with good health benefits over one with a bigger salary. Early on in your career, frequent business travel may appeal to you, whereas you may prefer less business travel at later stages in your life and your career. You must assess your own personal and professional needs each time you consider a job offer. Your life's circumstances are likely to change over time, causing you to develop different priorities at different points in your life.

As discussed throughout this chapter, when making a decision on your first job, you will want to consider the type of position, the salary, and the location of the job. As you seek your first job, it is not likely that you will get your first choices in all three areas. If your main concern is to stay in a particular geographic area, your salary may be less than what you could earn somewhere else. If your main concern is to get a certain type of position, you may have to be willing to relocate anywhere for that opportunity. Your first job will involve a choice.

ACTIVITY 13.5

Making the Best Job Choice

On the following lines, list these three components—location, type of position, salary—in order of their importance to you. Make this decision first before accepting a job.

1. _____
2. _____
3. _____

These aspects will change throughout your career, but as you gain experience, your chances of getting your first choice in all three areas will be better.

Review the following two job offers available to a new college graduate with a degree in marketing.

Job 1: Account Representative

Responsible for developing a new customer base for a new food product

Frequent travel

Company car

Two weeks of paid vacation

Base Salary: $35,000

Bonus potential: $5,000

Job 2: Telemarketing Representative

Responsible for developing a new customer base for a new food product

Company training program

Two weeks of paid vacation

Salary: $30,000

Tuition reimbursement

List the pluses and minuses of each job.

Job 1: Account Representative

Pluses   Minuses

Job 2: Telemarketing Representative

Pluses   Minuses

Complete the following, indicating which job you would take and why:

❏ Job 1

❏ Job 2

Your reasons:_____
_____
_____

COMMUNICATING YOUR DECISION

Once you have made your decision as to which job you will accept and which you will not, respond immediately to each employer. For the job you will accept, you should first call the person who extended the job offer. Tell the person you are pleased to accept the position, and ask what day and time you are to begin. If you are not sure of the location, ask your employer to forward directions. Follow up by sending a letter accepting a job offer (see Chapter 11).

If you are rejecting a job offer, you should call the employer directly and express thanks for the job offer if you can do so positively. Remember that it is important to maintain a good relationship with all employers. There may be a time, later in your career, when you will reapply to one of these companies and you will want to have made a favorable impression. Follow up your phone call with a letter refusing the job offer (see Chapter 11).

Many factors can influence your decision to accept or reject a job offer. If you attended college straight from high school and are accepting your first career position after graduation, your considerations will probably be different from an adult student with previous experience and more family and personal responsibilities.

Before deciding on whether a job offer is right for you, you need to think about what the employer offers you with regard to your long-term career development. You also need to review what you think you offer to that particular employer based on what you know about the specific job requirements and company culture.

Salary is always a major part of a decision to accept or reject a job. It is key that you do enough research about salaries in your field and geographic area so that you go into your interviews with realistic expectations. Learning to evaluate a salary offer based on the cost of living and your earning requirements is helpful to making a decision about a job based on salary. Also, understanding the best way to approach discussions about salary during your interviewing process can help you manage your desired outcome if it is at all possible.

Finally, knowing how to evaluate a job offer based on all major aspects of the job and company can help you make the best choice for you and the company. It is always preferable to make your decision based on what you can contribute to the company and learn from the job. Each job you take should help you build another set of skills that bring you closer to your ultimate career goal.

ACCEPTING OR REJECTING A JOB AND CAREER DECISION MAKING

Based on what you learned about accepting or rejecting a job in this chapter, answer the following questions:

What am I trying to decide?

_____

_____

What do I need to know?

_____

_____

Why do I need to know it?

_____

_____

How will it help me make a more informed decision?

_____

_____

Why do I need to know it now?

_____

_____

How can I obtain what I need to know?

_____

_____

    People _____

    Experience _____

    Research _____

Who are my best resources for the information I need?

_____

_____

Why do I think they are the right resources?

_____

_____

part three

Career Management

Growing Your Career

After completing this chapter, you will:

1 **Prepare** for your first day on the job

2 **Identify** the purpose of industry orientation and training programs

3 **Recognize** the importance of periodic review and assessment of your performance

4 **Develop** positive professional relationships

5 **Identify** skills to make you a more effective employee

6 **Determine** strategies to achieve a promotion

7 **Identify** ways to recession-proof your job

8 **Learn** how to make successful career moves

Your first months on the job set the stage for your long-term success with your job and your company. Even before you arrive, you will probably receive literature to describe the company's benefits and/or an employee manual or handbook or you will be told how to access it on the company's Website. The first few days offer several opportunities for you to become well established. A more in-depth training period, usually lasting one to three months, will follow. Some companies also implement a probationary period of one to three months to help confirm you are the right match for the job. Perhaps the most significant indicators and guides to knowing how well you are performing are your periodic performance reviews and assessments.

Once you have completed your adjustment period to your new job, you can focus on your professional development. Professional development is the process of establishing yourself in your career. This may include building your professional relationships, changing job responsibilities, improving your effectiveness on the job, and building skills that can survive economic swings.

CASE STUDY

Amanda was hired by a large, multinational food service company based in the United States. She had just received her degree in food service management and thought she would be assigned to one of the company's food service operations. Amanda made a positive impression on her first day in the training program. She was punctual, dressed professionally, and was very attentive to the program. She participated in sessions and interacted well with other trainees. At the social functions she networked well with managers and operators. By the end of the program, she decided that she might like to work in college relations instead of a food service operation. She saw herself doing everything from company presentations at college campuses, training new hires, and presenting recruitment plans and results at staff and management meetings. When she had her six-month progress review, she told her supervisor what she was thinking. She agreed that Amanda had the interpersonal skills to do the job and told her that she needed to rotate through several different functions where she could also demonstrate her time management, planning, and organizational skills. In these rotations Amanda would interface with customers, operations managers at the units, potential hires, and coworkers in the college relations department. Amanda proved herself through this opportunity and continued to be offered different responsibilities based on her reputation and results.

Within 6 years, Amanda was Director of College Relations for one of the units. Her plan was to be promoted in a few years to Assistant Director of Corporate College Relations responsible for recruiting for all U.S. operations and then on to a director's and vice president's job. She was well on her way.

Justin joined a small, new voice over IP (Internet protocol) company. There was no formal training or mentoring program at the company. Training and assimilation to the company took place through informal training and mentoring. Justin was assigned a peer to shadow and spend time with. He learned about the company's culture and policies and about the different types of assignments that could be available to him if he did a good job and created a positive impression at work. By shadowing his coworker he became familiar with different jobs. Eventually he started to fill in for his coworker and gained experience in different areas. In the process, Justin built relationships with employees at all levels of the company. He found that in this less structured environment he needed to focus himself on practicing his time management, planning, and organizational skills. His career path was less structured than Amanda's, but Justin enjoyed a series of successful career moves at the company, including two promotions.

Discussion Questions

1. What are some things you can do in a new job to make a positive first impression on others?
2. Can you think of a time when someone provided you informal training or mentoring?
3. Can you name the transferable skills that Amanda and Justin demonstrated on the job that contributed to their career advancement? Are these skills they could bring to another job if a recession caused them to lose their jobs?

 ## 14.1 YOUR FIRST DAY

Your orientation actually begins with your prearrival period. Use the time between acceptance of the job offer and the first day of employment to maintain contact with the company. Be sure you have taken care of as many final arrangements as you can before your first day. For example, ask if any benefit forms can be completed and be sure to ask if there are any organizational procedures you should be aware of before you start your job. Most often the company will provide you with literature that describes the company's benefits or otherwise welcomes you to the company. Read all this material carefully, and ask any questions you may have so there will be fewer questions on your first day. Know where and to whom to report on your first day.

The way in which you enter a new company and a new job will have a major impact on your success within that organization. First impressions are extremely important because they leave a lasting impression on those you interact with for the first time.

You can relieve the anxiety usually associated with your first day on the job by following some basic guidelines. Arrive a little early so that you are sure you are reporting to the right place. You may still have some paperwork to fill out before you start work, and an early arrival can give you more time to do this properly. Someone in the company will probably be responsible for guiding you through the day. While you should focus more on listening the first day, don't be afraid to ask any questions you may have.

Part of your day will probably be spent touring the area you are working in and meeting people in the organization. Focus on remembering the names of the people you will be working with most often. You may also be shown your work area and where and how to access the resources and supplies you need to get your job done. Someone may offer to take you to lunch as part of your welcome. If so, be sure to stick to your scheduled lunch time and avoid overindulging in food or drinks so that you will still feel alert throughout the afternoon. You will probably get a feeling for the company and the people who work there by the end of the first day. If something left you feeling unsure or uncomfortable, don't panic. This is normal. There is so much to get used to in a new job that you certainly won't feel totally adjusted after your first day. While you should feel excited about all that lies ahead, be sure to keep your goals and expectations realistic and stay focused on learning.

EMPLOYEE HANDBOOK

Most companies publish an employee handbook to help employees understand their relationship with the company in a variety of areas. The major objectives of an employee handbook are to present information on company policies and practices and to explain company standards for performance. By pointing out the company's strong reputation and commitment to its employees, the employee handbook can help build morale and team spirit. Finally, an employee handbook can answer routine questions and can be designed to comply with certain legal and procedural requirements. Some of the topics often covered in an employee handbook are the following: introduction to the company discharge procedures, general communication, work rules and standards, hiring policies, pay policies, the disciplinary program, benefits, and performance appraisals.

While the employee handbook is a good introduction to the company, it is also a handy reference guide for employees throughout their time with the company. The employee handbook is the most comprehensive tool used by employers to communicate company values and policies to employees.

 ## 14.2 ORIENTATION AND TRAINING PROGRAMS

Orientation and training programs are crucial to your success, especially in the early stages of a new job. Use these training sessions to your advantage, and learn as much about the company as possible.

FIRST FEW DAYS AND WEEKS

After your first day, your orientation may last anywhere from a couple of days to a few weeks, depending on the company. Some examples of information provided during these extended orientation periods are on-the-job safety instructions; an overview of the company's background, present operations, and products or services; and ways to get involved with employee programs (employee of the month, recognition programs, contests). Remember that your orientation period is focused mostly on getting you acquainted with your new environment and how it works. This differs from actual training programs, which may be longer (30–90 days) and are aimed at giving you the tools to actually perform your job better.

For your employer, a well-run orientation program can help reduce employee turnover. For example, Corning is a company that has successfully implemented an employee orientation program. Corning's primary objectives were to reduce early career turnover by 17 percent and to shorten by one month the time it takes a new person to learn the job.[1]

Training programs may be administered individually for new employees as they are hired or may be conducted periodically for small groups of employees who began their new jobs at approximately the same time. Training may be hands-on to teach or refine technical skills (drafting, machine operations), or classroom-style to reinforce interpersonal skills (teamwork, customer service). The following box is a sample of a basic retail training program.

Progress Check Questions

1. What do you think are the most important adjustments to make within a new company in the first 30 days? Why?

2. Are training programs only needed at large companies?

NOTES | Sample Training Program

Designed to help our management trainees achieve company objectives and identify individual store needs, our eight-month, three-phase training program comprises the following:

- Phase I, II, and III participant manual
- Product knowledge manuals
- Supplemental videos
- Management resource books
- Support materials (tests and evaluations)
- Graduation certificate

PHASE I

This 30- to 60-day intensive program trains participants in the fundamentals of salesmanship, customer service, in-depth product knowledge, and basic store operating procedures. Trainees will learn skills ranging from the proper methods of greeting customers, determining customer needs, and overcoming objections, to the correct techniques for fitting footwear.

PHASE II

Reinforcing the basics begun in phase I, this 90-day period gives the trainee hands-on experience in various aspects of retail store operations. During this phase most trainees will attain the position of assistant store manager and will take an active role in sales floor management. Skills covered include recruiting and hiring techniques, coaching for improved sales productivity, visual merchandising, training techniques, and advanced store operating procedures, including loss prevention, bookkeeping, and accounting.

PHASE III

Under the guidance of our most experienced store leader, the manager-trainer, trainees receive 90 to 120 days of hands-on experience in managing a total retail store operation. The skills taught during this phase are designed to fine-tune the MIT (manager-in-training) in the areas of communication, customer relations, delegation skills, recruiting and training, leadership, marketing, merchandising, and maximizing profits.

This program is divided into weekly lessons, each with clearly defined goals, discussion questions, and practice assignments. The objective of each lesson is reached through daily interaction on the sales floor and through one-on-one training with the store manager. The lessons are outlined in the *Management Training Development Manual*.

Upon successful completion of this program, trainees can expect to attain a store management position in the near future.

---

[1] Office of State Personnel. (2009). "From I do to happily ever after: The business case for onboarding." Retrieved September 1, 2009, from www.performancesolutions.nc.gov/staffinginitiatives/selection/Onboarding/fromido.aspx.

14.3 PROBATIONARY PERIODS, REVIEWS, AND ASSESSMENTS

Some companies have a period of formal probation for new employees. A probationary period is meant to give you the opportunity to demonstrate your skills, abilities, and overall fit with the company. Probationary periods may range from 30 to 90 days, depending on company policy. If your job involves this testing period, use it as an opportunity to demonstrate your abilities and positive attitude.

PERIODIC REVIEW AND ASSESSMENTS

During your first three to six months on the job, it would be helpful to you for your employer to conduct periodic reviews and assessments of your job performance. This will help you know whether or not you are on the right track and give both you and the employer a chance to discuss your strengths and weaknesses so that you can set immediate goals for improvement. Periodic reviews and assessments can help you adjust to your job during the first few months by setting and keeping you on a successful course. If these are not formally planned by your employer, you might want to ask your immediate supervisor to conduct these sessions because you think they may be helpful to both of you.

Look at the example of a typical performance appraisal checklist (see Figure 14.1) used by an employer to evaluate a staff member.

PERFORMANCE APPRAISAL

Company Name: _____

Job Title: _____

Department: _____

Directions: In Parts I and II, check all items relevant to the employee's position. Using the scale below, rate each item on a scale of 1 to 5, and circle the number at the right.

    Scale:
    1 = Needs much improvement
    2 = Needs some improvement
    3 = Satisfactory
    4 = Very good
    5 = Excellent

PART I: General Work Habits and Attitudes   **Scale**

	Scale
A. Attendance/punctuality/professional appearance	1 2 3 4 5
B. Meets deadlines	1 2 3 4 5
C. Cooperates with others	1 2 3 4 5
D. Accepts suggestions and criticism	1 2 3 4 5
E. Manages work schedule	1 2 3 4 5
F. Uses equipment properly	1 2 3 4 5

Comments: _____

_____

PART II: Job Performance   **Scale**

	Scale
A. Quality of work	1 2 3 4 5
B. Ability to solve problems	1 2 3 4 5
C. Uses original ideas	1 2 3 4 5

FIGURE 14.1

Sample Performance Appraisal Checklist

D. Communicates well	1 2 3 4 5
E. Time management	1 2 3 4 5
F. Technical/professional knowledge	1 2 3 4 5
G. Interpersonal skills	1 2 3 4 5
H. Learns new duties quickly	1 2 3 4 5
I. Ability to apply job knowledge	1 2 3 4 5

Comments: _____
_____
_____

What are this person's greatest strengths and weaknesses? _____
_____
_____

Suggestions to improve weaknesses: _____
_____
_____

What further training does this employee need? _____
_____
_____

What contribution has this person made to the company, department, or division beyond normal requirements of the position?
_____
_____

What is your overall evaluation of this employee? _____
_____
_____

Reviewed by: _____   Date: _____
Employee signature: _____   Date: _____

ACTIVITY 14.1

Appraise Your Own Performance

Using this sample performance appraisal as your guide to how you may be evaluated at your next job, rate your own work performance for the most recent position you held. In parts I and II, check all items relevant to your position. Using the following scale, rate each item on a scale of 1 to 5, and circle the number at the right.

Scale
1 Needs much improvement
2 Needs some improvement
3 Satisfactory
4 Very good
5 Excellent

PART I: GENERAL WORK HABITS AND ATTITUDES

A. Attendance/punctuality/professional appearance	1 2 3 4 5
B. Meets deadlines	1 2 3 4 5
C. Cooperates with others	1 2 3 4 5
D. Accepts suggestions and criticism	1 2 3 4 5
E. Manages work schedule	1 2 3 4 5
F. Uses equipment properly	1 2 3 4 5

Comments: _____

_____

_____

PART II: JOB PERFORMANCE

A. Quality of work	1 2 3 4 5	
B. Ability to solve problems	1 2 3 4 5	
C. Uses original ideas	1 2 3 4 5	
D. Communicates well	1 2 3 4 5	
E. Time management	1 2 3 4 5	
F. Technical/professional knowledge	1 2 3 4 5	
G. Interpersonal skills	1 2 3 4 5	
H. Learns new duties quickly	1 2 3 4 5	
I. Ability to apply job knowledge	1 2 3 4 5	

Comments: _____

_____

_____

What are your greatest strengths and weaknesses?

_____

_____

What suggestions do you have to improve weaknesses?

_____

_____

What further training do you need?

_____

_____

What contribution have you made to the company, department, or division beyond normal requirements of your position?

_____

_____

What is your overall evaluation of your performance this past year?

_____

_____

_____

14.4 BUILDING PROFESSIONAL RELATIONSHIPS

Throughout your career, you will be required to interact with people at different levels in your organization and with those outside the company. This interaction will range from dealing with your boss and associates to dealing with customers. Each of these situations always requires professionalism, but each requires a slightly different approach.

YOUR RELATIONSHIP WITH YOUR BOSS

A positive and productive working relationship with your boss can enhance your personal development as well as your professional growth. The following should help you:

- Loyalty sets the stage for trust. You can be loyal to your boss and to yourself even when you don't both agree. Be up-front and discuss the issue honestly—with him or her only.
- Don't talk negatively about your boss or the company you work for to other people.
- Don't waste your boss's time.

- Be aware of your boss's priorities.
- Help your boss get promoted. It may help you in the same way.
- Incorporate the boss's point of view in your decision making. Try to see his or her point of view, and you may make better decisions.
- Accept criticism from your boss as a learning experience. Criticism should not be interpreted as a threat. It should be seen as a desirable challenge.
- Admit your mistakes.
- Ask for feedback.
- Don't ever upstage your boss.
- Avoid presenting your boss with bad news early or late in the day or week.
- No surprises—keep your boss informed.

Remember you are part of the management team regardless of what position you hold. Your relationship with your boss should be mutually beneficial. You should foster an environment of cooperation so that you help each other achieve personal and company goals. Being a team player with your boss makes both your job and your boss's more productive and meaningful.

Handling Problems with Your Boss   Problems with your boss can stem from a variety of sources but most often will lie with your boss, with you, or a combination of both.

Common problems that lie with the boss include his or her inability to do the job, lack of experience with the job, poor communication skills, insecurity, or poor leadership skills. If you think your boss has one of these problems, you should be professional in your approach to resolving or improving the situation. First, you should avoid being disloyal and talking about the problem to others before you have the chance to talk directly to your boss about it. Before meeting with your boss, ask yourself what you expect from the meeting. Maybe you are looking for more direction, more authority, more responsibility, more involvement, or simply more support from your boss. Try to pin down the reason for your frustration so that you are able to tell your boss how the situation may be negatively affecting your productivity or morale. Also be ready to ask how the situation can be improved. Very often, differences between bosses and workers are the result of different expectations. Always take the high road, and let your boss know that you are eager to improve your relationship, and try to agree on a plan that will help both of you benefit from your meeting.

YOUR RELATIONSHIP WITH YOUR ASSOCIATES

Imagine that you are at the top of your graduating class and are used to being number one. You've earned the job you have now, but something is different. You've been hired along with a lot of other "number ones," and suddenly, the skills and talents that once put you on top now put you in competition. Yes, there are other people who are smarter, who can do it better, and who will challenge you. Learning to work with others and to respect their opinions, talents, and contributions to your organization can be difficult. Perhaps one of the hardest things you will face in your career is having to work with people you really don't like. Learn to separate your personal feelings and preferences about people and situations from your professional life. The person you dislike the most might be an important link in your team. Tomorrow's jobs require the ability to get things done with other people. You will actually be measured on team efforts as well as your individual accomplishments. You will be treated the way you treat other people. The following tips should help you learn to become part of a team:

- Be a team player.
- Build working relationships with those at your level and in other departments.
- Realize the power of praise. Compliment people for a job well done.
- Say thank you.

- Listen to what other people have to say.

- Respect other people the way you want them to respect you.

- Be objective; if there is a problem, ask yourself, What's wrong? Am I part of the problem? What can I do about it?

- Deal with pressure. Control your temper and emotions and remain level-headed when the going gets rough. Don't say or do something you'll be sorry for.

- Look at competition as an opportunity to do the best job you can. Above all, play fair as you compete to reach whatever goal you have set for yourself.

- Use common sense.

- Develop a genuine interest in other people. Show that you are sensitive to their individual needs.

- Be courteous.

- Cooperate. Work is more difficult when the climate is tense. Cooperation builds team spirit and is often more productive than individual effort.

- Be humble. If you are humble, you will still receive the credit you deserve. Don't be caught up in always needing to win, to have the best idea, or to be number one. You have a long career ahead of you, and if these are your goals, you will be disappointed many times.

Handling Problems with Your Associates   A large part of your professional development will depend on your ability to handle conflicts with coworkers. Problems with your coworkers are best dealt with immediately and professionally. You should focus on the person involved in the conflict with you. Go directly to that person and ask for a meeting to discuss the situation. You may want to do this over lunch so as not to interrupt your work. Also, being in a neutral environment usually helps diffuse a tense situation. In your discussion, take the initiative to state the problem between you and what you think the cause is. Do not place blame on the other person. Direct your comments toward the situation, not the person. Then ask for the other person's viewpoint. This is very important, because if you listen carefully, you may learn that the other person's perceptions are much different than you thought. Active listening is important to any conflict resolution, so work hard at it. After you have both explained your viewpoints, state that your goal is to come up with a resolution that is agreeable to both of you. Discuss what that might be, and resolve to make it happen. If the problem continues after you have truly tried to resolve it, seek the advice of your boss or another proper person at the company.

YOUR ROLE AS A LEADER

If you are in the position to lead a team, then your human relations skills will determine your success. People want to be led, not managed. You manage projects, things, and your time. You lead people.

Leadership can be developed if you know its essential ingredients and have a real desire to lead. The strong desire is important, because leadership requires much time, energy, commitment, and skill; and if you really don't want the responsibility, you will give up easily. If you really don't want a leadership role, don't accept it. You won't do yourself justice, nor will it be fair to the people looking for leadership. If you do think the leadership challenge is for you, here are some qualities of a good leader that you should master:

Vision	Intelligence
Courage	Enthusiasm
Self-starter	Character
Risk taking	Ability to motivate others
Positive attitude	Integrity
Energy level	Ability to plan and organize

Leaders create an atmosphere in which others can grow and develop their abilities. Effective leadership focuses on putting the people in your responsibility area first. Here are some guidelines for leaders:

- Recognize the power of people in your area.
- Empower commitment and loyalty by example.
- Recognize individual accomplishments as well as team efforts.
- Combine monetary rewards with other benefits, such as free time, a new opportunity, or additional authority.

ACTIVITY 14.2

What Makes a Good Leader?

A. Identify an influential leader that you know or work with. Think about what traits this person has that makes him or her such an effective leader, in your opinion. In the first column of the following table, write the traits down.

B. Share your story about this person with one or more other people and have them share a similar story with you. In the second column, list other leadership traits that result from your discussion.

In the third column, list the traits that appeared on both your own list and others' lists.

Use the information you have gathered to think about or discuss what makes a good leader.

Leadership Traits	Others' Leadership Traits	Common Leadership Traits
_____	_____	_____
_____	_____	_____
_____	_____	_____
_____	_____	_____
_____	_____	_____

YOUR RELATIONSHIP WITH CUSTOMERS

Good customer service is a major factor in allowing a company to remain competitive and stay in business. To provide good customer service, employees need to think about what the customer wants and how the customer wants to be treated. Being responsive to customers requires excellent communication skills (listening and speaking). Being able to talk with customers about their needs and preferences is helpful to the company in developing programs and products. If you are in a position that involves contact with customers, keep in mind that your reputation and your company's reputation are based largely on the customers' impression of you.

TEAMWORK

More and more companies are encouraging teamwork, as well as individual performance, as a means of professional development and as a technique for achieving company goals. As a member of a team, you are usually responsible for performing a specific role to help the team be successful. For example, the team's goal may be to win the perfect attendance award for its department during the month of September. For that to happen, everyone must have perfect attendance. If one person on the team does not fulfill his or her role, the team will not succeed. Teamwork is important because it is a way of bringing together individual ideas and opinions to create new ideas or solve a problem. In some cases, teamwork is more effective than individual effort. Teamwork is also intended to foster relationships among the team members by opening their minds to different perspectives.

Progress Check Questions

1. How have you successfully resolved a problem with a coworker or classmate?
2. Can you think of two people you know that fit the description of a leader presented earlier? Which of the leadership qualities describe them best?

 14.5 IMPROVING YOUR EFFECTIVENESS

You can be more effective in your job if you have good planning and presentation skills, exercise good meeting behavior, manage your time and organize your work well, and focus your performance on results.

PLANNING SKILLS

Planning is preparing for what lies ahead. If you know that you will assist with showing the company's office procedures to the new secretarial staff, you may set a goal now to prepare a procedures manual for that purpose. As an assistant sales manager, you may be required to help project the next year's sales in your area and establish strategies for reaching those goals. Being a good planner helps you set a direction for your job and keep yourself focused.

PRESENTATION SKILLS

Good presentation skills help you to be convincing about your ideas because they help the listener(s) be attentive to what you are saying. Many people feel nervous at the thought of making a presentation even to a small group. You can reduce your anxiety about making a presentation and increase your effectiveness by following these guidelines: decide on the main point you wish to convey and develop convincing information (articles, statistics, etc.) to use to illustrate your point. This will help you address any questions. Prepare a brief outline on index cards. Do your homework. Spending enough time preparing your presentation will help you be more confident about what you say. Look confident. Dress professionally, look alert and well groomed, and show enthusiasm for what you say.

PROPER MEETING BEHAVIOR

How you interact at company meetings reflects an image of you to others. Among the actions you can take to help to create a positive image are the following:

* Arrive on time. It is wise to arrive 10 to 15 minutes before the start of any meeting. This will give you time to become oriented to the room and the meeting agenda and to avoid having to sit on the perimeter of the room because all the best seats are taken.
* Introduce yourself to participants you may not know prior to the beginning of the meeting. Also, introduce yourself when you speak at the meeting if there are some attendees who may not know you.
* If the meeting is delayed, turn to someone and begin an informal conversation. You should be relaxed and prepared enough not to have to worry about any last-minute details by this time. This may give you an opportunity to communicate with someone you don't see on a regular basis.
* Arrive prepared. Don't count on being able to make last-minute copies or notes within 10 or 15 minutes before the meeting. Be prepared when you leave your own office.
* Rehearse your remarks well if you are to make a presentation. Bring a one-page list of key points you want to make at the meeting so you will be sure not to leave any out.
* Sit straight. Look interested, alert, and ready to participate.
* Pay attention, even when topics don't relate directly to you; don't shift to converse with others when the topic shifts. You should always listen to everyone who is speaking. Not only is this professional courtesy, but you may learn something important.

- Avoid interrupting. If you have questions or comments when someone else is speaking, try to wait until he or she has finished making the main point.

- Don't monopolize the time. Be concise and to the point with your remarks. You will be more effective this way and will allow others the opportunity to speak.

- Ask for clarification if you don't understand something. Don't be afraid of appearing stupid. If you don't ask for clarification, you may base an important decision on the wrong facts.

- Be positive and tactful when disagreeing. Even though it is right for you to express your disagreement with someone, make sure you make it clear that you are attacking the issue, not the person.

- Use we instead of I when talking to a group; we signifies being part of the group.

- Think before you speak. It is more important to focus on the quality of what you say at meetings than on the frequency of times you speak.

- Don't smoke in a room where it is not permitted. Not only would you violate a company policy, but you also may alienate some participants who may be bothered by smoking.

- Pour soft drinks into a cup. Never drink from a can at a business meeting; it looks unprofessional.

- Say thank you quietly and leave at the end of the meeting or when the chairperson indicates you should leave.

- After the meeting, congratulate anyone who performed exceptionally well in his or her presentation.

TIME MANAGEMENT AND ORGANIZATIONAL SKILLS

Improving your ability to manage your time and organize your work will help you become more productive and effective. It can also help you be recognized as someone who may be able to assume more job responsibilities.

Assess your workload and schedule on a weekly, then daily, basis. Be sure to identify the most important things you must get done during the workweek. Then look at your schedule for any meetings, appointments, or sales calls that might take away from the quality time you will have to work on important projects. To ensure that you can get to work on those projects, reserve at least two days during the week to devote large chunks of time for your work. Try to set aside 30 minutes a day to organize and complete some of your work in between lunches, meetings, and appointments. Create files for your projects and important information. Use the computer as much as you can to store information and finish projects. Keep a daily to-do list, and check off tasks as you complete them. Know when to say no! Keep a daily calendar. Plan on arriving at work on time every day. Be flexible enough to work through lunch, stay late, or come in for a few hours on Saturday morning to keep on top of your work.

There are great payoffs for being organized and managing your time well. Personally, you will reduce your stress and receive greater satisfaction from your work. Professionally, you will develop the image of a professional who is serious about getting things done and moving on to the next challenge.

In every job you have, you can increase your effectiveness by knowing what's important for you to do. Jobs exist because certain functions need to be performed and certain results are expected. For example, imagine that your job as a telemarketer involves selling cable TV service by telephone. You decide that you want to do better today than you did yesterday. Yesterday you made 25 calls and convinced eight clients to buy the service. You might decide to make 35 calls today, but what's really important is not making more calls but selling more cable subscriptions than you did yesterday. Therefore, a better goal might be to convince 10 clients to buy the service regardless of how many calls it takes. The workplace is becoming more and more structured toward individual workers' having yearly objectives, thus creating more accountability for job performance.

There will be many times during your daily job routine when the hectic pace and multitude of tasks that need to get done become overwhelming. By using good planning and presentation skills, exercising proper meeting behavior, managing your time effectively, and keeping focused on results, you can get things done both independently and with others. You can review more strategies for developing time management and organizational skills in Chapter 4.

 14.6 PROMOTIONS

As you progress in your job, you may demonstrate the ability and desire to take on other responsibilities in the company. This is a great way to build your career, because assuming new roles makes you more versatile and more valuable to your company. These growth opportunities can involve a new job or more responsibilities than you have in your current job. The following information and guidelines will help you establish and achieve your goals for promotion.

JOB ENLARGEMENT VERSUS JOB ENRICHMENT

You may be asked to perform more tasks at the same level of difficulty. This is job enlargement. Or you may be asked to assume more responsibility (for example, supervising other people). This is job enrichment. Either of these two instances could be described as a promotion.

The reason it is important to be aware of these two different types of promotion is that at some point, you need to decide what type of growth opportunity is best for you. If you enjoy the hands-on work you do and would be challenged by doing more of it, you may choose this as a way to grow professionally. Sometimes people who prefer to continue in their same job but expand upon it a little more don't see these additional responsibilities as a promotion. A promotion does not always have to involve supervising others or moving up to the next-higher job title and level of responsibility. For some people this works very well, while others do better growing in the existing job. What is most important about either of these forms of promotion is that you feel properly challenged in a job that suits your skills and personality. You and your employer are the best judges of which route suits you best.

Real Life Stories

Karen Katz, Neiman Marcus

Karen Katz[2] realized her career goal when she became the President and Chief Executive of Neiman Marcus Stores, based in Dallas, Texas. Her career path has been marked by a series of successful promotions that led her to her dream job with one of the most prestigious retail companies in the world.

Karen worked in retail positions during college. Her career goal was to be a lawyer, but her work in retail caused her to change her mind. At graduation, she applied to Neiman Marcus instead of applying to law school. She was rejected and took a management position at another major department store in Dallas.

While developing her buying skills, Karen went on to earn a master's degree in business administration. She was promoted and seven years later Neiman Marcus extended her an offer to join the company. She started as a merchandise manager. Her career sky-rocketed at Neiman's where she went on to become Vice President and General Manager, then Senior Vice President and Director of Stores. Karen moved into the role of Executive Vice President and before long became President. Her time to accomplish all of this at Neiman Marcus was about 15 years, not a long time for such a strong story of career progress. Karen's first rejection from Neiman Marcus made her more determined to explore her passion for the retail industry. While she was certainly disappointed that Neiman Marcus had not hired her at that time, she stayed committed to her goals and eventually found success back at the very place that had challenged her along the way.

"I have two rejection letters that I haven't thrown away: One is from Harvard Law School and the other is from Neiman Marcus."

—Karen Katz

---

[2] M. Halkias (October 24, 2007). "High end resumes." *Dallas Morning News.* www.dallasnews.com.

MENTORS

A mentor is someone with more experience than you who is willing to provide helpful advice for your professional development. If at all possible, find a mentor early in your career. This person can be a big help in setting and achieving your professional goals.

Selecting both a role model and a mentor can keep you on the right track with your personal and professional development. The one thing both have in common is previous experience and success. Role models can be selected from any walk in life, can be living or dead, or can be famous or unknown. Mentors are usually selected from within your career field, are living success stories, are usually employed within your own company, and are not necessarily famous people. You may or may not be able to consult with your role model, but you will be able to actually work with your mentor on an ongoing basis. In many ways your role model helps you believe in yourself and serves as your inspiration, while your mentor helps you develop hands-on strategies for success in the workplace and is a partner with you in your career success.

ACTIVITY 14.3

Selecting a Mentor

As you set goals for your own personal development, it will be helpful to choose someone who can be your mentor. While a student, you may consider someone from the company where you have a part-time or summer job, an internship, or a cooperative education assignment.

Think about some people who are possible mentors for you, and write their names in the space provided along with the reasons you would choose them.

Names   **Reasons Why**

_____

_____

_____

_____

_____

_____

_____

PERFORMANCE REVIEWS

Although you may have a three- or six-month assessment on your first job, performance reviews are conducted once a year in most companies. You should view your performance review as a chance to assess your professional strengths and weaknesses and to set goals for improvement. It is helpful to do your own pre-performance review prior to the actual scheduled time for your meeting with your supervisor. You should review the major responsibilities of your job, evaluate how many of those responsibilities you have met, evaluate the quality of the work involved, and think about why you were not able to fulfill some of your job responsibilities if this applies. You should also jot down a list of any of your unplanned accomplishments; these may range from winning an award to being asked to take charge of a special project. Be honest with yourself. By taking the time to reflect on your performance prior to your formal review, you accomplish two things: You reduce the chances of there being any surprises with your performance review, and you prepare yourself to discuss action steps for improvement. Even when your performance is satisfactory to both you and your employer, there is always room for improvement.

1. Have you ever been with a person who did not know how to behave properly at a meeting at school or at work? What was their biggest weakness and how did it affect the meeting?

2. How would you go about putting action steps in place for self-improvement after a performance review?

14.7 RECESSION-PROOFING YOUR JOB

In tough economic times, many businesses are faced with the decision to reduce their workforce. If you are properly prepared, you can handle these times should you become unemployed.

The key is to try to remain marketable to an employer. You can do this by having experience with a broad scope of responsibilities in your field, by being willing to take on many tasks, and by remaining flexible. You should also become comfortable with a little risk or uncertainty, because in a job transition you cannot be sure where you will end up or how long it will take to get there. Many times, a company may be willing to work at finding you a new role within the company, but there may be a long period of uncertainty in the process. Be patient and be open to a variety of job options.

ACTIVITY 14.4

Assess Your Transferable Skills

Below is a partial listing of transferable skills that employers value. The more transferable skills you develop, the easier it will be to move to another job and perhaps even change careers during downturns in the economy.

People Management	Sales and Marketing	Operation Management
Supervising	Negotiating	Planning
Teaching	Selling	Organizing
Training		Budgeting
Communication	**Leadership**	**Technical**
Public speaking	Coaching	Computer literacy
Writing	Direction setting	Desktop publishing
Foreign language	Inspiring	

After reviewing the preceding partial listing of transferable skills, list the ones you currently have:

_____

_____

_____

_____

Now review the list again and list the transferable skills you would like to acquire:

_____

_____

_____

_____

Write out a plan to develop each of the transferable skills you want to acquire.

Skill	Plan
Example: Selling	I will complete a sales training program offered next weekend on campus.
	_____
_____	_____
	_____

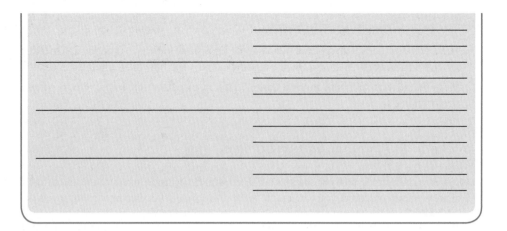

Build an account of all the transferable skills you have. Transferable skills are those that are acquired in one set of circumstances that can also be applied to a new set of circumstances. Examples of some transferable skills include organizational, budgeting, or interpersonal skills. Being able to show that you have talents to bring to a new situation and that you are willing to do so can help you keep your current job or be hired by a new employer. If you are laid off or fired from a company as a result of an overall staff reduction and have maintained a positive relationship with your employer, the company may provide you with outplacement assistance.

NOTES	Factors That Enable You to Recession-Proof Your Career
• Broad responsibilities • Many skills • Flexibility	• Ability to deal with risk or uncertainty • Transferable skills • Positive attitude

14.8 SUCCESSFUL CAREER MOVES

There are points in your career when you need to evaluate whether your current position within the company is where you should be at this time in your professional development. If you decide that you are not receiving the challenge, compensation, or recognition you really need, it may be time to leave the company and pursue a new career opportunity. When you decide to do this, do it right. Give proper notice to your employer that you are leaving. Depending on your job and the company, anywhere from two weeks' to two months' notice may be appropriate. It is better not to leave your job until you have a new one. Not only does this ensure a steady source of income for you, but, in general, prospective employers would rather interview candidates who are currently employed. This is because employed people tend to be more current with their skills and active in their profession. Always leave your job on good terms with your employer. Hopefully, both you and your employer have gained something from your professional relationship, causing your departure to be amicable. Remember that the company you leave may serve as a reference for you later on, so you want to leave a positive image of yourself. Every career change can be a new beginning for you if you approach it professionally and with a positive attitude.

If you decide to resign from your job, you should write a letter of resignation to your supervisor aimed at informing your employer of your decision to leave and stating the benefit of your experience with the company. You can find a sample letter of resignation in Chapter 11.

Getting off to the right start can make a big difference to both you and your employer. If you learn what is important to functioning well in your organization, the chances of your feeling comfortable and doing well will be greater.

During your first months on the job you should be familiar with how the company operates, how to perform your job well, how you will be evaluated, and how well you are doing. The goal is to use this time to become a productive member of the company. You should focus on your contribution to company goals and objectives as well as on your own professional development.

Positive relationships with others on the job will help you grow professionally and create new opportunities for you. This is because organizations are made up of people, and much of the success and failure of a company is contingent upon the ability of its people to achieve company goals. When you are viewed as someone who can work with your peers, your supervisor, those you supervise, and—most of all—customers, you become a valuable company resource.

In addition, learning how to improve your own personal production and effectiveness helps you grow toward greater responsibility and greater personal satisfaction with your career.

GROWING YOUR CAREER AND CAREER DECISION MAKING

Based on what you learned about growing with your job in this chapter, answer the following questions:

What am I trying to decide?

What do I need to know?

Why do I need to know it?

How will it help me make a more informed decision?

Why do I need to know it now?

How can I obtain what I need to know?

People

Experience

Research

Who are my best resources for the information I need?

Why do you think they are the right resources?

Contemporary Issues in the Workplace

After completing this chapter, you will:

1 **Describe** employee assistance programs

2 **Identify** how health-related issues affect you in the workplace

3 **Recognize** family care issues that affect you in the workplace

4 **Assess** the role of personal ethics in the workplace

5 **Explain** some laws that protect employees from workplace discrimination

The world of work is changing toward increasing integration between personal and professional aspects of life. The overlap of personal and professional interests is a result of changing personal value systems. For example, there is a trend for workers to value free time more than ever before. Changes in society also influence contemporary issues in the workplace. For example, men and women who want to raise families are faced with conflicts in work-life priorities. Unethical behavior by many business leaders is a societal concern that frequently disrupts the workplace. As a result, many corporations are implementing new codes of conduct for workers at all levels in a wide range of areas. Because contemporary issues in the workplace affect the way we live and work, you should be aware of some that will affect you during your career.

CASE STUDY

Jenny worked as an office manager for the local performing arts center for two years. She supervised four other employees and worked independently most of the time. Her boss came in one hour later than Jenny every day and then spent most of her time out of the office at meetings and community events, planning and promoting the center's work.

Jenny's morning routine started with organizing her work for the day. Within the first hour, she was sure to clean up any personal tasks that needed to be done. On any given day, this might have included paying some personal bills online, sending an e-mail confirming her weekly dinner plans with her friends, or ordering a birthday present or other items online as needed. There were days, such as when planning her family vacation, that she needed to spend that time researching best air fares online. Her boss was satisfied with Jenny's work and did not dictate how she managed her time at the office, as long as she got the job done.

Jenny moved on to accept a new job as the Assistant Director of Human Resources at a large insurance company. When she participated in the new employee orientation program, she learned that the company had an Internet/e-mail policy that was published in the employee handbook. She was aware of issues with employees spending time social networking at work, but never really thought about other abuses of technology at work.

The policy outlined specific uses of technology that were not acceptable during work hours. These included personal e-mails, sharing confidential company information, and sending e-mails that were potentially discriminatory. The policy prohibited the use of online activities during business hours including use of entertainment, sports, gambling, and online shopping sites. One of her first assignments involved providing reports to the legal department for an employee lawsuit. The employee was suing the company for allowing e-mails containing discriminatory jokes about her ethnic background to be circulated within her department. As Jenny was preparing to hire a job candidate she learned through a friend in human resources at another company that the person had been dismissed from a previous job because of sharing confidential information about the company's new product line to a friend who worked with a competitor. At her previous job, she never realized how serious misuse of the Internet, including e-mails, could be for a company or for its employees. While the company had an Internet policy in place, there was not a system in place for formally monitoring it. Jenny's boss was now considering monitoring employee use of the Internet and had her research several computer and Internet monitoring services. When she worked at her previous job, she would have thought this type of oversight by her employer to be unnecessary, but now she saw things from a much different perspective. She understood that individuals have a different sense of what is right and wrong. The company needed to provide the policy to spell out exactly what was acceptable and unacceptable for that company so that each employee knew what was expected of them. This would protect the company from lost productivity and possible damage to its reputation from employee misuse of technology.

Jenny also realized that managing Internet use at the company would benefit individual employees as well.

Discussion Questions

1. Do you think Jenny was wrong to use the Internet for personal use at her job at the performing arts center? Why or why not?
2. Do you think that companies should monitor employee Internet use at work? Why or why not?
3. Was it right for Jenny's friend in human resources to tell her why the job candidate Jenny was about to hire was fired from his last job? Why or why not?

 ## 15.1 EMPLOYEE ASSISTANCE PROGRAMS

The many types of employee assistance programs (EAPs) that companies offer serve as a benefit to employees and a retention tool for the company. Employee assistance programs provide help to both supervisors and employees in responding to personal problems that could affect job performance. "Over 82 percent of companies with more than 500 employees have EAPs, and 62 percent of small business owners with 25 or more employees offer EAPs. Employers are increasingly offering EAPs because recent analyses have shown a return of $15 for each $1 spent on an EAP."[1] The extent of these programs may vary

---

[1] Jorgenson/Brooks Group. (2005). "Why use an employee assistance program (EAP)?" Retrieved July 14, 2005, from www.jorgensenbrooks.com/.

substantially by company. Most include assistance to employees with issues that range from substance abuse, family care, and stress management, to financial planning and legal assistance.

⦿ 15.2 HEALTH-RELATED ISSUES

By being better informed on these issues, you can understand why certain company policies are in place and what assistance is available to you to help you deal with these issues personally or with coworkers.

Health-related issues affect employees in the workplace in many ways. Substance abuse may affect an employee's productivity and attitude and can result in increased absenteeism. Laws requiring more accommodations are opening up new career opportunities for special-needs employees. As a result of the emergence of these health-related issues, more companies are committed to formal health education programs for their employees.

SUBSTANCE ABUSE

Overuse of some drugs and alcohol can produce behavioral problems for employees that disrupt either their own productivity or the environment they work in. An increasing number of employers—including the U.S. Postal Service, General Motors, Alcoa, The New York Times, and American Airlines—are requiring preemployment urine or blood tests to screen for the presence of cocaine, barbiturates, amphetamines, marijuana, and opiates. Federal experts estimate that in excess of 10 percent of all U.S. workers have used illegal drugs on the job.[2]

The effects of substance abuse problems are profound on both the employer and the employee, and that is why they have become a major focus of attention. Employers report a higher incidence of problems with productivity, accidents, medical claims, absenteeism, and employee theft among employees with substance abuse problems. These all result in higher costs to the employer. As a job candidate or an actual employee, you can be affected by these problems whether you are a substance abuser or not. Drug and alcohol abuse costs U.S. business as much as $140 billion a year in lost productivity.[3]

If you test positive for drugs when looking for a job, you will almost certainly not be hired. Once you are employed, detection of drug or alcohol use can cause you to be fired if you show any kind of work-related problem because of it.

STRESS MANAGEMENT

Nearly one third of employers report that high stress levels cause conflict between their work responsibilities and personal priorities. The same report cited other factors that contribute to work-related stress:

- Long hours 25%
- Fast-paced environment 14%
- Inflexible schedule 13%
- Personal values conflict with my company's core values 9%
- Highly competitive environment 7%[4]

---

[2] Abbott Laboratories Diagnostics. (2005). "Drug abuse." Retrieved July 14, 2005, from www.abbottdiagnostics .com/YourHealth/Drug_Abuse/.

[3] Ibid.

[4] Deloitte & Touche. (2007). "Leadership counts." Retrieved from www.deloitte.com/dtt/cda/doc/content/us_ ethics_workplace2007a.pdf.

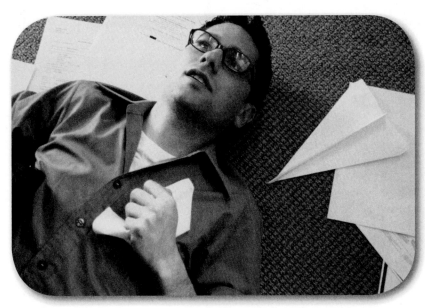

There are many ways employees can learn to manage their own stress by developing better discipline for healthier lifestyles. Four basic lifestyle tips are helpful in managing stress:

- Maintain a healthy diet and weight.
- Maintain a daily exercise routine.
- Prioritize your schedule every day.
- Ask for help if you need it.

In addition to these lifestyle practices, EAPs may offer the assistance you need to get back on and stay on track at home and in the workplace. Some companies are even more committed to promoting healthy lifestyles than others and offer employees lifestyle benefits that may include memberships to health clubs, fitness centers, or weight-loss programs. Education and assistance with managing debt, buying a car, or planning savings and investments are other examples of assistance companies may provide to help employees manage the stress that is a natural outcome of daily living.

HEALTH EDUCATION

As a result of some of these health-related issues, there is an increased effort to provide health education in the workplace. Many employers have implemented such programs to familiarize employees with how their substance abuse or that of their coworkers can affect them on the job. The programs are also aimed at prevention.

Another major component of health education involves wellness programs, which promote overall good nutrition and exercise as a way of life. These wellness programs instruct employees on how to keep fit and may recommend individual fitness programs as well. For companies, the major reasons for offering wellness programs are that they are cost effective (their cost often is outweighed by savings in health care costs), are responsive to employees' demands, and offer a sense of social responsibility. For the employee, participation can result in reduced absenteeism because of improved physical health and mental attitude, reduced expenses from joining outside fitness programs, stress reduction, and assurance that one's work life can be a positive factor contributing to an overall healthy lifestyle.

ACCOMMODATIONS FOR SPECIAL-NEEDS EMPLOYEES

The Americans with Disabilities Act (ADA) has required employers to make accommodations for employees with special needs. The act bars employment discrimination against the disabled and mandates access for the disabled to public spaces. Companies that fail to meet these standards are subject to civil actions for noncompliance. The Americans with Disabilities Act makes it easier for job candidates and employees to get to and from work and move about safely in the workplace.

 15.3 FAMILY CARE ISSUES

Today the participation rate in the workplace of women ages 25 to 64 exceeds 76 percent.[5] At the same time, the 65-and-over population is expected to grow by more than 80 percent and represent 21 percent of the population by 2030.[6] Of the "sandwich generation"—ages

---

[5] I. S. Wolfe. (2004, January). "What's in store for 2004?" *Success Performance Solutions.* Retrieved from www .super-solutions.com/whatsinstorefor2004_employeeproductivity.asp.

[6] I. S. Wolfe. (2005). "The perfect labor storm–facts." Retrieved July 14, 2005, from www.perfectlaborstorm .com/facts.html.

45 to 55—44 percent have children under 21 years of age and living in-laws and/or parents.[7] Parental leave for child care and leave for elder care are the two fastest-emerging work-family conflicts. Caring for the family often means taking care of older parents as well as children. This, coupled with job demands, puts tremendous pressure on many workers, who often experience stress trying to keep everything balanced.

PARENTAL LEAVE

The Family Medical Leave Act (FMLA) requires companies to allow eligible employees up to 12 weeks' leave during any 12-month period for childbirth, adoption, or foster child care; serious illness of a spouse, child, or parent; or a personal serious health condition. Many leaves are nonpaid, although employees are entitled to continue their company-provided medical coverage during their leave. Despite the strong interest many men and women have in staying home to care for their children, many of them simply cannot afford to. The trend of men taking leave or reducing hours has been slow to surge, experts say, since most employers do not offer paternal leave. Accounting giant Ernst and Young provides two weeks of paid paternal leave.[8]

CHILD CARE

DuPont Company surveyed its employees and learned that 80 percent would have missed work if not for its emergency/backup care program. One year, that program saved nearly 1,500 employee days.[9]

The quality of day care varies enormously. States license and monitor the private for-profit and not-for-profit centers. In some states, important matters such as learning activities or the teacher-child ratio are ignored. The tremendous amount of time being spent by workers on child care and the inconsistent quality of day care centers are creating a new push toward the corporate on-site day care center. There are advantages to such centers. Parents can drop in anytime. Companies benefit in the recruitment and retention of employees. One of the most innovative efforts was made by Levi Strauss & Co. When children get sick, traditional day care centers are not the answer for working parents, because sick children are not allowed in day care centers. To enable parents of sick children not to miss work, Levi Strauss & Co. funded a 17-bed children's infirmary that is attached to an independent day care center in San Jose, California.

Companies are realizing the advantages of day care centers. Many companies offer subsidized day care centers, financial assistance for child care, or child care referral services.

All of this means that the pressure for caregiving is increasing for employees, resulting in an unprecedented investment by employers to attract and retain employees.

Most companies are willing to accommodate employees' special needs, especially the need for a more flexible work schedule, to properly care for elderly family members. As child care and elder care become a concern for more employees, some employers are considering innovative ways to address individuals' unique situations. The fact that these options are available to you demonstrates companies' commitment to attracting and retaining competent workers by assisting them with family issues that may have a direct impact on their work life. This should reduce the number of workers who need to quit working for extended periods of time to take care of their family responsibilities.

---

[7] C. Aoyagi. (2005) "Sandwich generation: Pulling double duty." Retrieved July 14, 2005, from www
.imdiversity.com/Villages/Asian/family_lifestyle_traditions/pc_sandwich_ generation_0505.asp.

[8] B. Torres. (2005). "Dads on leave." *Mail Tribune Online.* Retrieved April 21, 2005, from www.mailtribune
.com/archive/2005/0421/life/stories/01life.htm.

[9] Work Options Group. (2005). "Workplace impact—child care." Retrieved July 14, 2005, from www
.workoptionsgroup.com/Default.aspx?tabid 157#child.

FLEXTIME

Employee assistance programs or a company's general benefits program can offer some unique solutions to employees for managing their work-life balance. One practice that is gaining popularity in many firms is offering flextime to employees. Flextime creates the opportunity for employees to perform the functions of their jobs outside the traditional 8:30 a.m. to 4:30 p.m. or 9:00 a.m. to 5:00 p.m. workday, and sometimes outside the traditional office setting.

Here are several types of flextime:

- Part-time management professionals. The number of part-time management professionals grew from 5.7 million to 6.4 million between 2000 and 2004.[10] This trend among mid-level professionals has grown in direct relationship to work-life balance needs among American workers. Employers find the use of part-time management professionals attractive when there are specific projects requiring outside expertise for a limited period of time. The professional needs to balance the sacrifice from a financial standpoint with the gain in personal time and overall balanced lifestyle.

- *Job sharing.* Job sharing is an arrangement in which the responsibilities and hours of one job position are carried out by two people. It permits two part-time workers to divide one full-time job. While job sharing is another flextime option, it is much more difficult to find. Job sharing is more readily available at small firms, start-ups, nonprofits, and colleges or universities.

- Telecommuting. Another way of describing work at home, telecommuting has been gaining in popularity in recent years as another response to employees' work-life balance issues. In a May 2008 Society for Human Resource Management (SHRM) poll, 18 percent of responding employers said they offered telecommuting as a way to help employees deal with rising fuel costs. By September 2008, the number had risen to 40 percent.[11]

While flextime is a growing option offered by many U.S. employers, it is not yet common practice, especially with large firms. For this reason, many flextime opportunities are not advertised. Networking is the best way to learn about available positions or the best companies to approach for flextime career opportunities.

NOTES | Top Three Positive Influences of Overall Job Satisfaction

- Compensation
- Flexible work
- Benefits

Progress Check Questions

1. What advantages and disadvantages do you see to telecommuting?

2. Do you think that you, personally, would be a more productive or satisfied employee working with a flextime arrangement at work? Why or why not?

---

[10] C. Larson. (March 21, 2005). "Family balance: More professionals opt to go part time." *U.S. News.com.*

[11] L. Zamzow. (Winter 2009). "Penny-pinching at the pump: How employers can help employees with higher fuel costs." Retrieved September 2, 2009, from www.fredlaw.com/bios/attorneys/zamzowlindsay/20ANSWR_Winter2009.pdf.

15.4 ETHICS

Although the practice of good business ethics has always been important, as we have entered the 21st century, we must make a stronger commitment to both the practice and enforcement of ethics. The prevalence of unethical behavior in the workplace, and in society, requires stricter enforcement of laws against such behavior to stop it. Many individuals or companies have become comfortable with behavior with which they should be uncomfortable. Theft, fraud, discrimination, and harassment are a few examples of unethical behavior that exist in today's workplace.

PERSONAL ETHICS

Being an ethically responsible employee involves consistently making good choices with both big and small decisions on a daily basis. Here are some behaviors that show a general lack of concern about ethics at work:

Misuse of company finances

  Stealing petty cash

  Cheating on an expense report

  Improper accounting

Using company technology for personal use

  Personal e-mails

  Social networking

  Online activities: shopping, gambling, entertainment

Misuse of company property

  Telephones

  Copy and fax machines

  Stealing supplies

  Company vehicles

Misuse of company benefits

  Calling in sick when you are not sick

  Applying for disability without eligibility

  Approving employee vacations beyond their eligibility

If you observe someone at work demonstrating unethical behavior, you should report it to your supervisor or to the human resources department. It might be unproductive to confront the employee directly, since, in all likelihood, that person will be defensive with you and put you in an uncomfortable situation. Doing nothing is even more nonproductive. Take some responsibility and arrange to speak appropriately to someone who can take appropriate action with the company.

Real Life Stories

Isabella and Max

Isabella was a working mother and part-time student at the local community college. She had a flextime arrangement at her current job that allowed her flexibility in the morning and at the end of the day to juggle getting her daughter to and from day care and attending her 4:00 p.m. class on Tuesdays and Thursdays. When she was offered a promotion with an attractive salary increase, she had a lot to think about. Her husband, Max, had just received word from his employer that because company revenues were declining, a decision had been made to cut the hours of one-third of its workforce, while keeping salaries level, instead of cutting people from the payroll. Many companies were doing this to try to preserve people's jobs during the ongoing recession. Max's schedule was cut from 40 to 25 hours per week for an undefined period of time. His boss worked hard to convince Max that the company valued his work and wanted to ensure he would still be one of its employees once the economy improved. Max obtained a temporary position to fill in the hours he would be losing because he wanted to keep his job.

Isabella's new position would require her to be at early morning meetings and occasionally attend social events a few nights each month. She felt conflicted as she processed her decision to stay in her current job or accept the promotion. After all, her goal for furthering her education was to advance in her career and this seemed like a perfect opportunity. She asked herself, "Should I delay my education to concentrate on a new job?" "Would the salary increase be offset with the additional hours per week I will have to spend on daycare?" "How will the extra time needed to invest in the new job affect my personal life?" "If I refuse this offer, will there be a similar opportunity down the road?" Isabella talked with her family and with two of her teachers about her option. While everyone was excited for her, both her family and her teachers advised her to stay with her current job and finish school. Max agreed. Right now, Isabella felt she had a good balance with her family and work life and she was doing well in school. While the increase in salary certainly would make her family's financial situation easier, she was worried that if she accepted additional responsibility at this stage in her life, that she would add stress to herself and to her family. She also might become too distracted from completing her college degree, which was key to achieving her career goals. She decided she could make her best contribution, at the current time, to her family and to her job by keeping her current position.

FIGURE 15.1

Why People Make Unethical Decisions

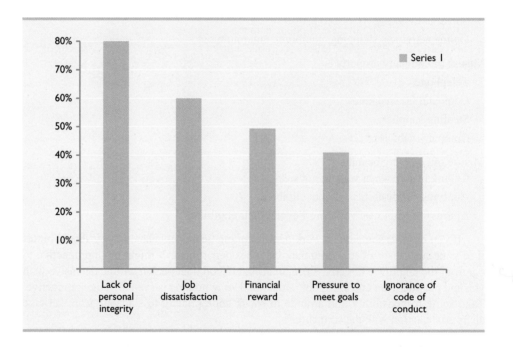

MISUSE OF TECHNOLOGY AT WORK

Misuse of technology among employees has become a major concern for employers, especially within the past few years.

Internet and E-mail   Gartner Gray reports that non-work-related Internet surfing results in up to a 40 percent loss in productivity at American businesses each year.[12] It is

[12] Links on SpectorSoft. (2009). Retrieved September 2, 2009 from www.facebook.com/posted.php?id=44523071199&share_id=127034967288&comments=1&ref=mf.

easy to damage a company's reputation, and yours, misusing sites like Facebook, Twitter, and YouTube, especially at work.

Most companies have an Internet/e-mail policy published for employee access in their company employee handbook. While employers know they cannot totally control employee use of the Internet and e-mail at work, they intend to minimize damage by enforcing the policy. It is important to first let the employees know a policy exists at the company and provide them with the details. Violations occur without the employee knowing they have done something wrong if the policy is not clear. Once the employee knows what is acceptable or unacceptable, it is up to the individual to honor the policy. Consider some of the potential damage to a company:

- An employee has sent confidential company information out to a competitor and is charged with trade secret theft.
- A discriminatory e-mail provokes an employee or a group of employees into a lawsuit against the company.
- False financial information or workplace violence threats are sent, requiring unnecessary resources to be spent avoiding an unreal threat.
- An employee disparages the company name on a blog or social networking site.
- A company's productivity falls each hour one employee spends on the Internet or e-mails not related to company business.

Telephones   Inappropriate use of cell phones and office phones at work can also be problematic:

- Leave a professional sounding recorded message on any phones you use for work. There is a risk with the use of phone cameras at work or at work-related events.
- Be careful not to speak loudly in public places about confidential business at the office.
- Your presence on the phone should replicate the professional image you present in person.

ABUSE OF PRIVILEGE

Abuse of privilege occurs when someone takes a privilege that is given to her or him, such as a company expense account, and extends its use beyond what is acceptable or expected by the company. In this case, an individual may use a company expense account to be reimbursed for personal expenses that are not company related.

Most companies have policies prohibiting the removal of company property without written permission from the supervisor responsible for the property in question. Company property can include tools or equipment; confidential literature; computer disks, tapes, and other storage media; or information identified as proprietary or a trade secret.

Removing or attempting to remove company property without permission can be grounds for disciplinary action. If you are not sure whether an action will be considered an abuse of privilege, review any written company policies in your employee handbook or ask a responsible person in the company about the proper use of company policy or property. If you are still not sure whether you are acting appropriately, do not take the risk of making a mistake that could negatively affect your reputation and possibly your career.

CONFLICT OF INTEREST

Conflicts of interest sometimes occur between company and personal interests or goals. A drafter who has a private consulting business outside of the job with his or her employer may experience a conflict of interest if trying to consult during the employer's work hours.

Most companies expect all employees to avoid activities that create conflicts of interest with their responsibilities to the company. Employers may ask employees to refrain from activities that may conflict or interfere with company operation or with others with whom the company does business. Conflicts of interest include, but are not limited to, the following:

1. *Outside employment.* A second job with a competitor is usually prohibited because of the danger that exists for sharing procedures, business plans, and product development techniques, especially if the second company is competing for the same customers.

2. *Gifts and entertainment.* Some companies have strict policies prohibiting employees from accepting gifts of more than nominal value from people or companies that do business, or want to do business, with the company.

3. *Legal issues.* All companies prohibit employees from doing anything in the conduct of business that would violate any local, state, or federal law.

4. *Fair competition.* Companies generally encourage their employees to conduct business fairly and ethically, with consideration given to the needs of customers, fellow workers, and suppliers.

PREFERENTIAL TREATMENT

Preferential treatment is when an employee shows special treatment to certain groups of people or takes shortcuts for one person and not another. An example would be an account representative at a bank who processes a loan for a friend without following the prescribed waiting period for approval or without checking all the necessary references.

These are just some examples of how day-to-day work activities can lead an individual into an ethical dilemma. When faced with an ethical decision, most people follow their own personal code of behavior, as opposed to the behavior of others or any formal company policy. Ultimately, you are in control of your own actions.

. . . .

Progress Check Questions

1. What would you do if you knew a coworker constantly used online entertainment sites during working hours?

2. How would you handle an e-mail sent to you containing an ethnically discriminatory joke?

. . . .

 ## 15.5 NONDISCRIMINATION LAWS

The U.S. Department of Labor is charged with the responsibility of regulating workplace activity to ensure fair treatment of individuals and groups of employees in a wide range of areas. The following are some of the more commonly known laws that are in place to accomplish this goal.

EQUAL EMPLOYMENT OPPORTUNITY

Fairness in hiring practices is the goal of the Equal Employment Opportunity Act. Companies that maintain a policy of nondiscrimination in all phases of employment must also comply in full with all applicable laws. The following practices ensure that companies properly implement their nondiscrimination policy. The company will:

- Recruit, advertise, hire, transfer, and promote without regard to race, religion, color, national origin, physical handicap, sex, age, or any other legally protected classification.
- Base all employment decisions on candidates' qualifications to do the job.

Despite the widespread attention given to this issue nationwide, few U.S. corporations can be proud of their minority hiring and promotion records to date. This is because issues not related to performance keep entering the hiring process and prevent us from realizing equal employment opportunity. As the number of available minority workers will be increasing over the years, measures must be taken now to revisit this issue and set the law in practice. Minority workers may find more attention given to this effort in future years as the potential workforce continues to include more minority candidates.

AFFIRMATIVE ACTION

Today's American workplace looks much different than it did in the 1960s when minorities were often discriminated against in the hiring process and in the daily work environment. Women were also often discriminated against when seeking employment or working outside the home.

The affirmative action law was instituted to improve the participation of more minority and female workers in the workplace. Today, attitudes about affirmative action range from supportive to opposed. Those in favor believe that because of affirmative action, women and members of racial and ethnic minority groups play a larger role in the workplace. Those opposed say that as affirmative action has evolved, there is now too much emphasis on meeting "goals and timetables" for hiring or promoting women and minorities.

Most employers are engaged in some sort of affirmative action program. As they implement these programs, employers must be careful to maintain a balance in their hiring practices for first hiring the most qualified candidates and then ensuring there is a good mix of workers from all backgrounds in their workplace.

SEXUAL HARASSMENT

Awareness of sexual harassment in the workplace was heightened by incidents in the 1990s that were publicized nationally. As a result, companies are reviewing their policies on sexual harassment and setting in place programs to teach people what it is and what harm it can do. Sexual harassment issues in the workplace are costly to employers. It is reported that sexual harassment has cost some Fortune 500 companies up to $6.7 million a year in absenteeism, lower productivity, and turnover.[13] Legal fees for defending a sexual harassment charge average $250,000, and judgments routinely exceed $1 million. As a result, employers openly publish policies to make it clear to employees that sexual harassment is inappropriate workplace behavior that is not tolerated.

[13] J. E. Johnston. (2005). "Dear human resources professional." Retrieved July 15, 2005, www.workrelationships .com/site/awb/awb.php.

Sexual harassment policies in many companies read as follows: "All unwelcome sexual advances, requests for sexual favors, and other such verbal or physical conduct are prohibited by the company." These policies exist so that all employees can share a work environment free of potentially harmful comments or actions. Employees who feel they have been harassed usually have the option of complaining to someone in the company (human resources department, supervisor's boss, etc.) other than the harasser. This provides them a more comfortable form of communication.

Tips for Dealing with Sexual Harassment

1. Tell the harasser to stop the offensive behavior.
2. Document all incidents of harassment.
3. Notify your supervisor or other appropriate person of the harassment.
4. Know your company or school policy on sexual harassment and follow its procedures.
5. Consider filing a forward grievance or complaint if the preceding steps do not remedy the situation.
6. Stay on the job.
7. Find support from family, friends, or other groups to help you through the situation.

CHAPTER SUMMARY

As you navigate your career, there may be times when you feel some conflict between work and personal priorities. As you try to maintain the right balance between the two, take advantage of resources that your employer may offer. Employee assistance programs vary from company to company but basically are there to provide you support in a number of ways, ranging from financial advising, educational assistance, to advice on child care and stress management. Think of the employee assistance program as your safety net at work, providing you tools to achieve your goals and maintain work-life balance in the process.

Part of the services available to you might be advice on health and wellness and family care related issues. Support to help you reduce stress and maintain healthy habits at work vary from a fitness club membership to health assessments with advice on a variety of health-related issues. Staying healthy at work is important to being productive and enjoying your work. There are many support programs to help you balance family responsibilities at the same time.

A major part of your career success will depend on how well you can bring your good judgment and common sense to ethical decisions you may need to make. Making sound ethical decisions is important to your personal reputation and can impact your company's reputation. Having a sense of fairness in the way you deal with others and avoiding behavior that is discriminatory will help you develop strong working relationships, including the trust and respect of people in your company.

Managing yourself and your family and building a solid reputation as an ethical and fair professional will improve your chances of success in your career, while balancing other important aspects of your life.

CONTEMPORARY ISSUES IN THE WORKPLACE AND CAREER DECISION MAKING

Based on what you learned about contemporary issues in the workplace, select a topic that represents an issue that you think will impact your career decisions the most. Think about a career decision you are trying to make and how this issue might influence you.

What am I trying to decide?

_____

_____

What do I need to know?

_____

_____

Why do I need to know it?

_____

_____

How will it help me make a more informed decision?

_____

_____

Why do I need to know it now?

_____

_____

How can I obtain what I need to know?

_____

_____

   People _____

   Experience _____

   Research _____

Who are my best resources for the information I need?

_____

_____

Why do I think they are the right resources?

_____

_____

Credits

Index